An Introduc
to Instrumei
Phonetics

An Introduction to Instrumental Phonetics

by

COLIN PAINTER, Ph.D.

Director of the Robbins Speech and Hearing Laboratory
Emerson College, Boston
Research Affiliate in the Speech Communication Group
Research Laboratory of Electronics
Massachusetts Institute of Technology, Cambridge
and
Associate Professor, Faculty of Medicine
University of Toronto, Ontario

University Park Press
Baltimore

UNIVERSITY PARK PRESS
International Publishers in Science, Medicine, and Education
233 East Redwood Street
Baltimore, Maryland 21201

Typeset by The Composing Room of Michigan, Inc.
Manufactured in the United States of America by Collins Lithographing and
Printing Co., Inc.

The illustrations on the cover of this book are of the author
saying "An introduction to instrumental phonetics."

Library of Congress Cataloging in Publication Data

Painter, Colin.
    An introduction to instrumental phonetics.

    Bibliography: p.
    1. Phonetics—Instruments.   I. Title.
P221.P22   414   79-1497
ISBN 0-8391-1330-7

Contents

Gratias ago
Atque Habeo

It has been my very good fortune to work especially under two phoneticians graced by humility, courtesy, and good humor as well as scholarship and I would like to extend my thanks to Fred Householder and Ken Stevens for their support, encouragement, and stimulation over the years.

To these two, to Stefanie Shattuck Hufnagel, and to the students who acted as guinea pigs I am indebted also for prepublication readings of earlier drafts. I am most grateful for their comments.

And last but not least to Robin Thelwall who, one evening in Leeds, aided by a couple of pints of Tetley's ale, finally persuaded me to write this book.

1
Introduction

1.1 THE INTENDED READERSHIP

This book is intended primarily for senior undergraduates or M.A. students in departments of or programs in general linguistics, audiology, and/or speech pathology. In broad terms, they fall into two groups and will have to be taught in different ways in the tutorials even though institutional economics may put them together in the course work. The first group comprises research workers in the making. They may already have taken a whole sequence of speech science courses: general phonetics, the anatomy and physiology of speech, acoustic phonetics, and speech perception, and probably intend to pursue a Ph.D. later on. It is recognized, however, that most students will at best have taken only one cover-all speech communication course and possibly merely an introductory course in general phonetics and/or one in the phonetics of English or some other language. We might call this second group the "applied phoneticians," since their expertise will lie elsewhere and they are mainly interested in knowing what can be done in a phonetics laboratory and how. The instruments themselves should hold their interest while they are learning that, although very easy to produce, data are just so much wallpaper if the phonetician cannot interpret them.

A third group, sometimes pure and sometimes applied, sometimes advanced and sometimes not, consists of those students with a major in a department or program other than general linguistics, audiology, or speech pathology, but then, as we shall see in a moment, phonetics is at the point of overlap of so many disciplines: modern languages, music, singing, experimental psychology, otorhinolaryngology, orthodontics/oro-facial anomalies, and electrical engineering as well as its principal homes.

1.2 THE INTENDED LEVEL OF THE BOOK

An introduction to instrumental phonetics is not an introduction to phonetics. Indeed, by definition, it is either an intermediate or an advanced level course in that it is implied that the student already has at least some background in general phonetics or communication science; this textbook has been designed to be useful at both the intermediate and advanced levels. It takes nothing for granted except the fact that the student's science background is probably rather weak and that the linguist will know no engineering and the engineer no linguistics, etc. What is already familiar can be skipped over but what is new will need no further explanation than that which is in the text.

1.3 KNOB-TURNING AND DATA INTERPRETATION

Few institutions have a large phonetics laboratory and many have no laboratory at all, but it has always been the author's belief that it is possible to teach a worthwhile course in instrumental phonetics even in the absence of a laboratory, providing that there is a textbook available that contains a suitably large corpus of instrumental data for examination. This is not to say that such an approach is to be desired, but it can be done and it should be emphasized that the larger task is to teach students how to interpret data so that they can read the literature with understanding. The mere manipulation of knobs is of lesser importance, although great fun.

1.4 HOW MANY KINDS OF PHONETICS?

Speech has to be produced, it has to be propagated from speaker to listener, and it has to be heard and processed. In the United States, particularly in the literature of speech pathology, it is common to call these three stages "speech production," "speech acoustics," and "speech perception," whereas in the United Kingdom, and more generally in the literature of linguistic phonetics, it is more usual to talk of "articulatory phonetics," "acoustic phonetics," and "auditory phonetics." Each set of terms has a certain symmetry and each reflects something of the differing histories of the discipline on opposite sides of the Atlantic.

In the United States speech science has a double origin in anthropological linguistics with its study of American Indian languages and speech pathology, but in Europe phonetics developed from modern language teaching, the study of non–Indo-European languages in the old colonies, and historical linguistics. *Speech production* is undoubtedly a better term than *articulatory phonetics,* since the production end involves respiration and phonation as well as articulation in the strict sense of the word, although the term *acoustic* unfortunately tends to be used very broadly in the United States to cover both the acoustic and auditory aspects of speech. On the other hand, "auditory phonetics" suggests only a study of the ear, of reception, whereas "speech perception" implies an interest only in what goes on beyond the ear.

However, one's choice of terms is less important than the realization that there are three kinds of phonetics and that one ignores any one of them at one's peril. In addition, all three may be studied by the use of instrumental techniques, i.e., instrumental phonetics, although it should be noted that the best instrument we have at our disposal is the human ear. There is no replacement for the ear and the connections it has with the brain and the production mechanism. Above all the student should begin his work in phonetics with an ear-training course. He should learn to discriminate and identify sounds by ear and be able to describe and transcribe them accurately on the basis of what he has heard. This aspect of the science is strongly developed in the European tradition but poorly so in the United States, where many otherwise knowledgeable and well-known scholars in the field often make errors because of their weak ear-training and try to cover up by claiming either that ear-training is unimportant or that claims to expertise are spurious or that instruments are more precise and reliable. The fact is, however, that instruments are often precise just when one does not want them to be so, i.e., they "hear" things that the ear does not, and as to being reliable—well, they *usually* are, but one has to know how to interpret what they tell us.

The reader may be confused at this stage. Is the author trying to play down the role of instrumental phonetics? Obviously not, since he is about to expand on the joys and usefulness of the phonetics laboratory, but he *is* trying to say that one should not walk into a laboratory with an untrained ear[1] and expect to solve one's problems merely by speaking into one end of a machine and getting the answers out at the other. The ear must be trained, used, and trusted. Instruments merely confirm and quantify.

The last sentence is undoubtedly an overstatement but, for all that, it is not a bad motto for the student to carry around over his heart.

1.5 INSTRUMENTATION AND THE SPEECH CHAIN

It is convenient to conceptualize the field of phonetics in terms of the speech chain, which may be represented as a series of cause and effect relationships (see Figure 1). To do so is to oversimplify matters because there are so many built-in feedback mechanisms and because certain stages are in fact simultaneous rather than sequential, but it does give the student an overview and provides a framework for showing what instrumental techniques can do and for distinguishing between linguistics, speech production, acoustics, audiology, and perception.

All speech events have their origin in the brain—the black box of our system. The neural organization of the brain is still poorly understood but it is now believed that some aspects of its structure are innate to man and reflect the point that *Homo sapiens* has reached in the evolutionary chain. One such aspect is man's capacity for language. Insects, reptiles, and lower mammals do not have it, as far as we know, and even in the apes it is not well developed, but man *does* and, regardless of the language community he is raised in, he will show fea-

---

[1]While it is true that one cannot, strictly speaking, train an *ear,* the term *ear-training* is firmly rooted in the literature, so I shall maintain the metaphor.

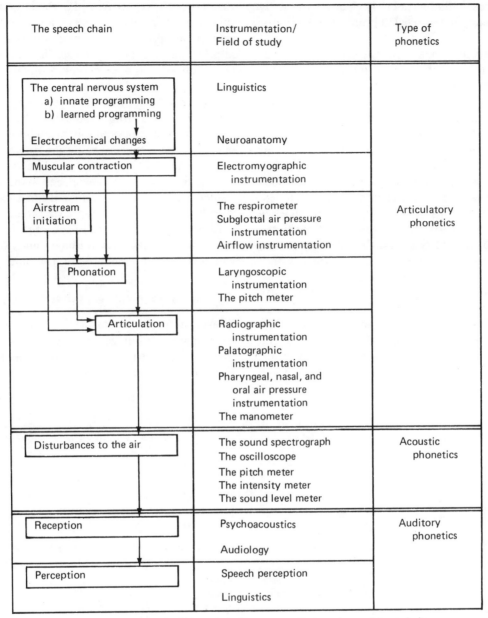

The speech chain	Instrumentation/ Field of study	Type of phonetics
The central nervous system a) innate programming b) learned programming Electrochemical changes	Linguistics Neuroanatomy	Articulatory phonetics
Muscular contraction	Electromyographic instrumentation	
Airstream initiation	The respirometer Subglottal air pressure instrumentation Airflow instrumentation	
Phonation	Laryngoscopic instrumentation The pitch meter	
Articulation	Radiographic instrumentation Palatographic instrumentation Pharyngeal, nasal, and oral air pressure instrumentation The manometer	
Disturbances to the air	The sound spectrograph The oscilloscope The pitch meter The intensity meter The sound level meter	Acoustic phonetics
Reception	Psychoacoustics Audiology	Auditory phonetics
Perception	Speech perception Linguistics	

Figure 1. The speech chain and the instruments that can be used to study it.

tures common to all mankind, those features which are now called "linguistic universals." Other aspects of the brain reflect learned behavior, for example details of one's native language which are not necessarily to be found in other linguistic communities. There is at present no instrumental technique for studying linguistic behavior directly and what we do know comes from the practical and theoretical work of linguists.

The brain sends the messages that initiate speech down neural pathways to the muscles of the speech mechanism, i.e., the brain initiates neural impulses and the impulses cause muscle contractions, gestures that set up ever-changing articulatory configurations. The gestures may be studied by electromyography and the configurations by radiographic techniques, although it would be wrong to think only of the former technique as being used for dynamic events while the latter has static applications. However, respiration, phonation, and articulation, in other words the various aspects of speech production, are amenable to a variety of instrumental procedures, including not only electromyography and radiography but also palatography and laryngoscopy.

Furthermore, once the lungs begin to force air out through the speech tract it also becomes possible to make measurements at different places within the body of air pressure and airflow, and the techniques for doing this give us additional useful information on speech production.

A message must be propagated through the air from the lips of a speaker to the ears of a listener. The medium changes. It is no longer nerves or muscles that we are studying but disturbances to air particles, the field of acoustics, and the instruments that we use for this purpose—the sound spectrograph, the oscilloscope, the pitch meter, the intensity meter, and the sound level meter—pick up signals with a microphone and subject them to analysis.

Vibrating air particles cause the eardrum of a listener to vibrate and the task of the ear is to change mechanical motion into nervous impulses again. The study of audiology is a study of reception and the transformation of energy into yet another medium. The ear, it is now believed, is intimately connected to not only the receiving end of the brain but also the speech production mechanism, and the study of perception, as opposed to reception, still has a long way to go since we know relatively little about how the brain actually handles incoming signals. Direct evidence is sparse and what we *do* know comes largely from people with brain damage, from experimental psychology, and from linguistics.

Most of our phonetic instrumentation, then, is used to study speech production and acoustics, although much of our acoustic knowledge can be turned from the analysis of speech to the synthesis of speech signals, i.e., artificial machine-produced speech, in order to set up experiments in speech perception. At either end of the speech chain is the brain, about which we still have much to learn and which is still not amenable to instrumental study.

1.6 THE WORLD OF THE PHONETICIAN

Everyone thinks he knows a little about history, geography, and physics, for example, but, to judge from cocktail party questions, most people have no idea what a phonetician does. There are occasional

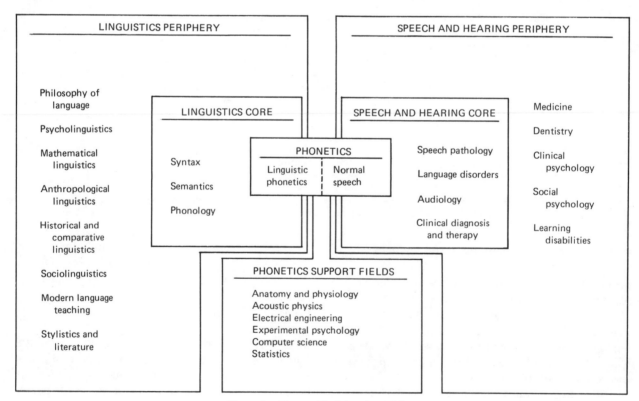

Figure 2. The world of the phonetician.

gropings in the direction of *Pygmalion* and the teaching of reading, but on the whole the phonetician has to begin his answers from suitably phrased remarks about the articulatory possibilities of man. Then comes the difficult part, because we do not seem to have a home; some of us are in the department of linguistics, some in communication disorders, some in electrical engineering, others are in specially designed programs, and so on. We have to explain that we conceive of ourselves as being at the center of a fascinating world at the point of overlap of many disciplines.

General linguistics has a core that all linguists study: syntax, semantics, phonology, and linguistic phonetics and a periphery comprising the philosophy of language, psycholinguistics, mathematical linguistics, anthropological linguistics, historical and comparative linguistics, sociolinguistics, modern language teaching, and stylistics and literature, which they may or may not become involved with. Likewise, communication disorders has a core that all practitioners master: normal speech and language, speech pathology and language disorders, audiology, and clinical diagnosis and therapy, and a periphery comprising aspects of medicine and dentistry, clinical and social psychology, and learning disabilities. Sitting right at the center of these two fields is linguistic phonetics/normal speech with anatomy and physiology, acoustic physics, electrical engineering, experimental psychology, computer science, and statistics as support disciplines.

Figure 2 tries to give some indication of the nature of this octopus, phonetics, and the student should try to feel his way into what the world of the phonetician[2] involves. In an age when students are expected to learn "nothing about everything" the author finds it refreshing to know that there are still disciplines where one may learn "everything about nothing." The problem of what to take for one's "all-college requirements" is solved automatically by branching out systematically from one's central core of interest.

---

[2]The term *speech scientist* tends to refer to someone well grounded in communication disorders and/or what I have called above "phonetics support fields" but without those interests and skills that characterize the linguistic phonetician. Ladefoged makes the following comment on p. 409 of *Dynamic Aspects of Speech Production* (see subsection 4.2.1, item 6): "There is an essential difference between the aims of linguists and the aims of speech science. What the linguist is trying to do is to describe the patterns that occur within each language. Speech scientists, on the other hand, . . . want to explain what people are doing when they talk and listen . . . The goals of these two groups of scientists are related, but they are by no means identical."

1.7 THE STUDENT IN THE LABORATORY

The beginning student is typically fascinated by but fearful of the laboratory. The fascination makes life easier for the teacher since the student is faced not by work but by bank upon bank of new toys that do wonderful and beautiful things, to say nothing of being useful. In all probability this fascination will remain until the end of the course and even grow stronger.

The apprehension, however, is not helpful. The student probably has a poor scientific background and imagines that even if he avoids electrocuting himself he will undoubtedly push the wrong button one day and break some frightfully expensive instrument. At the very least he fears he will ruin a group experiment 2 days before the grades are due in and incur everyone's wrath. He should not worry, however, since everyone learns to operate the equipment satisfactorily and instruments tend to die of old age rather than misuse providing that supervision is strict.

I have made the assumption throughout this book that each laboratory will have a printed set of instructions to give students, telling them exactly what settings to make for a particular task, what buttons to push and in which order, although there are those who refuse to do this on principle because it smacks too much of stifling initiative. This objection, however, ignores the fact that students with a weak science background can easily be discouraged when things fall apart and they are left face to face with a silent, unresponsive machine. It is comforting to them to know that there is always a baseline to return to; that they can start again rather than having to give up in despair. It is easy to produce a competent technician and, as has been pointed out, it is in the interpretation of the data that the challenge lies.

1.8 THE ORGANIZATION OF THE BOOK

The two major chapters in the book are concerned with acoustic and physiological instrumentation, respectively, and we might distinguish between the two by saying that acoustic signals are picked up by a microphone placed somewhere between the speaker's lips and the listener's ears in order to analyze them using the available instrumentation, whereas physiological data are obtained by placing something in or on a speaker's body. This "something" covers a range from tubes and face masks to fine wire electrodes, x-rays, false palates, and mirrors.

The examples that illustrate what can be done with each technique have been chosen to cover a wide range of problems in linguistics and speech pathology and, as a matter of policy, the same utterances have been used again and again in different sections to show what new light a different technique can throw on an already familiar problem. The net result should be strongly reinforcing and leave the student with a good grasp of those questions that constantly arise in the course of his work.

An attempt has been made to present most of the demonstration projects in a manner that will stimulate the joy of discovery. The problem is stated as if the answer were not known; i.e., the problem is presented as it would be in a research methods course. The interpretation then grows out of the data and little by little the student learns how to set up an experiment.

On the whole problems are illustrated by only one example, and we should all be aware that one cannot generalize from one example or even from many examples recorded by one speaker. However, care has been taken to choose illustrations that are either representative of results reported again and again in the literature or in agreement with isolated but large-scale studies.

Most of the data illustrated here were made by the author especially for this book using himself as a subject, although some (particularly those for African languages) were taken from previously published articles by the author. In all, five laboratories were used to produce these data: Indiana University Medical School (Indianapolis), The University of Wisconsin (Madison), The Haskins Laboratories (New Haven, Connecticut), RLE MIT (Cambridge), and Emerson College (Boston). Of the 441 illustrations, 26 are taken from the published work of other authors and recognized as such on the appropriate page. I would like to extend my thanks to those scholars for their cooperation. The illustrations themselves have been placed together at the end of the book with their pages perforated so that the reader may detach them and place them side by side on a table for comparison if so desired.

The book is seen as being appropriate for a one-term course of 3 hours a week for 12 or 15 weeks.

Furthermore, the book does not set out to review work in the anatomy and physiology of speech, acoustic phonetics, or speech perception, but, ranging as it does through those problems that can be usefully examined in a phonetics laboratory, it cannot help but touch briefly on much that one would learn in courses devoted to them. However, an effort has been made to cut down on new information that is not directly relevant to instrumental techniques. For example, source-filter theory has been presented in the simplest of terms and only when necessary, and physiological information has been presented in a manner that is largely self-explanatory.

Finally, it should be noted that not only is there a classified bibliography at the end of the book in Chapter 4 but also a subsection entitled "Readings" at the end of each technique. There are usually three items listed for each section, one being a "state of the art" paper or a general survey of the technique and the other two being articles that are fairly easy to read and, above all, that contain data to look at. This may mean, although it usually does not, that the article is of no great theoretical interest, but it should be borne in mind that our task is to get used to looking at and interpreting data. Furthermore, in most cases I have chosen articles that are readily available at most universities, e.g., articles in *The Journal of the Acoustical Society of America* or *Journal of Speech and Hearing Research*.

1.9 DEMYSTIFICATION

One of my main aims has been to demystify the subject and to the degree that I have succeeded much of the material may seem simple. However, by the end of the book it should all add up to a fairly large body of knowledge. The choice of details to be made explicit, even sometimes to the point of seeming to overstate the obvious, has been based largely on the questions which, predictably, year in and year out, will be asked by someone in the class.

Most beginners, even the brightest of them, find the research literature as a whole too forbidding since the bulk of it is presented in a manner that takes so much for granted and because some of it is pedagogically unsound, whatever its scientific merits. However, by the end of this course, students do come to realize that, if the subject is taken in small doses, it is not so difficult after all.

1.10 STATISTICAL PROCEDURES

The author spent a considerable amount of time trying to decide whether or not to deal with the question of statistical procedures. There is no doubt at all that students must at some stage learn what to do with all the measurements they have made, but it was decided, first, that a separate section on the question would stick out like a sore thumb and not fit in well with the present organization of the book; second, that to spread a treatment of statistical procedures around the book so as to make it less obtrusive would require problem sets at the end of each topic and increase the "work" at the expense of the "fun"; third, that the readings at the end of each section do, in any case, introduce the student to a wide variety of methodological and statistical procedures; and, finally, that there is a relatively large body of students who are anxious to gain insights into speech events but whose enthusiasm is dampened considerably at the very mention of the word "statistics"; I would like to keep up that enthusiasm, whatever the cost. Consequently, it is suggested that students wait until they have reached the stage where they have run an experiment such as the one the author reports in *Phonetica,* volume 33, pages 334–352, and come up with a large body of data that needs sophisticated statistical treatment. At that point they might look at Frederick Williams' book *Reasoning with Statistics* (see subsection 4.2.8) and learn, for example, how to apply the chi-square test "on the job." Such an approach to statistics seems to be less artificial and more acceptable to the student.

Of course, not all problems of experimental design are statistical in nature and students should always discuss the setting up of an investigation *before* embarking on hours of work in the laboratory, because a decision on what to measure is just as important as a knowledge of what to do with the measurements once they have been made.

1.11 NUMBERING

The following numbering system is used throughout this book: the first (leftmost) number is used for *chapters,* of which there are four. The second number is for *sections* and in Chapters 2 and 3 each section deals with a different instrumental technique. The third number is for *subsections* and in Chapters 2 and 3 almost all sections have the structure: 1. The instrumentation, 2. Operation, 3. Demonstration projects, 4. Reading, and 5. Student projects. The fourth number is for *topics* and examples from Chapters 2 and 3 are "vowels," "consonants," and "fundamental frequency." The fifth number is for *parts,* examples from Chapters 2 and 3 being "plosives," "liquids," and "intonation." The sixth number is for *items* and refers to: 1. The problem, 2. The data, and 3. The interpretation.

Some people are put off by numbering systems of any kind and to these I can only say, "Try to pretend they are not there." At least they cannot do any harm. However, most students welcome an explicit indication of the way the material has been organized and will note that it is possible to build up hierarchical branching "trees" from the present decimal numbering system, with the more general "chapters" at the top of the tree and the most specific "items" at the bottom.

2

Acoustic Instrumentation

2.1 A BEGINNING: TRANSDUCERS, VOLUME CONTROLS, DISPLAYS, AND TAPE RECORDERS

When students walk into a phonetics laboratory for the first time they are usually quite perplexed as they glance round at the meaningless collection of knobs, buttons, dials, and wires. Even in a highly technological age, it will be with some relief that they pick out a few familiar objects such as a microphone, a loudspeaker, or a tape recorder.

Experience suggests, however, that it would be wrong either to assume that even these basic tools are as well understood as the screwdriver or to hope that the student will learn to use them without instruction. Therefore, before embarking on the next 12 sections, each of which deals with a specific piece of instrumentation used in phonetics, a few words are said about a number of all-purpose pieces of equipment.

2.1.1 Transducers

Since the instruments we use to analyze sound are largely the products of the electrical engineer, we constantly need devices that will change sound energy into electrical energy or vice versa. Such devices are called transducers and we use them to transform disturbances in the air into changing voltages and currents which may then be amplified, displayed, or recorded. Two types of transducer that are discussed later (sections 3.1 and 3.2) are the air

pressure transducer, which converts changes in air pressure into a varying current, and the airflow transducer, which indirectly converts changes in airflow into an electrical current.

2.1.2 Microphones

The most common kind of transducer is the microphone, which converts air pressure into an electrical voltage or current. All microphones have a diaphragm, which is a tightly stretched membrane that vibrates backward and forward in response to the changes in air pressure which characterize an incoming speech signal. Behind the diaphragm, and directly connected to it, there may be a pack of carbon granules with an electrical current running through it. As the incoming sound pressure changes, so too does the pressure on the carbon and the resistance of the granules to electrical flow. Alternatively, the diaphragm may be connected to a type of crystal that gives out a voltage when squeezed or to a small coil of wire suspended in a magnetic field such that it generates a voltage as it moves backward and forward together with the diaphragm. Another kind is the condenser microphone, which has a metallic plate fixed close to the back of the diaphragm such that the current flowing through the plate varies with the pressure on the diaphragm.

In all cases a pressure input is converted into an electrical output, the condenser microphone being the most accurate of them all, but expensive, whereas the carbon microphone is inexpensive and, as one might expect as a result, the least accurate. The other two both have a fairly uniform response throughout the frequency range used in speech, the crystal microphone being the cheaper but less reliable of the two.

2.1.3 Volume Controls

The electrical output from a transducer is usually quite small, too small in fact to drive either a display unit, a loudspeaker, or an analyzer. In such cases it is necessary to make the signal larger by the use of an amplifier, which allows the small input current from the transducer to control a much larger flow within a vacuum tube or transistor. The output from the amplifier will sound louder when played back through a loudspeaker than it would unamplified.

On other occasions, however, an electrical signal may be larger than is needed; it may, for example, have a voltage large enough to damage a piece of equipment and in such cases the signal must be scaled down by an attenuator, the output from which will sound softer when played back through a loudspeaker than it would unattenuated.

2.1.4 Loudspeakers and Headphones

We have seen how it is possible to convert an acoustic pressure into an electrical voltage or current. The loudspeaker does the opposite; it converts an electrical voltage or current into an acoustic pressure and is also a transducer. In principle, only the carbon granule microphone could not in reverse function as a loudspeaker, but in practice only the coil is commonly used for playback purposes. The coil travels backward and forward around a fixed magnet as the input signal arrives and controls the movement of a large diaphragm made of thin cardboard. Since the diaphragm covers a considerable area, it sets a large number of air particles into vibration and the listener will hear a sound wave.

Headphones, or earphones, are merely small loudspeakers positioned over the listener's ears by a support structure. It should not be assumed, however, that earphones, because of their size, are necessarily of poorer quality than loudspeakers. Moderately expensive earphones, in fact, usually give better results than similarly priced loudspeakers and, in addition, have the advantages of shutting out external noise and of delivering a controlled signal more accurately to the ears.

Sometimes the phonetician will need to listen in stereo, not quite as we do for music when we have the signals from two differently placed microphones delivered separately to two loudspeakers or two headphones, microphone A to loudspeaker A and microphone B to loudspeaker B, but dichotically, i.e., the signal from channel A to the right headphone is totally different from that from channel B, which goes to the left headphone. Stereo headsets have both their input leads entering the support structure near the left ear.

2.1.5 Meters

Once an acoustic pressure has been converted into an electrical analog it is often desirable to measure the strength of the signal. This can be achieved by the use of a meter, which is a device that enables a needle to be deflected around a scale as the input current changes. The current flows through a coil suspended between two magnets and, since the coil has a hinge at one end and the needle at the other, the needle will move around the scale as the coil is attracted by a magnet when the current flows. Some meters measure changes in current whereas others handle voltage; some have a needle on a scale but others are digital, i.e., numbers appear on a screen.

2.1.6 Display Screens

Section 2.3 examines the use of the oscilloscope, but it is useful at this stage to point out that an electrical signal may not only be measured on a meter but also displayed on a screen for temporary or permanent inspection. The cathode ray tube, or TV monitor screen, amplifies an incoming signal and projects it, left to right in time and up and down in amplitude, onto a screen which lights up when struck by a stream of electrons. Once the image has moved with time from the left-hand side of the screen to the right, it dies out and the tracing begins again on the left. Thus the visual representation of the changing electrical signal is of brief duration and is useful only for monitoring purposes. If a permanent record is desired, either the screen must be photographed or a memory must be built in to retain the image.

2.1.7 Tape Recorders

The tape recorder is an instrument that enables one to make a permanent record of an acoustic signal and play it back. As such it performs the same task as a disk-cutter and gramophone.

When the phonetician wishes to record a sample of spoken material he speaks into a microphone and puts the signal into the tape recorder through the connection labeled "microphone input" (Mike). The input signal is amplified and the current is led to a recording head, where the flow creates a magnetic field that imprints an analog of the sound wave onto magnetically coated plastic tape moving at 7½, 3¾, or 1⅞ inches per second (sec) across the head. The tape passes an erase head before arriving at the recording head, thus removing any previously recorded signal, and may subsequently be passed over a playback head once the desired signal has been recorded.

The student thus has a choice of tape speeds, although 7½ inches per sec gives a higher quality recording, such as is normally needed in phonetic research and obligatory for instrumental work. He must also select either "record" or "play," although in order to record one must first push the "record" button and then the one marked "play" while "record" is still pressed down. This double procedure is a safeguard against accidental erasure.

One should take care not to twist the tape from back to front while threading it onto the recorder at the beginning of the session. Most tape has a shiny side and a dull side, the former facing the outside and the latter passing across the heads. Tape should be quite thick, i.e., 1.0 or 1.5 mil, to avoid recording on adjacent channels of the tape, i.e., to avoid ending up with one recording partly superimposed on another. Although thin, long-playing tape may be cheaper, it has its disadvantages.

Most tape recorders have a voltmeter, or VU meter, which indicates the strength of the incoming signal. Since most signals need to be amplified before recording, it is necessary to turn up the volume by adjusting the "record level" knob until the needle deflects to no higher than −1, i.e., just before entering the red zone, at maximum deflection. If the needle *does* enter the red zone the recording will be distorted, but if it deflects only to a point well below zero, even at maximum deflection, the recording will not be loud enough. This principle holds true for the use of all instruments with an input level dial.

Before actually recording the sample, one should have a trial session during which the best loudness level is set and the trial is played back in order to see that everything is as it should be.

Stereophonic tape recorders have two separate inputs for recording on the right and left channels of the tape and either one output into which stereo headphones may be plugged, plus a "mono"/ "stereo" selector switch, or two outputs, one for the right channel and one for the left. Leads from the latter pair may be connected directly to two separate loudspeakers or indirectly to a single stereo headset,

in which case the output leads and the headphones are plugged into a junction box having two switches, one of which is capable of delivering the signal from the right channel either to the right ear only, the left ear only, both ears, or neither, and the other switching the signal from the left channel in similar fashion.

The student is urged to read through the manufacturer's operation manual, which is usually written for the layman, before embarking on a recording session.

2.2 THE SOUND SPECTROGRAPH

2.2.1 The Instrumentation

The sound spectrograph is the single most important instrument in the phonetics laboratory because of its versatility and because it is easy to operate and relatively inexpensive. When a laboratory is being set up it is usually the first piece of equipment to be ordered, and in institutions with small budgets it is often the only instrument.

Koenig, Dunn, and Lacey gave the first published account of the sound spectrograph (see Illustration 1) in 1946, describing it as follows: "The sound spectrograph is a wave analyzer which produces a permanent visual record showing the distribution of energy in both frequency and time." Frequency (which we perceive as musical pitch) is represented on the vertical axis of the paper and covers the speech range from 0 to 8000[1] Hertz (Hz, cycles per second, cps, c/s or ⁓), whereas duration (time) is represented on the horizontal axis and normally covers 2.4 sec. Intensity (which we perceive as loudness) is represented by the degree of darkness of the marks on the paper and is thus a third dimension. Since all speech events are ultimately analyzable into their frequency, duration, and intensity components, the sound spectrograph gives us information on all the parameters of speech and enables us to carry out an acoustic analysis of both segmental and suprasegmental features. Acoustic information can be obtained on vowels, consonants, fundamental frequency, intensity, and duration.

The instrument is sometimes known by the trade name Sona-Graph and the visual record presented on paper is called a "spectrogram," "sonagram," or "voice print." In fact, the reader will note

---

[1] When phoneticians are talking, they tend to give figures over 999 in hundreds unless they are exact multiples of 1000, e.g., "... harmonics at 29 hundred, 3 thousand and 31 hundred Hz..."

throughout this book many words ending in either "-graph," "-gram," or "-scope," and it is useful to point out at this early stage that words ending in "-graph" refer to instruments that produce pieces of paper with data written on them, whereas words ending in "-gram" refer to the pieces of paper produced. Words ending in "-scope" refer to instruments that display the data not on pieces of paper but on a monitor screen.

In order to understand what the spectrograph is capable of doing, we should begin by examining data from an oscilloscope (see section 2.3). Four basic wave types are of interest to us in phonetics: a) the sine wave, b) the complex wave, c) the damped wave, and d) white noise.

Illustration 2 shows a 200-Hz sine wave recorded at 2 milliseconds (msec) per division and 5 volts (V) per division (see subsection 2.3.1). The sine wave is a representation of the motion of a vibrating body, such as a pendulum, backward and forward about its rest position with constant amplitude and frequency, i.e., it moves the same distance on either side of the rest position and repeats the cyclic motion in identical periods of time forever and ever in the absence of friction. Amplitude is shown on the vertical axis and time on the horizontal axis. The tuning fork approximates this condition, and a sustained whistle looks very like a sine wave on the oscilloscope. Sine waves, however, are not found in speech.

Illustration 3 shows a complex wave with two components from two oscillators set at 200 Hz and 2500 Hz, respectively. It was recorded at 2 msec per division and 5 V per division. The complex wave is a representation of a vibrating body moving backward and forward about its rest position in a non-simple fashion with momentary reverses in direction one or more times per cycle, although, like the sine wave, with each cyclic motion repeated in identical periods of time to infinity in the absence of friction. A complex wave may normally be approximated merely by striking two or more different sized tuning forks at the same time.

Illustration 4 shows a complex wave very like the one described above (i.e., it was put together from the outputs of two oscillators set at 200 Hz and 2500 Hz, respectively) except for the fact that it grows in amplitude over the first four divisions only to be damped over the final six. It was recorded at 5 msec per division and 1 V per division and the total signal had a duration of 60 msec, with a rise-fall time

of 30 msec, i.e., 30 msec of amplitude growth (rise) and 30 msec of damping (fall). A damped complex wave is to be seen between 20 and 50 msec as measured from the leftmost side of the photograph. Both simple and complex waves may be damped, i.e., they may lose energy and show ever smaller amplitude across time, finally dying out altogether, although their frequency will remain constant, other things being equal.

Vowels and sonorant consonants have wave forms of this kind. Each cycle of vibration of the vocal folds produces a complex wave that loses energy so rapidly that a second vibration is necessary a moment later, which produces a second complex wave. A fundamental frequency of 100 Hz means 100 vibrations of the vocal folds per sec or the production of 100 damped complex waves—nonrepetitive but repeated.

Illustration 5 shows white noise recorded at 5 msec per division and Illustration 6 the same signal recorded at 1 msec per division. White noise is a representation of the random motion of a vibrating body and may be synthesized by combining an infinity of components of equal amplitude at all frequencies. White noise is not found in speech, but speech noise is of a similar nature and represents random motion which, when analyzed, shows that the components in a restricted frequency range are of greater amplitude than those elsewhere in the spectrum. The energy in fricatives may be described in this way.

In short, a given wave form with displacement/amplitude/intensity plotted on the vertical axis and time on the horizontal axis represents the backward and forward motion of any air particle between the lips of the speaker and the ear of the listener.

Fourier analysis is a mathematical tool for analyzing a complex wave into its sine wave components. If we allow ourselves the liberty of an analogy that is not quite correct, we may visualize the components as a set of tuning forks, let us say a set of 177 tuning forks spaced out every 45 Hz or a set of 27 tuning forks spaced out every 300 Hz throughout the speech range (0–8000 Hz) and conceive of a set of instructions for which forks to hit and how hard to hit them at a given moment in time. The combined musical "chord" would sound rather like the complex wave being subject to Fourier analysis.

What the sound spectrograph essentially does is to carry out a frequency analysis across time of a speech sample and present it visually on paper with time on the horizontal and frequency on the vertical axis, i.e., it sorts out the individual tuning forks in the "chord." Intensity is a third dimension realized as the darkness of the marks on the paper.

From an articulatory point of view, vowels, fricatives, and plosives are the products of an open, a narrowed, and a closed vocal tract, respectively, and the acoustic end products of these articulations are very different. Vowels, and the in many ways acoustically similar nasals, liquids, and nonsyllabic vocoids (semi-vowels), have a clear formant structure, a formant being a region of the spectrum where the frequency components are relatively large in amplitude. If intensity were physically represented as a third dimension, a spectrogram of an utterance would look like a contour map with mountain peaks and valleys. An utterance comprising a series of connected vowels would look like a series of ridges with valleys between them, the high peaks corresponding to the high energy regions of the spectrum, i.e., the formants.

The fricatives show random energy distributed unevenly throughout the spectrum and the plosives are characterized by the acoustic consequences of their pressure and release stages, viz., no energy during the pressure period followed by a brief burst of energy at the moment of release.

The spectrograph usually offers a choice between two filter settings: wideband (or broadband) (300 Hz) and narrowband (45 Hz). Since the use of a wideband filter for an utterance on a fundamental frequency between 80 Hz and 150 Hz will cause two or three harmonics to be analyzed together at any moment in time, the print-out blends harmonics together into the broad dark bands which represent the formants. Formants stand out clearly but individual harmonics do not. A wideband filter is imprecise with respect to frequency. Conversely, however, it is precise with respect to time and is therefore capable of representing individual vocal fold pulses discretely as vertical striations. It is particularly good for low-pitched adult male voices.

A narrowband filter has the opposite characteristics. It is precise with respect to frequency and therefore separates the harmonics on the print-out, although formants are more difficult to read, particularly when the harmonics are rising and the formants falling or vice versa. It is imprecise with respect to time and therefore does not sense individual vocal fold pulses. It is particularly good for high-pitched adult female voices. On the whole the instrument exhibits a degree of sex and age bias since data from adult males are easier to analyze than data from adult females. Data from children are often relatively difficult to handle.

In addition to a choice of filter, the spectrograph offers a means of representing intensity as a function of frequency at a given moment during an utterance: the section. If, for example, a section is taken in the middle of the steady state portion of a vowel, and the spectrogram is turned so that the left-hand side is at the bottom, the intensity/frequency analysis of that vowel will look just like the mountain peaks and valleys mentioned earlier.

2.2.2 Operation

The instrument is composed of two parts: a recorder and an analyzer. Illustration 7 shows a schematic representation of the basic method of the sound spectrograph.

When the spectrograph is set to "record," the microphone or tape recorder input is connected to a recording surface which, for most instruments, is around the edge of a large wheel. The wheel, as it is turned by the motor, first passes an erase head and then a record head; 2.4 sec elapse before the wheel turns full circle, at which point it begins to erase the beginning of the utterance and to record again. This limits the use of the instrument to utterances of no more than 2.4 sec (about four lexical items or one small sentence).

When set to "reproduce," the analyzer is connected to a stylus or needle which tracks automatically up a revolving spindle in such a way that the chosen filter analyzes low-frequency components when the stylus is at the bottom and high-frequency components when the stylus is at the top of the spindle. On top of the recording wheel is a drum, around which the recording paper is fastened. When the stylus is pressed against the paper and tracks upward, energy in the signal causes the paper to blacken.

Since the spectrograph in its modern form is a self-contained unit, no other equipment is required except a microphone or a tape recorder and connecting leads. Choices have to be made such as "sectioner on"/"sectioner off" or "wide band"/"narrow band," "linear scale"/"logarithmic scale," and record and reproduce levels have to be set by using the voltmeter, but operation is very simple and limited to turning the "record"/"reproduce" controls. In practice, the biggest problems for the learner are to gauge 2.4 sec and to maintain an appropriate speaking rate and volume once the levels have been set.

We are now ready to look at and interpret data for representative vowels and consonants and for suprasegmental features.

2.2.3 Demonstration Projects

2.2.3.1 *Vowels*

2.2.3.1.0.1 *The problem* From a pedagogical point of view it is probably still most satisfactory to use as a first approximation in introductory courses an older articulatory/auditory approach to vowels, which classifies them according to the highest point of the tongue in the mouth. Such a classification is best illustrated by the traditional vowel quadrilateral, which displays vowels on a two-dimensional matrix, with front/back on the horizontal axis and open/close on the vertical axis (see Illustration 8).

It is also necessary to state whether the lips are spread or rounded. Not even implicit in such an approach is the fact that pharynx width changes considerably from vowel to vowel, changes that are on the whole, especially in languages that do not use variations in pharynx width for specific linguistic purposes such as vowel harmony, predictable once we know the position of the highest point of the tongue in the mouth. Close vowels, for example, have a wide pharynx, whereas open vowels have a narrow pharynx.

These parameters, however, do not make complete acoustic sense, particularly with respect to the set of back vowels. From an acoustic point of view, it is preferable to classify vowels according to: a) A: the cross-sectional area at the point of maximum constriction in the vocal tract (x min) between the glottis and the lips, b) V: the volume of air behind x min, and c) le: the length of the vocal tract between x min and the lips.

The acoustic results of a variation in A are well seen in a set of front vowels [i], [e], and [ɛ][2], which have a rather similar point of maximum constriction,

---

[2]Throughout this volume all examples will use either normal English spelling, shown in quotation marks, e.g., ''part''; a phonemic transcription, shown in obliques, e.g., /pɑːt/, which indicates contrastive units within the sound system of the language in question; or a phonetic transcription conforming to the ''Principles of the International Phonetic Association'' (IPA), shown in square brackets, e.g., [pʰɑːt]. Since the author is a native speaker of R.P. British English (with some reflexes of his earlier Black Country dialect from the Midlands), examples from English will usually reflect this rather than General American or regional dialect forms.

where an increase in A results in a rise in the value of the first formant (F_1).

A set of back vowels such as [u], [o], [ɔ], and [ɑ], however, has a rather constant A but very different points of maximum constriction such that V varies considerably within the set. Since x min for [u] is at 9 centimeters (cm) from the glottis, whereas that for [ɑ] is at only 4 cm, the value of V for [u] is greater than that for [ɑ]. The acoustic results of an increase in V are a fall in the value of F_1. For any give x min, the value of le may be increased merely by rounding and protruding the lips, the acoustic result of which is to lower all formants, particularly F_3 for alveolars and F_2 for palatals. It is clear that there is some merit in talking about palatal vowels (e.g., [i]), velar vowels (e.g., [u]), and pharyngeal vowels (e.g., [ɑ]).

2.2.3.1.0.2 *The data* Almost all the illustrations in this section are presented as paired wideband/narrowband spectrograms, the former placed first on a page and the latter immediately below them for comparison. This has been done because wide- and narrowband spectrograms highlight different aspects of the same speech event and the student will profit from looking at different representations of the same utterance.

Furthermore, a majority of the illustrations have been grouped into twos or threes and placed in one of two carrier sentences, ''Say . . . please'' with the intonation contour [‿---‿] or ''Say a . . . again'' with the intonation contour [‿‿.---.‿], in order for the student to see what the utterances look like in a natural speaking environment. The exceptions are, first, the nasal and liquid consonants whose characteristics are not always easy to identify in the middle of a piece of running speech and are more conveniently illustrated by rather carefully spoken utterances, and, second, the phrases and sentences that constitute most of the illustrations after number 173.

Illustrations 9–16 show a set of front vowels, all with lips spread, which show the acoustic effect of an increase in A. In reading this set, [i], [e], [ɛ], [a], the vowels are progressively more open, the position of the highest point of the tongue in the mouth becomes ever lower, and the distance between the front teeth becomes greater as the lower jaw falls. For [a], in fact, the tongue becomes so low in the mouth that the narrowest point in the vocal tract is in the pharynx.

Illustrations 17–24 show a set of back vowels, [ɑ] with lips neutral to spread, and [ɔ], [o], and [u] with lips rounded, which show the acoustic effect of an increase in V. Since [ɑ] has an x min at only 4 cm from the glottis, whereas [u] has an x min at 9 cm from the glottis, the values of *V* increase throughout the set. These values are compounded by the fact that the pharynx is wider for [u] than for [ɑ], since the low tongue position of the latter thrusts the root of the tongue back into the pharynx.

Illustrations 25–28 show two half-close front vowels, [e] and [ø], which have identical tongue positions and differ only in that [e] has spread lips whereas [ø] has rounded lips. They show the acoustic effect of an increase in *le*.

2.2.3.1.0.3 *The interpretation* Formant frequency measurements may be made by placing a transparent ruler across the spectrogram from a calibration mark on the left-hand margin to the corresponding calibration mark on the right-hand margin. The black marks in the margins are to be taken as the center of the calibration frequencies and are spaced out every 500 Hz (0.5 kHz) in this book. The abbreviation kHz stands for kiloHertz, which equals 1000 Hz. Alternatively, a transparent grid showing the frequency scale on the vertical axis and the time scale on the horizontal axis may be placed over a spectrogram to obtain measurements of vowel formants. Furthermore, it will be noted that the author prefers to set the sound spectrograph so that there is a mirror image around the zero line, i.e., the marks below 0 Hz are a perfect mirror image of those above it. In this way one can be absolutely certain where the zero line is.

Measurements should be made during the steady state of the vowel, not during the transition from the previous consonant or to the following consonant. This task is made much easier when the vowel is of long duration. Spectrograms of vowels uttered at a fast tempo tend to have little or no steady state so that one has to take the highest value when the initial transition rises and the final transition falls in frequency or the lowest value when the initial transition falls and the final transition rises in frequency. When both the initial and the final transitions rise, or both fall, and the tempo is fast one is often reduced to making an estimate of the formant frequency at some midpoint in time.

It has been noted that most of the illustrations throughout this section are of both wide- and narrowband spectrograms. The wideband spectrograms are produced using a 300-Hz wideband filter for analysis and therefore harmonics spaced less than 300 Hz apart (such as they are for most utterances by male speakers, who usually have a fundamental frequency below 300 Hz, and some female speakers, who often have a fundamental frequency below 300

Hz) are blended together into a broad horizontal formant band. Measurements should be made at the center of the formant.

The narrowband spectrograms are produced using a 45-Hz narrowband filter for analysis, and therefore all harmonics are kept separate and seen as narrow horizontal lines for both male and female speakers. Since the harmonics are a reflection of the fundamental frequency, whereas the formants reflect the resonance chambers in the vocal tract, and since the two are on the whole independent of each other, a prolonged vowel uttered on a rising fundamental frequency will show the harmonics rising through the constant formant areas, and a diphthong uttered on a level fundamental frequency will show the formants rising or falling through constant harmonics.

One should at this stage mention the often neglected fact that we all have different eyes and that therefore when several students look at the same spectrogram, from the same distance, in the same light, they see different things. As a result, students should during the course of the demonstration projects in this section look at the illustrations with their glasses on and their glasses off, from close up, from a middle distance, and from relatively far away until they have found the conditions under which they see what the discussion suggests they should be seeing. The process involves being able to see enough detail, but not too much. It is difficult to interpret a spectrogram when you cannot see the wood for the trees.

The vowel illustrations also show sections taken at points in time in the middle of the steady state of the vowel. Whereas spectrograms give us information on frequency as a function of time, i.e., the frequency components of a vowel at any moment in time, sections give us data on amplitude as a function of frequency, i.e., on the intensity of the harmonics at different frequencies throughout the speech spectrum. The sections themselves may use either a wide- or a narrowband filter, in this case wideband sections on the wideband spectrograms and vice versa.

Table 1 shows measurements made from these illustrations and gives us data on the vowels under investigation. The formant frequency data may then be plotted on an acoustic vowel chart[3] as in Illustration 29.

---

[3]Such as the one on page 51 of Joos, M. 1948. Acoustic phonetics. *Language, monograph 23* (Suppl.).

Table 1. Formant frequency and intensity measurements taken from the illustrations

Illustration number	Vowel	Formant frequency (Hz)		Intensity (in arbitrary units—mm— from the narrowband spectrograms)	
		F_1	F_2	F_1	F_2
11	i	250	2250	28	21
12	e	400	2050	29	27
15	ɛ	550	1975	29	20
16	a	800	1600	28	26
19	ɑ	700	1000	29	29
20	ɔ	500	850	29	21
23	o	375	800	29	24
24	u	300	700	28	23
27	e	400	2200	28	23
28	ø	350	1750	27	23

2.2.3.2 *Consonants*
2.2.3.2.1 *Plosives*
2.2.3.2.1.1 *The problem*

From an articulatory point of view plosives may be said to have five stages: stop, pressure, release, aspiration, and transition. During the brief stop stage an upper (passive) and a lower (active) articulator, e.g., the upper and lower lips, are brought completely together in such a way as to prevent the airstream from moving through the oral cavity, the nasal cavity being shut off by raising the soft palate against the posterior wall of the pharynx. In the pressure stage it is generally assumed that air is being forced out of the lungs so that pressure builds up behind the stop. A definition of this kind would not include the implosives, ejectives, and clicks, which would be described in similar but not identical terms. In the brief release stage, the two articulators forming the stop are drawn away from each other, allowing the compressed air to escape. A fourth stage, aspiration, may be considered in those cases when voicing does not begin until sometime after the release and this in its turn is followed by a brief transition stage, during which the articulatory configurations are changing rapidly from those of the consonant to those of the following vowel.

Each stage is also marked by relatively discrete acoustic events. Segmentation of the speech continuum is not always easy and often quite impossible but plosives are fairly amenable to segmentation.

The pressure stage is sought for first. Since the vocal tract is shut off during this stage there will be no disturbance to the air beyond the lips for a microphone to pick up. No energy will be recorded and the spectrogram will show blank paper for a period that is in marked contrast to the formant structure of the surrounding vowels. There may or may not be voicing during the pressure stage. If the vocal folds are vibrating, vertical striations will be seen on the baseline (i.e., at very low frequencies) on a wideband and the first harmonic on a narrowband spectrogram. These disturbances are propagated through the body tissue.

The stop stage is marked at the moment in time when the formants of the preceding vowel cease. It is normal for the first formant to continue in time a little beyond higher formants.

When the air compressed behind a stop is released it is forced through an initially very small gap and turbulent noise is generated, which excites the small cavity at the place of articulation and the larger cavity between the place of articulation and the lips. This release stage lasts for only 20 msec and is marked on the wideband spectrogram by a sudden vertical spike, which often runs through the whole frequency spectrum in the case of dental and alveolar plosives but is confined to certain frequencies for plosives at other places of articulation. The energy in the spike, which is called the burst, is not of equal intensity throughout all frequencies and, although the alveolars show energy throughout the spectrum, the region above 4000 Hz often predominates. The fronted velars have an energy peak between 2000 Hz and 4000 Hz, whereas the retracted velars have a burst with a rather lower frequency concentration. The bilabials have a burst peak between 500 Hz and 1500 Hz and often so little energy above 1500 Hz that it is not detected at all by the spectrograph.

Once the pressure has been released, air from the lungs begins to excite the whole vocal tract and the aspiration stage, when present, is characterized by brief duration random noise after the release spike and the transition by the onset of formant structure, a structure which has values changing over time until the steady state of the following vowel is reached. Transitions can begin during the aspiration stage. When one traces backward in time through the steady state formants of a vowel and through the transitions from a preceding consonant a point will be reached, although sometimes only by extrapolation, on the release spike of the consonant which is called the locus (plural, loci ['loʊsaɪ]). Loci (L) are useful cues to place of articulation in spite of the fact that they are not physical events but only places from which formants appear to come or toward which they point.

2.2.3.2.1.2 *The data* Illustrations 30–47 show voiceless plosives and Illustrations 48–65 voiced plosives at three places of articulation (bilabial, blade-alveolar, and velar), each followed by three vowels, [i], [a], and [u]. These three vowels are chosen because they represent articulatory and acoustic extremes: maximally front/back, maximally open/close, and with extreme F_1 and F_2 values.

2.2.3.2.1.3 *The interpretation* The stop is well seen in Illustration 55 [da] and the pressure stage in Illustration 54 [ba]. This pressure stage has a typical duration of 80 msec. The release is clearly seen in Illustration 31 [ti] and less clearly in Illustration 38 [ka]. Bursts are seen in Illustrations 36 [pa], 37 [ta], and 38 [ka]. The burst for [p] has most of its energy below 2000 Hz, that for [t] covers most of the spectrum between the baseline and 8000 Hz, and that for [k] spans the lower and middle part of the spectrum up to 4700 Hz. Aspiration may be seen in Illustration 31 [ti], but sometimes all we see is a gap between the release spike and the onset of the transition as the random energy after the release is of such low intensity.

The F_1 transitions (see Illustrations 54 [ba], 55 [da], and 56 [ga]) are similar for all plosives since they all have a very low locus 1 at about 200 Hz. Hence there is a rising transition to a following vowel and a falling transition from a preceding vowel. Since [a] has a much higher F_1 than [i] and [u], the extent of the transition will be greater to the open vowel than to the close vowels (compare Illustrations 53 [gi] and 56 [ga]).

F_2 transitions (see Illustrations 48–50 [bi], [di], [gi], 54–56 [ba], [da], [ga], and 60–62 [bu], [du], [gu]) differ depending on the place of articulation of the plosives and are therefore good place cues. Bilabials have a low locus 2 at about 800 Hz so the F_2 transitions rise to all vowels. Alveolars have a locus 2 at about 1800 Hz so the F_2 transitions rise a little to [i], stay level to [ɛ], and fall to other vowels. Velars do not have an invariant locus 2 but rather one as high as 3000 Hz before front vowels, with a resultant falling transition, and another much lower one before back vowels, with transitions that rise or fall depending on the vowel. It will be seen from Illustrations 55 [da] and 56 [ga] that the blade-alveolar and velar plosives are distinguished from each other more by the F_3 and F_4 transitions than by the transitions to and from F_2.

The voice bar is well illustrated in Illustrations 50 [gi] (wideband) and 51 [bi] (narrowband) and its absence is apparent in Illustration 43 [tu], although in none of these supposedly voiceless plosives are the vocal folds totally inactive, and, as a consequence, it is best to make voicing judgments by looking for the first and second harmonics on the narrowband spectrograms. A study of voice onset time (VOT) in English would normally show that voicing starts immediately at the release for the so-called voiced plosives in word initial position in English, a language where truly voiced plosives are usually found only in word medial and final position. However, the speaker for these illustrations (the author) usually exhibits features of a dialect that has voicing before the release, during the pressure period, even in word initial position (see Illustration 217, ''a bid''). Voicing starts 55 msec after the release for the voiceless plosive in Illustration 47 [ku].

2.2.3.2.2 *Fricatives*

2.2.3.2.2.1 *The problem* From an articulatory point of view fricatives are characterized by the bringing together of an upper and a lower articulator in such a way that, although there may be considerable contact laterally between the two, there is a narrow channel, usually down the midline, through which the air from the lungs is forced. Perceptually, we hear what is known as friction in such cases. Acoustically, we find random noise, which is of maximum intensity only within a certain frequency range of the spectrum. These random disturbances of the air are caused by turbulence set up at the front end of the narrow tube which is the point of maximum constriction. In the absence of voicing this turbulence is the sole energy source for the fricative, and the resonating cavities of the vocal tract respond to it. As a result, even in the absence of vibrating vocal folds, one may sing a song on the fricatives, using their natural resonance frequencies to give the impression of pitch. For example, the sequence [x], [ʃ], [s], [ç] forms a rising sequence. Try singing "Three Blind Mice" on various allophones of /s/ and /ʃ/, once allowing the lip position to change from "note" to "note" and again with the lips spread throughout the song. For each articulatory position there are different natural resonance frequencies and hence a different distribution of energy within the spectrum. This can easily be seen on a spectrogram, especially in a section.

Lip rounding will lower the resonance frequency of a fricative and palatalization will raise it. In addition, the central groove through which the air is forced may be either "broad," i.e., extensive from side to side but not deep, as in [ʃ], or "narrow," i.e., not extensive from side to side but deep, as in [s]. Other things being equal, a narrow groove will raise the resonance frequencies and a lengthening of the groove from front to back will lower them. Furthermore, the overall energy of the random noise across the spectrum may be high, as in [s] and [ʃ], or low, as in [θ] or [f]. Finally, it should be noted that the range of variation for the various allophones of /s/ and /ʃ/ is quite wide such that, for example, /s/ before /u/ may have a natural resonance frequency lower than /ʃ/ before /i/.

The majority of articulation cases in speech clinics involve a rather small misplacing of the articulators, resulting in either the wrong type of grooving, the wrong length of the groove front to back, or the wrong place of articulation. Inappropriate labialization or palatalization or the lack of it may compound the effect, as may lateral rather than central direction of the airstream.

The presence or absence of a voice bar and of vertical striations through the random noise marks fricatives as being either voiced or voiceless.

2.2.3.2.2.2 *The data* Ilustrations 66–83 show voiceless fricatives at three places of articulation, labio-dental, blade alveolar, and blade post-alveolar, each followed by [i], [ɑ], and [u]. [f] is low energy whereas [s] and [ʃ] are high energy fricatives. [ʃ] has some lip rounding and a long constriction

whereas [f] and [s] have spread lips and a short constriction. [s] has a narrow groove, whereas [f]] and [ʃ] have a broad groove.

Their voiced counterparts [v], [z], and [ʒ] are shown in Illustrations 84–101 also followed by [i], [ɑ], and [u], but with the ordering of the consonants and vowels changed for comparative purposes.

The voiceless fricatives have sections superimposed—wideband sections on the wideband spectrograms and vice versa.

2.2.3.2.2.3 *The interpretation* Spectral energy peaks are good place cues and the sections show that [s] has random energy between 3 and 8 kHz and above, with peaks at about 4500 Hz and 7500 Hz, whereas [ʃ] has random energy between 2 and 6 kHz, with a peak at about 4000 Hz. Since female vocal tracts are smaller than those of males, the resonance frequencies for a given fricative will be higher and an [s] uttered by an adult female may have peak energy at frequencies as high as 12,000 Hz, which is off the spectrogram when the spectrograph is set at 0–8000 Hz, as it usually is.

A comparison of [v] (and [ð]) with either [s] or [ʃ] shows that the overall energy level of the former is much lower than that of the latter.

Illustrations 67 and 79, 68 and 80 show that the energy distribution of [s] before [i] (2800 Hz to 8000 Hz) is higher than that of [s] before [u] (2300 Hz to 8000 Hz) and that of [ʃ] before [i] (1900 Hz to 6700 Hz) is higher than that of [ʃ] before [u] (1200 Hz to 6500 Hz) because of the effects of both the lip position and the tongue position of the following vowel. A comparison of [ç], the narrow groove palatalized post-alveolar fricative, with [ʃ], the broad groove post-alveolar fricative, or of [s], the narrow groove dental fricative (a common form of lisp), with [θ], the broad groove dental fricative, would show that the narrow groove versions have their energy distributed higher up in the frequency spectrum.

Transitional cues are useful for determining the place of articulation of fricatives too, and Illustrations 88, 94, and 100 show that the F_2 transition in [vɑ] rises, whereas those in [zɑ] and [ʒɑ] fall.

The lack of a voice bar, i.e., energy in the first or first few harmonics, in Illustration 69 [fi] and the presence of one in Illustration 87 [vi] show [f] to be voiceless and [v] to be voiced.

Finally, it should be noted that the Kay sound spectrograph boosts the amplitude of the higher frequencies in the speech spectrum. Otherwise the relatively weak energy immediately below 8000 Hz would not be represented on spectrograms at all. As a result, energy peaks at 7000 Hz that appear to be of equal intensity to those at 3000 Hz are in fact not so. It is not always clear in the literature whether this correction factor has been taken into account or not.

2.2.3.2.3 *Affricates*

2.2.3.2.3.1 *The problem* From an articulatory point of view an affricate may be described either as a plosive immediately followed by a homorganic fricative (i.e., one made at the same place of articulation) or as a slowly released plosive. [tʃ] and [dʒ] are considered units in English phonology, while [ts] and [dz], although they are affricates phonetically speaking, are not, since they almost always contain a morpheme boundary, as in [kæt-s]. [tɹ] and [dɹ] on the other hand might well be considered affricates in English, although they rarely are. A reading of affricates on spectrograms presents few problems, because they are seen quite obviously to be plosives followed by a fricative, the place of the former determined largely by the transitions from the preceding vowel and of the latter by the spectral distribution of energy. The random energy often overlaps the following vowel in the time dimension (see Illustration 114 [dzi]).

2.2.3.2.3.2 *The data* Illustrations 102–125 show voiced and voiceless blade alveolar and blade post-alveolar affricates, each followed by [i], [ɑ], and [u].

2.2.3.2.3.3 *The interpretation* Illustrations 114 and 115, [dzidzɑ], show a falling transition from the high F_2 of [i] to the locus 2 of [d], and Illustrations 124 and 125, [dzɑdzu], show a rising transition from the relatively low F_2 of [ɑ] to the locus 2 of [d]. The post-release stages show a higher frequency distribution of random energy for [s] (3400 to 8000 Hz in Illustration 106 [tsɑ]) than for [ʃ] (1800 Hz to 6000 Hz in Illustration 112 [tʃɑ]). Also, the F_2/F_3 transitions to the following vowels differ from [dz] (Illustration 115, with a locus 2 at 1700 Hz and a locus 3 at 2500 Hz) to [dʒ] (Illustration 121, with a combined locus 2/locus 3 at 2100 Hz). The voiced and voiceless pairs differ by the presence or absence of a low-frequency voice bar (see Illustrations 106 [tsɑ] and 118 [dzɑ]).

2.2.3.2.4 *Nasals*

2.2.3.2.4.1 *The problem* From an articulatory point of view the nasals are characterized by an obstructed oral cavity and a lowered soft palate, which leaves a free passage of the air through the nose. The acoustic consequences show certain parallels with plosives and certain differences. Since there is no pressure buildup in the mouth or pharynx during the production of a nasal consonant, an external microphone will pick up a signal throughout the utterance, i.e., nasal consonants are in this respect continuants with a well-defined formant structure that reflects the nasal resonance. On the other hand the transition cues for plosives and nasals at the same place of articulation are similar, reflecting the part played by the oral cavity.

2.2.3.2.4.2 *The data* Illustrations 126–143 show nasals at three places of articulation, bilabial [m], blade alveolar [n], and palatal [ɲ], each followed by three vowels, [i], [ɑ], and [u].

2.2.3.2.4.3 *The interpretation* Nasal consonants exhibit certain acoustic features which characterize them as a class as opposed to orals and others which distinguish one nasal consonant from another.

Features that characterize nasals as a class: All nasals have a very low frequency straight low energy first formant at about 250 Hz, with no transition to a neighboring vowel. This is what I have called a "fault transition" since there is a sudden break between the first formant of the nasal and that of an adjacent vowel that looks like a geological fault line in a rock layer (see Illustration 130 [mɑ]). Laterals also have this fault transition. In addition, the formants of all nasals are heavily damped and the valleys between the formants tend to be filled (see Illustration 126 [mi]). Up to 3000 Hz there is a fairly even distribution of energy throughout the spectrum with neither prominent energy peaks nor wide or deep spectral valleys. This valley-filling and peak-lowering effect is caused by filtering through the resonances of the nasal passage, whose function is more like that of a damping channel than that of a resonance chamber, particularly for the higher frequencies. The dull complex resonances of a velar nasal are essentially a speaker-dependent pure nasal resonance that is much the same for all nasal consonants and all nasalized vowels.

Finally, the presence of anti-formants in regions where they would not be found in the corresponding oral sounds characterizes all nasals as a class. Anti-formants (or anti-resonances or zeros) are seen on a spectrogram either as considerable damping of a formant with a resultant wide band of low energy (see Illustration 138 [ɲi] for a wide low frequency band from 0 to 1500 Hz comprising F_1 and a special "nasal formant" (see below)) or as the complete elimination of energy in a given region (see Illustration 132 [ni], where there is no energy at all above 2750 Hz). They are found either when there is a side chamber to the oral tract (as in the case of the nasals) or when the source of disturbances to the air is not the larynx (as is the case for the turbulence of voiceless fricatives). Finally, nasal consonants usually exhibit a special "nasal formant" at about 800 Hz such as is well seen through both the consonant and vowel in Illustration 132 [ni].

Features that distinguish one nasal consonant from another: The F_2 of nasal consonants and the transitions to the following vowel are the most important place cues, although care should be taken to distinguish the F_2 from the "nasal formant" mentioned above. [m] has a low F_2 at about 1000 Hz and as a result the F_2 transition rises from the nasal consonant to a front vowel (see Illustration 126 [mi]). [n] has an F_2 at about 2000 Hz, so the F_2 transitions to close front vowels are straight (see Illustration 132 [ni]), while the F_2 transitions to back vowels fall (see Illustration 134 [nu]). Palatal nasals have an even higher F_2 at about 2200 Hz so that the F_2 to all vowels except [i] fall steeply (see Illustration 140 [ɲu]). Transitions from velar nasals are small (since there is no oral resonance) and not especially useful as place cues. It is often possible to separate nasal consonants on the basis of the location of the zeros. [m] often has a sharp anti-formant immediately above F_1 at about 500 Hz, which cuts beneath the very low F_2 (see Illustration 128 [mu]). [n] has a wideband anti-formant above 1250 Hz (see Illustration 134 [nu]) and a palatal nasal has no energy around 1500 Hz or around 2400 Hz (see Illustration 139 [ɲa]), the F_2 and F_3 of adjacent vowels being displaced steeply around the zeros to high nasal formants at about 2100 Hz and 3200 Hz. Most velar nasals, and often other nasals too, have a broadband zero above 3000 Hz (see Illustration 132 [ni]).

2.2.3.2.5 *Liquids*

2.2.3.2.5.1 *The problem* Like vowels, nasals, and syllable-margin vocoids (semi-vowels), the liquids have a well-defined formant structure. From an articulatory point of view they are essentially vowel-like, although in the case of the laterals there is a total primary constriction down the center line, which allows the air to flow past only over one or both sides of the tongue. In the case of the velarized laterals, e.g., [ɫ] in "world," the air will escape only through the buccal cavity between the teeth and cheeks. The front, back, and root of the tongue, however, can simultaneously adopt configurations appropriate for a large selection of vowels. As a result, the distribution of energy for laterals gives us evidence both for the blade alveolar central stop and for the overall configuration of the tongue.

The central liquids form a complex group. Some are labio-dental, some alveolar, and some uvular. Some are rolls, i.e., formed by two articulators being repeatedly sucked together and blown apart again; some are taps, i.e., a lower articulator is raised against an upper articulator and immediately lowered again so that there is no time for pressure to build up behind the stop; some are flaps, i.e., the tongue tip is curled back behind the alveolar ridge and then thrown forward, striking the ridge briefly in passing; and some are approximants (or frictionless continuants), i.e., a lower articulator is placed close to but not against an upper articulator. As a result, rolls, taps, and flaps might be considered to be single or multiple plosives without a pressure period, whereas the approximants are rather like vowels. All of them have extensive transitions to a following vowel, transitions that are rather rapid in the case of the rolls. In spite of the differences there are considerable acoustic similarities within the group.

2.2.3.2.5.2 *The data* Illustrations 144–149 show the blade alveolar lateral [l] and Illustrations 150–155 the blade alveolar central approximant [ɹ] before [i], [a], and [u]. Illustrations 156–161 show the blade alveolar tap [ɾ], the tip alveolar roll [r], and the voiced uvular central approximant [ʁ], all before [a].

2.2.3.2.5.3 *The interpretation* The laterals have a low steady state F_1 between 250 Hz and 350 Hz (see Illustration 149 [lu]) and a fault transition to a following vowel (see Illustration 145 [la]. F_2 is variable, being as high as 1500 Hz or 1800 Hz for the more palatalized (clear) forms (see Illustration 144 [li]) and as low as 850 Hz for the more velarized (dark) ones (see Illustration 149 [lu]). F_3 is high, between 2500 Hz and 3500 Hz (see Illustration 146 [lu]).

The Rs, although they have a low steady state F_1 similar to those of the laterals (see Illustration 154 [ɹa]), usually have a somewhat lower F_2 as high as 1600 Hz before front vowels and as low as 600 Hz before back vowels, a variation in F_2 that is lacking in our data, where F_2 is a rather constant 800 Hz (see Illustration 153 [ɹi]). F_3 is low, between 1500 Hz and 2000 Hz (see Illustration 151 [ɹa]). It will be seen from the next part that whereas F_1 is low for [l] [r], [j], and [w], F_2 divides [j] (F_2 high) from both [w] (F_2 low) and [l] and [r] (F_2 mid), and F_3 divides [r] (F_3 low) from [l], [j], and [w] (F_3 high). It is the retroflexion of the tongue tip that is responsible for the F_3 or [r] and the F_3 of a uvular [ʁ] is as high as that for [l], as can be seen in Illustration 158]ʁa]. The tap (Illustration 156 [ɾ]) shows a brief (20 msec) single discontinuity,

fundamental frequency carries the whole functional load, but it is easy to make measurements of the fundamental frequency from spectrograms and it is found that the preferred patterns in sentence final position are: [⌐.] [stressed high fall + unstressed low level] for the noun and [.⌐] [unstressed low level + stressed high fall] for the verb.

2.2.3.3.4.2 *The data* Illustrations 188–191 show the pair "a súbject" and "to subjéct."

2.2.3.3.4.3 *The interpretation* "Súbject" has 15.5 vertical striations for a measured $^1/_{10}$ sec in the first syllable and 12 in the second for a contour of 155 Hz and 120 Hz. Furthermore, the striations in "súb-" are closer together at the beginning than at the end of the syllable, indicating a falling tone. The word "subjéct" has 12 vertical striations for a measured $^1/_{10}$ sec in the first syllable and 14–10 in the second for a contour of 120 Hz and 140–100 Hz. Furthermore, the second syllable has a falling tone. The same results are obtained by tracing the fifth harmonic on the narrowband spectrograms.

2.2.3.3.5 *Sentence Stress*

2.2.3.3.5.1 *The problem* Sentence stress can be examined using the techniques illustrated under part 2.2.3.3.1 (Intonation) and part 2.2.3.3.4 (Word Stress); in fact, since an utterance like "subject" is both a word and a sentence at the same time, it will carry sentence stress. The dominant feature of the syllable bearing sentence stress in English is the fact that it has a contour, i.e., a rising or falling pitch, and not just a full vowel quality or extra duration or a pitch that is different from its neighboring stressed syllables. For example, "He put the photograph in the tray" [hɪ 'pʊt ðə 'foʊtə,grɑ:f ɪn ðə 'treɪ] [.⌐'-·-··⌐] has three stressed words, each of which begins on a new pitch level. The second one also has a syllable with secondary stress that has full vowel quality but no pitch change. The unstressed

syllables (the dots) have vowels with a centralized quality and no pitch change. Only the syllable bearing sentence stress (the last one) has full vowel quality, pitch change, *and* a moving pitch (see Table 2).

2.2.3.3.5.2 *The data* Illustrations 192–199 show the sentence "Joe broke the plate" uttered first with a neutral intonation pattern [⁻-·⌐], second as a reply to "Who?" [⌐_._], third as a reply to "Did what?" [_⌐._], and finally as a reply to "Broke what?" [__.⌐].

2.2.3.3.5.3 *The interpretation* Illustrations 192 and 193 have a contour 180 Hz, 160 Hz, 140 Hz, and 130–80 Hz; Illustrations 194–195 have 180–140 Hz, 110 Hz, 110 Hz, and 110 Hz; Illustrations 196–197 have 125 Hz, 180–160 Hz, 120 Hz, and 110 Hz; and Illustrations 198–199 have 140 Hz, 130 Hz, 120 Hz, and 180–105 Hz. The syllable with the sentence stress has the highest pitch in the sentence and a pitch that moves. Notice that the general intonation contour is most easily read off from the narrowband version.

2.2.3.4 *Intensity*

2.2.3.4.0.1 *The problem* While it is possible to make measurements of intensity from spectrograms, there are difficulties in doing so unless one has a Kay Sona-Graph with a built-in Amplitude Display Unit. However, the latter does not differ in kind from the intensity trackers discussed in subsection 2.5.1, so the technique is not discussed here. First, it can only be done from sections, and not only is this time consuming but it also places limitations on measurements of running speech, since sections cannot be taken for vowels close together. Second, one always runs up against the problem of inherent intensity. Close back vowels have less overall energy than close front vowels, and open vowels have more energy still. Therefore, in a word like "ímport," where one might expect more energy on the first, stressed syllable, it is just as likely that one

Table 2. Degrees of stress in English

Degree	Type	Peripheral vowel quality	Pitch change	Moving pitch
1	Sentence stress	+	+	+
2	Primary word stress	+	+	−
3	Secondary word stress	+	−	−
4	Unstressed	−	−	−

will find less because the inherent intensity of the open vowel is so much greater than that of the front vowel that it may outrank the stress placement.

Relative measurements can be made on narrowband sections in unspecified units of intensity (we could even call them "millimeters of intensity," mm I) at each harmonic up to the 30th. The figures for a given vowel are then added to give an estimated relative intensity.

2.2.3.4.0.2 *The data* Illustrations 200–202 show narrowband spectrograms with sections for [i], [ɑ], and [u] and Illustration 203 shows in the same way the relative intensities of the vowels in "discharge."

2.2.3.4.0.3 *The interpretation* The three vowels examined in Illustrations 200–202 are rank ordered as follows: [ɑ] 158 mm I, [i] 151 mm I, and [u] 108 mm I. These figures might be compared with those given by Lehiste (see subsection 4.3.8) on page 120 of *Suprasegmentals* for the mean intrinsic intensity of syllable nuclei in American English for one speaker: [a] 85.7 dB, [u] 80.4 dB, and [i] 80.1 dB.

Illustration 203 shows that, in spite of the fact that the stress is on the first syllable, [ɑ:] (568 mm I) has more energy than [ɪ] (512 mm I) because of the inherent intensity of the two vowels. A comparison of Illustrations 201 ([ɑ] = 158 mm I) and 203 ([ɑ] = 568 mm I) shows clearly that such measurements are relative, depending very much on speaking level and/or settings on the volume control.

2.2.3.5 Duration

2.2.3.5.1 Contrastive Vowel Length

2.2.3.5.1.1 *The problem* Many languages have constrastive vowel length as part of their phonology, and English has a number of vowel pairs like [i:]/[ɪ] (e.g., "beat"/"bit"), [u:]/[ʊ] (e.g., "cooed"/"could"), and [ə:]/[ə] (e.g., "earned"/"and"), where the contrast is realized as much by quantity as by quality, even though vowel pairs like [aɪ]/[ɪ] (e.g., "decide"/"decision") and [eɪ]/[æ] (e.g., "page"/"pagination"), where both quantity and quality play a role, are more important in the grammar. The measurement of duration is easily made from spectrograms, usually in milliseconds.

2.2.3.5.1.2 *The data* Illustrations 204–207 show the pair "to beat"/"a bit."

2.2.3.5.1.3 *The interpretation* In an identical environment "b__t" [i:] is much longer, here 174 msec, than [ɪ], here 95 msec.

2.2.3.5.2 Allophonic Vowel Length

2.2.3.5.2.1 *The problem* Some durational differences are not contrastive but dependent on the environment of a vowel. In English, a given vowel is at its shortest when followed by a voiceless consonant, longer when followed by a voiced consonant, and longest of all (in most dialects) when word final, e.g., "beat," "bead," and "bee." Hence, a long, phonologically short vowel, e.g., "bid," may be as long as or longer than a short, phonologically long vowel, e.g., "beat." Measurements of duration are easily made from spectrograms.

2.2.3.5.2.2 *The data* Illustrations 208–213 show the duration differences in "to beat"/"a bead"/"a bee" and Illustrations 214–217 those in "a bit"/"a bid."

2.2.3.5.2.3 *The interpretation* The five vowels examined have the following durations: "bit" 115 msec, "beat" 152 msec, "bid" 155 msec, "bead" 226 msec, and "bee" 272 msec.

2.2.3.5.3 Inherent Duration

2.2.3.5.3.1 *The problem* Not only do vowels have inherent pitch and intensity but also inherent duration. Lehiste (see subsection 4.3.6) in *Suprasegmentals* shows on page 68 that the open vowels have lower inherent pitch than the close vowels: [a] 163 Hz, [u] 182 Hz, and [i] 183 Hz (see part 2.2.3.3.3), on page 120 that the open vowels have greater inherent intensity than the close vowels: [a] 85.7 dB, [u] 80.4 dB, and [i] 80.1 dB (see item 2.2.3.4.0.3), and on page 47, in a table of average durations of long vowels in the first syllable of dissyllabic words in Estonian, that the open vowels have longer inherent duration than the close vowels: [ɑ] 223.5 msec, [u] 195.9 msec, and [i] 182.1 msec.

2.2.3.5.3.2 *The data* Illustrations 218–223 show representative utterances of [i], [ɑ], and [u] in word final position ("tea," "tar," and "too").

2.2.3.5.3.3 *The interpretation* [i] has a duration of 202 msec, [ɑ] of 315 msec, and [u] of 255 msec.

2.2.4 Reading

It is suggested that the student now read the following items before proceeding with the projects below.

Fant, G. 1970. Analysis and synthesis of speech processes. In B. Malmberg (ed.), *Manual of Phonetics*, pp. 173–277. See especially pp. 243–253. North-Holland Publishing Company, Amsterdam.

Koenig, W., Dunn, H.K., and Lacey, L.Y. 1946. The sound spectrograph. *The Journal of the Acoustical Society of America* 17: 19–49.

Ladefoged, P. 1975. *A Course in Phonetics*, pp. 168–191. Harcourt Brace Jovanovich, Inc., New York.

Peterson, G.E., and Barney, H.L. 1952. Control methods used in a study of the vowels. *The Journal of the Acoustical Society of America* 24: 175–184.

Potter, R.K., Kopp, G.A., and Green, H.C. 1947. *Visible Speech*. D. Van Nostrand Company, Princeton, N.J. See illustrations only.

2.2.5 Student Projects

2.2.5.1 *Replication Projects*

a. Make spectrograms of yourself saying "beat," "bit," "bet," "bat," "Bert," "bart," "bought," "but," and "boot" and plot the formant frequencies of the vowels. Try to keep the fundamental frequency, intensity, and speaking rate constant.

b. Make spectrograms of yourself saying "pea," "tea," "key," "bee," "dee," and "Guy" [gi:] and plot the consonant loci.

c. Make spectrograms of yourself saying "súbject" and "subjéct" and plot the fundamental frequency and duration of the vowels.

2.2.5.2 *New Projects*

a. Find a speaker of a language other than English or of a dialect of English rather different from those normally described in textbooks and make spectrograms of a dozen words with different vowels. Make formant frequency measurements and compare them with standard British or American English.

b. Find a speaker with a misarticulated /s/ or /r/ and make spectrograms of selected words containing it. Make appropriate acoustic measurements and compare them with those in normal speech.

2.3 THE OSCILLOSCOPE

2.3.1 The Instrumentation

If the sound spectrograph is the single most important instrument in a phonetics laboratory then the oscilloscope (see Illustration 224) is probably the second most valuable piece of equipment.

In section 2.2 we spoke of the four wave types that are of interest to us in phonetics: a) the sine wave, b) the complex wave, c) the damped complex wave, and d) white noise, and related them to three major sound types. The first was the frictionless continuants—the vowels and sonorants—characterized by considerable overall energy distributed in a well-developed formant structure over a relatively long period of time. The second was the fricative continuants—the fricatives and voiceless vowels—characterized by relatively little overall energy distributed in rather random fashion throughout the frequency spectrum over a relatively long period of time. The third was the frictionless noncontinuants—the plosives—characterized by relatively little overall energy distributed in a formant-like manner over a rather short period of time. The vowels and fricatives are similar with respect to duration, the vowels and plosives with respect to frequency, and the fricatives and plosives with respect to intensity (see Figure 3).

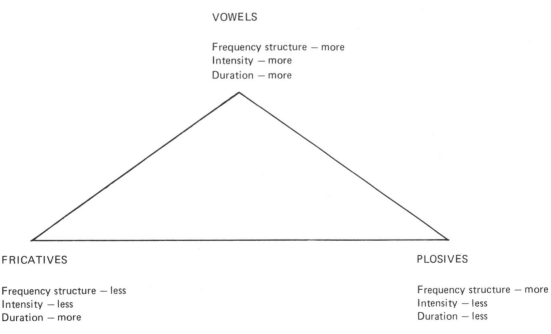

VOWELS

Frequency structure — more
Intensity — more
Duration — more

FRICATIVES

Frequency structure — less
Intensity — less
Duration — more

PLOSIVES

Frequency structure — more
Intensity — less
Duration — less

Figure 3.   Three major sound types.

The oscilloscope shows this as clearly as the spectrograph but it is less useful to us in that, whereas the spectrograph analyzes the signal for us, the oscilloscope merely presents the unanalyzed wave form, which is more difficult to interpret. Furthermore, the spectrograph shows frequency on the vertical axis and time on the horizontal axis with intensity as a third dimension, but the oscilloscope shows only intensity on the vertical and time on the horizontal axis—frequency being represented only indirectly. The wave form is called an oscillogram and it is displayed on a monitor screen for a pre-chosen time span, from as little as 50 microseconds (millionths of a second; μsec) for the whole screen, which gives considerable detail but of only a very brief signal, to as much as 50 sec, which gives very little detail but does capture long utterances. In practice one uses only a small range of time settings for phonetic research: 5 to 200 msec for the whole screen when analyzing structures the length of a vocal fold period or of one segment and 500 to 1000 msec for the whole screen when analyzing syllable or word length structures.

When a signal is picked up by a microphone, amplified, and displayed as a wave form on a continuous piece of paper, it is called a "microphone tracing" ("Mike") or more loosely an "audio tracing" ("Audio"). It is customary when gathering physiological data (see Chapter 3) to put a microphone tracing automatically on the bottom of the paper underneath tracings of other parameters, since it is fairly easy to segment an utterance with the help of a wave form. However, a very fast paper speed of 8 inches per sec, which is too fast for most tasks and too expensive (at \$24 for a 100-foot roll of paper) for most institutions, is equivalent to only the slowest oscilloscope settings mentioned above, so the paper write-out should be used for segmentation purposes and the oscilloscope for detailed analysis.

In addition, the microphone tracing is in practice limited to a fraction of a paper width, whereas, when one uses the oscilloscope, a voltage setting may be chosen that spreads the signal from top to bottom of the screen. The microphone at the input end turns acoustic pressure into a voltage which can be displayed on the oscilloscope over a range of 400 microvolts (millionths of a volt; μV) to 40 V for the whole screen.

The oscilloscope screen is divided into a grid of small squares, each of which is called a division, and one might, for example, find eight divisions on the intensity (= voltage) and 10 on the time axis. Settings are made per division, so that 10 msec per division (10 m/div) would handle an utterance of 10 msec $\times$ 10 divisions = 100 msec = 10 vocal fold cycles at 100 Hz. Furthermore, the wave form of a given signal would have twice the amplitude at a setting of 1 volt per division (1 V/div) than at a setting of 2 V/div where 1 V equals only a half a division.

In addition, it should be noted that the terms *fast setting* and *slow setting* should be interpreted as follows: 10 msec/div is to be considered a relatively fast setting since the beam travels faster across the oscilloscope screen than it would at a setting of 100 msec/div. Since the former gives detail but of only a short duration speech event it may be compared with a microphone tracing made at a fast paper speed, whereas the latter gives little detail but of an utterance of longer duration and may therefore be compared with a microphone tracing made at a slow paper speed.

Finally, it should be noted that the oscilloscope is the most accurate and finely calibrated instrument in the laboratory, so that all other instruments can be checked against it. If, for example, you want to know whether your sine wave generator is working well, set it to 1000 Hz and put the signal through the oscilloscope at a setting in 1 m/div. There should be exactly one cycle each division.

2.3.2 Operation

When it is necessary to analyze live speech, the utterance is picked up by a microphone and sent to an amplifier before being put into the oscilloscope, although care should be taken not to amplify the signal to a voltage that is in excess of what the oscilloscope can handle. However, a tape recording can be put into the oscilloscope directly, as can other inputs, such as sine waves, complex waves, and white noise. Sine waves are introduced from a sine wave generator, alternatively called a function generator or oscillator. Two or three oscillators may be joined together to produce a complex wave as input. White noise is brought in from a white noise (or thermal noise or Gaussian noise) generator. These instruments are used to illustrate basic principles in acoustic phonetics (see Illustrations 2–6 and subsection 2.2.1).

On some oscilloscopes it is possible not only to adjust the voltage and time settings but to display the same signal twice, once at the top of the screen with one time setting (e.g., 0.1 sec/div) for a longer utterance and once at the bottom of the screen with another setting (e.g., 10 m/div), which will give more detail but for a shorter utterance. Furthermore, the tracing with the greater detail can be made to begin at any predetermined point in the longer utterance by the use of a "time delay" control. In this way detail can be seen within the context of the larger utterance.

Furthermore, some oscilloscopes have a built-in memory which can receive and permanently display one utterance of pre-chosen length. This can subsequently be photographed by a special Polaroid camera which is hooked over the screen; all the illustrations cited in this section were made in this way. A simple push button erases the picture and another push button readies the memory for a second utterance.

2.3.3 Demonstration Projects

2.3.3.1 *Vowels*

2.3.3.1.0.1 *The problem* The wave forms of different vowels may be distinguished by their gross gestalt patterns when uttered by the same speaker under the same conditions, but even what we perceive to be identical vowels may look very dissimilar when uttered by different speakers, at different intensities, or under different vocal fold conditions, such as breathy or harsh voice.

When the pattern representing the results of one vocal fold pulse filtered through the mouth is examined closely, it is usually possible to see certain gross subpatterns. For example, the wave form for [i] has something which, by simple visual inspection, is seen to happen with large amplitude twice per cycle, and superimposed on this is something that is seen to happen with small amplitude about 20 times per cycle. These events are a reflection of what a spectrogram shows as the first formant at about 200 Hz and the second formant at about 2000 Hz. An examination of the wave form of [ɑ] shows rather obviously that something is happening about six times per cycle and this is a reflection of the first formant at about 600 Hz.

Smaller variations on these more obvious patterns and subpatterns for a given vowel reflect individual, age, and sex characteristics or health and emotional states.

2.3.3.1.0.2 *The data* Illustrations 225–227 show the vowels [i], [ɑ], and [u], respectively, uttered by a healthy adult male and recorded at 2 msec per division. Illustrations 228–230 show the same vowels uttered by the same speaker when recorded at 10 msec per division.

2.3.3.1.0.3 *The interpretation* Illustrations 225–227, taken at 2 msec per division (= 20 msec, or

2 cycles at 100 Hz, for the whole screen), show that the vowels [i], [ɑ], and [u] do have characteristically different wave forms, as would be expected for a set of vowels that are maximally differentiated from each other. [i], it will be recalled, is close front and lip spread, [u] close back and lip rounded, and [ɑ] open and back with lips neutral to spread. [i] has a palatal place of articulation and a wide pharynx, [u] a velar place of articulation and a wide pharynx, and [ɑ] has a pharyngeal place of articulation and thus a narrow pharynx.

The wave forms for [i] and [u] are the most grossly similar of the three, since for each cycle there are two major events with a resultant up-down-up-down pattern. This is indicative of acoustic energy in the area of 200 Hz, and we have already seen (Table 1, item 2.2.3.1.0.3) that close vowels have an F_1 at about 250 Hz.

[u] has very little fine structure superimposed on this pattern, indicating that F_2 is close to F_1 in frequency, whereas [i] has a fine structure of small amplitude waves, about 20 per cycle in number, superimposed on the large amplitude two-event pattern. This is indicative of acoustic energy in the area of 2000 Hz, and we have already seen (Table 1) that [i] has an F_2 at about 2250 Hz. It is instructive at this point to look back to the two-component complex wave in Illustration 3 and forward to the vowel [i] in Illustration 272.

[ɑ], on the other hand, is characterized by about six ups and downs each cycle, which reflects an F_1 at about 600 Hz and an F_2 close to it in frequency. We have already seen (Table 1) that [ɑ] has an F_1 at about 700 Hz and an F_2 at about 1000 Hz.

The wave forms for front vowels other than [i] fall between the extremes shown for [i] and [ɑ] and those for the remaining back vowels fall between the extremes shown for [ɑ] and [u].

Although it is easy to recognize the wave forms for these three pivotal positions, it is much more difficult to comment on the wave forms of intermediate vowels than it is to give formant frequency values for a given set of vowels on the evidence of spectrograms. The spectrogram should be used to obtain formant frequency values and the oscillogram reserved for detailed studies of voice quality and intensity and for precise measurements of the duration of vocal fold cycles.

Finally, it will be seen that oscillograms taken at 10 msec per division (Illustrations 228–230) give us much less detail than those made at 2 msec per division, but they do enable us to make statements about the onset and offset characteristics of vowels, since at this speed it is possible to capture 10 or 20 cycles of a syllable center.

2.3.3.2 *Consonants*

2.3.3.2.1 *Plosives*

2.3.3.2.1.1 *The problem*
Since a microphone placed in front of the lips will not pick up any energy during the pressure stage of a plosive except for low energy voicing radiated through body tissues, most of the evidence of the wave form will relate to the release stage, the explosion, the burst. As a result, we were able to state (in subsection 2.3.1) that the energy in the wave form of a plosive was less than that seen in vowels and of smaller duration, but that like vowels it was highly structured. The brief duration of a burst is easily seen on an oscillogram, although particularly weak explosions are manifested only by a few irregular cycles at the beginning of the following vowel.

However, the structure of a burst is seen only on a spectrogram section, the unanalyzed wave form being of little use to us. This is because the burst is merely one brief, heavily damped wave, and it will prove useful to compare this with other burst-like transient waves.

2.3.3.2.1.2 *The data*
Illustrations 231–235 show typical wave forms of various types of transient: an electrical click caused by switching on an amplifier attached to the oscilloscope and then turning it off and on again; a series of pencil taps on a table top; a series of lateral clicks produced with a velaric ingressive airstream mechanism such as one finds in a number of southern African languages; a series of exploded [k]s; and two glottal stops. Illustrations 231 and 235 were recorded at 100 msec/div and 0.1 V/div and Illustrations 232–234 at 50 msec/div and 0.2 V/div. Illustrations 236–239 show voice onset time for word initial /p/ and /b/ in English as recorded from utterances of "a pea" (Illustrations 236 and 237) and "a bee" (Illustrations 238 and 239). Each utterance is recorded from an A source (Illustrations 236 and 238) at 5 msec/div and 1 V/div and a B source (Illustrations 237 and 239) at 50 msec/div and 1 V/div. The A source is, in each case, delayed by four divisions; that is to say that the A source tracing begins at the same moment in time as the beginning of the fifth division of the B source tracing. A representation of this kind is called a dual-beam time-delayed tracing.

2.3.3.2.1.3 *The interpretation*
A transient is a nonrepetitive complex wave, one that may be analyzed into many components and is so damped that it dies out quickly and does not repeat itself.

Illustration 231 is an electrical simulation of a highly damped wave. When an electrical circuit is switched on or off there are sudden fluctuations in the voltage. Here the amplifier is turned on at the beginning of the first division, off at the end of the third, and when it is turned on again at the beginning of the eighth the voltage surges momentarily, causing a high amplitude peak to be registered on the oscilloscope. The peak is quickly followed by a few low amplitude quasi-sinusoidal modulations and the signal dies out.

Illustration 232 is a series of pencil taps produced at a rate of about five per second (180 msec each). The wave form for each tap has a triangular shape with the base to the left. Energy is lost quickly and the apex represents the point in time when the signal dies out. If the taps do not follow each other quickly there will be silence between each pair of transients, but the tap rate may be increased to the point where a second tap will arrive before the energy in the first tap has died out. In such cases, the triangular wave forms will overlap. Vocal fold vibrations produce trains of pulses that are in this respect very much like trains of accelerated pencil taps. Depending on the fundamental frequency of vibration, there will be more or less overlapping of the damped waves. On the other hand, the pencil taps are also like the explosion bursts of plosives and, since both vocal fold taps and plosive bursts have their energy structured in frequency, these two classes of sound have one feature in common which neither shares with fricatives.

Illustration 233 shows a series of lateral clicks. Clicks are not common in the languages of the world but are excellent examples of heavily damped transients. Their wave forms are even sharper than those of the pencil taps.

Illustration 234 is a series of exploded voiceless velar plosives and Illustration 235 is two glottal stops, the former recorded at 50 msec/div and the latter at 100 msec/div. Weakly exploded lenis plosives produced by releasing a relatively low positive pressure from behind two articulators that move slowly apart are marked not so much by a transient as by an irregular onset to the following vowel.

In most dialects of English, vocal fold vibrations begin at the moment of release for the so-called voiced plosives in word-initial position, whereas for the voiceless plosives the vocal fold vibrations begin only 40–60 msec after the release. Illustration 237, "a pea," shows precisely this: the release comes at 190 msec[4] on the 50 msec/div tracing (and at 0 msec at 5 msec/div) but voicing does not start until after the aspiration stage 70 msec later at 260 msec. However, Illustration 239, "a bee," shows a dialect (or strictly speaking an idiolect) which, like French, has voicing throughout the pressure stage (from 50 msec to 225 msec on the 50 msec/div tracing), the lenis release coming at 11 msec on the 5 msec/div tracing in Illustration 238. Information on voice onset time (VOT) is, it will be seen, easy to obtain from the wave form.

2.3.3.2.2 *Fricatives*

2.3.3.2.2.1 *The problem* In subsection 2.3.1 we saw that fricatives have durations comparable to those of vowels although they have less energy and the wave form is random and nonrepetitive. Within the class of fricatives it is possible to distinguish between those like [f] and [θ], which have relatively little energy, and others like [s] and [ʃ], which have considerably more, but in other respects the wave forms of fricatives look identical at oscilloscope settings of more than 0.5 msec per division because of the random nature of speech noise.

White noise is analyzed as an infinity of components of equal amplitude at all frequencies and by definition such waves never repeat themselves. Fricatives may be synthesized merely by filtering out white noise above and below certain frequencies, leaving band-passed noise in that part of the spectrum where the random noise of a given fricative is of greatest intensity. For example, noise passed only between 6000 Hz and 9000 Hz is perceived as [s], whereas noise passed only between 3000 Hz and 6000 Hz is perceived as [ʃ]. When the wave forms of fricatives are examined at 0.5 msec per division or faster, pseudo-periodicities appear which correspond to those parts of the frequency spectrum where the random noise is of greatest intensity, and it becomes possible to distinguish one fricative from another even to the point where one can recognize fairly minor misarticulations.

2.3.3.2.2.2 *The data* Illustration 240 shows "Sasha" recorded at 0.1 sec/div. The recording was triggered by a pencil tap (the tail end of which can

be seen in the first division) so as to not have the onset of the word cut off. Illustrations 241 and 242 show "thigh" and "sigh" recorded at 0.1 sec per division and Illustrations 243–249 show a set of fricatives: a narrow groove tip dental [s̩], a narrow groove tip alveolar [s-], a broad groove tip dental [θ], a narrow groove blade alveolar [s], a broad groove blade post-alveolar [ʃ], a velar [x], and a uvular [χ] recorded at 1 msec/div and 0.2 V/div. Illustrations 250–256 show the same fricatives recorded at 0.2 msec/div and 0.2 V/div.

2.3.3.2.2.3 *The interpretation* Illustration 240 shows that, although both [s] (200–300 msec) and [ʃ] (480–590 msec) are easily recognized as fricatives by their small amplitude and random form, it is not possible at this speed to distinguish the one from the other. On the other hand, it is possible (see Illustrations 241 and 242, "thigh" and "sigh") to distinguish [θ] (100–220 msec) from [s] (500–600 msec) by the intensity of the random noise, [θ] having much less energy than [s]. When, however, the speed is increased to 1 msec/div pseudoperiodicities appear (see Illustrations 243–249) which, when the speed is increased even more (see Illustrations 250–256 at 0.2 msec/div), are quite easily counted. This enables us to characterize the natural resonance frequencies of a set of fricatives produced at various places of articulation from front to back. By counting peaks as best we can on Illustrations 243–249 we see that [s̩] has eight peaks per division and when we multiply this figure by 1000 (since there are 1000 divisions per sec) we are able to determine that the energy maximum for [s̩] is at about 8000 Hz. The figures for the whole set are approximately as follows: [s̩] 8000 Hz, [s-] 7000 Hz, [θ] 6000 Hz, [s] 5000 Hz, [ʃ] 3000 Hz, [x] 1000 Hz, and [χ] 750 Hz. Illustrations 250–256 show clearly that the duration of each pseudo-cycle gets longer for each fricative from top to bottom of the photograph.

2.3.3.3 **Fundamental Frequency**

2.3.3.3.0.1 *The problem* It is very easy to make statements about fundamental frequency by examination of the oscillographic record; furthermore, measurements can be made with great accuracy when necessary. All one has to do is count the number of vocal fold pulses per time period. If, for example, a vowel is seen to last 200 msec and to have 20 cycles, then each cycle will have an average duration of 200 ÷ 20 = 10 msec, which is a fundamental frequency of 1000 msec (i.e., 1 sec) ÷ 10 msec per cycle = 100 cycles per sec or 100 Hz. This technique

---

[4]Throughout this section the segmentation of utterances is calibrated from the beginning of the first division, i.e., from the leftmost edge. So, for example, the end of the fourth division for a recording made at 50 msec/div would be given as 4 × 50 = 200 msec and halfway through the third division for a recording made at 5 msec/div would be given as 2.5 × 5 = 12.5 msec.

is quite satisfactory for handling texts one short sentence at a time, and when utterances do not exceed 1 sec one can maintain both speed and reasonable accuracy merely by using a setting of 100 msec per division (where 10 cycles per division = 100 Hz) and counting the number of spikes for a given 100-msec duration within each syllable center. This figure multiplied by 10 gives the fundamental frequency.

However, there are times when one is interested in rapidly changing fundamental frequency, for example at the beginning of a vowel after the explosion of a plosive. In such cases one has to balance the need for accuracy, which implies shortening the duration of the piece being recorded, with the fact that it takes 50 msec or more for fundamental frequency to stabilize after the release. A setting of 5 msec per division is recommended and measurements are made not in Hz, but in msec for each separate period.

Finally, one may be interested in comparing the wave forms of vowels differing only in fundamental frequency. It is well known that muscle forces creating tension from front to back, from top to bottom, and from side to center of the glottis, plus subglottal pressure and airflow, are implicated in changes in both fundamental frequency and intensity (see topic 2.3.3.4), so it is not surprising to see changes in fundamental frequency reflected in the wave form.

2.3.3.3.0.2 *The data* Illustration 257 shows how to specify the intonation contour for the sentence "Joe bróke the plate." It is recorded at 200 msec per division. Illustrations 258–261 give post-release data for the pair [bɑ] (top) and [pɑ] (bottom) recorded on dual beam, with the B source delayed by one division, at 5 msec/div for source B (Illustrations 258 and 260) and 20 msec/div for source A (Illustrations 259 and 261). Illustrations 262–265 show wave forms for [ɑ] spoken at low frequency/low intensity (top tracing), low frequency/high intensity (second tracing), high frequency/low intensity (third tracing), and high frequency/high intensity (bottom tracing). The recordings were made at 10 msec/div.

2.3.3.3.0.3 *The interpretation* Illustration 257 shows that the sentence "Joke bróke the plate," which could be segmented as follows: [dʒ] 320–365 msec, [ou] 365–640 msec, [br] 640–700 msec, [ou] 700–920 msec, [k] 920–1000 msec, [ð] 1000–1120 msec, [ə] 1120–1200 msec, [pl] 1200–1360 msec, [ei] 1360–1560 msec, and [t] 1560–1640 msec, has the fundamental frequency contour 150 Hz, 162–125 Hz, 100 Hz, and 100 Hz [⁻ ˎ ˏ]. Fundamental frequency is obviously a major cue for the perception of sentence stress on the second word.

The fundamental frequency data on the transition between consonant and vowel in Illustrations 258–261 show, quite typically for a pair of cognate voiceless/voiced plosives, that the voiceless plosive has the higher inherent frequency, because soon after the release of the [p] (Illustrations 260 and 261) the following vowel has a fundamental frequency of 154 Hz, whereas the vowel following [b] (Illustrations 258 and 259) has a fundamental frequency of only 139 Hz. The measurements were made from the tracings at 5 msec/div, although a simple visual inspection of the same wave forms counting cycles from trough to trough shows that [b] has six complete cycles and two partial ones, whereas [p] has six complete cycles plus two almost complete ones.

Illustrations 262–265 show that an increase in either fundamental frequency or intensity has the result of making the wave form less flat, i.e., the peaks and troughs within each cycle become more pronounced. Greater amplitude, of course (see Illustrations 263 and 265) is equivalent in perceptual terms to "louder" and more cycles per division (see Illustrations 264 and 265) to higher pitch. Compare the low frequency/low intensity with the high frequency/low intensity recordings and the low frequency/high intensity with the high frequency/high intensity ones and it will be seen that a higher fundamental frequency is achieved by physiological mechanisms which result in more differentiated curves.

2.3.3.4 *Intensity*

2.3.3.4.0.1 *The problem* It was noted earlier that it is customary to add an oscillogram at the bottom of a page of physiological data to help segment the material. However, it is not quite true that it is easy to segment once one has a running wave form. What is true is that it is easy to mark syllable centers. Syllable margins are much more difficult to pinpoint—an old problem in syllabification and a phonetic definition of the syllable.

Nonetheless, vowels do have more energy than sonorants and fricatives and the latter do have more than the pressure stage of plosives. However, the picture is complicated somewhat when we take into account the inherent intensity of the various vowels and consonants and the changes introduced by different word and sentence stress patterns. For example, other things being equal (and they rarely are), open vowels like [ɑ] will have larger amplitude wave forms than close vowels like [i], and fortis plosives like [p] will have larger amplitude explosions than lenis plosives like [b]. Furthermore, strongly accented syllables will have larger amplitude wave forms than the same syllables in unaccented position.

A somewhat different problem was touched on in item 2.3.3.3.0.2: How is the wave form of an individual cycle changed under varying conditions of intensity?

2.3.3.4.0.2 *The data* Illustration 266 shows the wave form of the utterance ''two small clean pans'' recorded at 0.2 sec/div and 0.2 V/div and triggered by a pencil tap, the tail end of which can be seen in the first division. The intonation contour was [_ ‾ ‿]. The reader is referred back to Illustrations 258–265 for further discussion.

2.3.3.4.0.3 *The interpretation* Illustration 266 shows how easy it can be to identify syllable centers in running speech. The sentence might be segmented as follows: [t] 50–200 msec, [h] 200–235 msec, [u:] 235–360 msec, [s] 360–400 msec, [m] 400–495 msec, [ɔ:] 495–680 msec, [l] 680–720 msec, [k] 720–755 msec, [h] 755–780 msec, [l] 780–835 msec, [i:] 835–1000 msec, [n] 1000–1040 msec, [p] 1040–1085 msec, [h] 1085–1160 msec, [a] 1160–1300 msec, [n] 1300–1600 msec, [z] 1600–2000 msec, and it will be seen that the four vowels have greater amplitude than the other segments. Although it is also easy to identify the absence of energy corresponding to the pressure stages of the three plosives, the fricatives and sonorants are rather more difficult to segment out, particularly when they follow each other, as in [sm] and [nz].

This phrase was uttered with approximately equal stress on each syllable, but it may be seen that the open vowels [ɔ:] and [a] have greater inherent intensity than the close vowels [u:] and [i:]. The inherent intensity of the fortis/lenis pair [p]/[b] may be seen in Illustrations 236–239, where the burst for [p] is of much greater amplitude than that for [b].

Finally, Illustrations 262–265 show that, if one compares low frequency/low intensity with low frequency/high intensity and high frequency/low intensity with high frequency/high intensity, greater intensity is achieved by means that result in wave forms with more pronounced peaks and troughs within each cycle.

2.3.3.5 *Duration*
2.3.3.5.0.1 *The problem* It is possible to achieve greater accuracy for durational measurements by using an oscilloscope than one normally needs. In fact, the details provided by the wave form can be a problem. For example, the onset and offset of voicing does not occur instantaneously and one has to make some principled decision as to when one should consider voicing to have begun and ended in the presence of low amplitude cycles of irregular periodicity.

Nevertheless, one can handle problems such as the duration of vowels in open as opposed to closed syllables and before voiceless as opposed to voiced consonants, the length of long as opposed to short vowels and consonants and the duration of vowels in stressed as opposed to unstressed syllables. The faster the time setting of the oscilloscope, the more accurate the measurement of duration.

2.3.3.5.0.2 *The data* Illustrations 267–270 show wave forms for the phrases ''a bit'' and ''to beat,'' ''to bid'' and ''a bead'' recorded at 0.1 sec/div and 1 V/div. Each is triggered by a pencil tap, the tail end of which can be seen in the first division.

2.3.3.5.0.3 *The interpretation* Illustrations 267–270 may be segmented as follows: ''a bit'' [ə] 270–350 msec, [b] 350–460 msec, [ɪ] 460–580 msec, [t] 580–665 msec; ''to beat'' [t] 150–285 msec, [h] 285–335 msec, [ə] 335–405 msec, [b] 405–530 msec, [i:] 530–720 msec, [t] 720–770 msec, [h] 770–825 msec; ''to bid'' [t] 150–280 msec, [h] 280–330 msec, [ə] 330–410 msec, [b] 410–545 msec, [ɪ] 545–750 msec, [d] 750–880 msec; ''a bead'' [ə] 180–270 msec, [b] 270–440 msec, [i:] 440–780 msec, [d] 780–860 msec.

It can be seen from the illustrations that the vowel in ''bit'' is shorter (120 msec) than that in ''beat'' (190 msec) and the vowel in ''bid'' shorter (205 msec) than that in ''bead'' (340 msec) but that the vowel in ''bit'' (120 msec) is shorter than that in ''bid'' (205 msec), and the vowel in ''beat'' (190 msec) shorter than that in ''bead'' (340 msec). Furthermore, the short ''long'' vowel in ''beat'' has a duration (190 msec) less than that of the long ''short'' vowel in ''bid'' (205 msec).

2.3.3.6 *Voice Quality*
2.3.3.6.0.1 *The problem* Whereas the sound spectrograph is preferable to the oscilloscope in all respects except accuracy and detail for most of the topics so far dealt with, the oscilloscope is able to display material on voice quality which the sound spectrograph handles less well.

For example, those phonation types that we call voiceless, voiced, breathy voiced, and creaky voiced are well suited to analysis on the oscilloscope. They are produced by adjusting the tension and configuration of the vocal folds. In the case of ''voiceless'' the vocal folds are either not positioned close enough or are held too tightly together for them to vibrate as air flows, or tries to flow, between them from the lungs. For "voiced," the conditions for vocal fold vibration are established by a proper balance between tension along the length of the vocal folds (longitudinal tension), and appropriate bringing together of the folds (medial compression), subglottal pressure, and airflow. The same holds true for "breathy voice" and "creaky voice," but in the former case the vocal folds are rather slack and never come completely together whereas in the latter case the muscles of adduction are more than normally tense so that the folds vibrate irregularly and along only part of their length. Such different laryngeal settings not surprisingly result in different wave forms.

Other voice quality differences are the result either of training or of laryngeal pathologies and the wave forms of the trained and untrained speaker can differ radically as can those for healthy as opposed to unhealthy larynges.

2.3.3.6.0.2 *The data*

Illustrations 271–278 show a single speaker uttering the vowel [i] first voiced, then voiceless, and finally with breathy and creaky voice.

Illustrations 279–290 contrast three different speakers uttering the vowels [i] and [ɑ]. The first speaker (Illustrations 279–282) is a well-trained male phonetician, the second (Illustrations 283–286) is an untrained female speaker with a strong voice but a slightly breathy quality, and the third (Illustrations 287–290) is an untrained female speaker with a bad cold and a touch of laryngitis. Each utterance was recorded on dual beam at two speeds, slower at the top and faster at the bottom.

2.3.3.6.0.3 *The interpretation*

The voiced vowel in Illustrations 271 and 272 is characterized by clear periodicities and the pronounced peaks and troughs within each cycle that we expect from a strong, healthy voice. Illustration 271 was made at 10 msec/div and Illustration 272 at 2 msec/div, both with an amplitude setting of 0.2 V/div. The fundamental frequency is 124 Hz and the intensity 0.36 V peak to peak.

The voiceless vowel in Illustrations 273 and 274 has no periodic structure. It is in fact a glottal fricative with oral resonances superimposed. Illustration 273 was made at 2 msec/div and Illustration 274 at 0.5 msec/div, both with an amplitude setting of 0.2 V/div. There is, of course, no fundamental frequency and the intensity is 0.12 V peak to peak.

The breathy voiced vowel (Illustrations 275 and 276), although periodic in nature, lacks pronounced peaks and troughs. It was recorded at 10 msec/div and 2 msec/div with an amplitude setting of 0.2 V/div, and it will be seen that the fundamental frequency is 120 Hz although the intensity is only 0.2 V peak to peak.

Finally, the creaky voiced vowel (Illustrations 277 and 278), which was recorded at 20 msec/div and 5 msec/div with an amplitude setting of 0.2 V/div, has a wave form like that of a series of glottal stops, each followed by a rapidly damped disturbance of the supraglottal air, which was exactly what this particular kind of creaky voice sounded like. The fundamental frequency is as low as 50 Hz (hence the slower time setting) and the intensity is 0.4 V peak to peak.

Even well-trained voices may show variation of up to 5% in the duration of successive cycles of vocal fold vibration and, indeed, the exactly equal pulse repetition rate of machine-synthesized speech gives it a slightly unnatural quality. Variation of 10% or more is perceived as creaky (harsh) voice and in Illustration 277 successive cycles have durations of 22, 22, 21, 20, 21, 21, 22, and 21 msec with a mean of 21.25 msec and a range of variation of 2 msec (9.4%).

Whereas Illustrations 271–278 showed a single speaker using different phonation types, Illustrations 279–290 show three different speakers using what was, on the day of the recording, normal voice. However, the kind of variation noted in Illustrations 271–278 is seen again in the latter set.

The first speaker is a well-trained male phonetician saying the vowels [i] (Illustrations 279 and 280) and [ɑ] (Illustrations 281 and 282), each recorded at 10 msec/div (top tracing) and 2 msec/div (bottom tracing) with an amplitude setting of 0.5 V/div. [i] has a fundamental frequency of 110 Hz and 8 of the 10 cycles have the same duration. The amplitude is 0.55 V peak to peak. [ɑ] also has a fundamental frequency of 110 Hz, and 7 of the 10 cycles have the same duration. The amplitude is 0.7 V peak to peak. The trained voice produces little variation in duration from cycle to cycle, pronounced peaks and troughs, and considerable intensity, all marks of control strength and the efficient use of natural resources.

The second speaker is a female student with a strong but slightly breathy untrained voice also saying the vowels [i] (Illustrations 283 and 284) and [ɑ] (Illustrations 285 and 286), each recorded at 5 msec/div (top tracing) and 1 msec/div (bottom tracing) with an amplitude setting of 0.1 V/div, compared with 0.5 V/div for the first speaker. [i] has a fundamental frequency of 210 Hz with a range of variation in duration of about 5% from cycle to cycle and the amplitude is 0.14 V peak to peak. [ɑ] has a fundamen-

detail but for a shorter utterance. Furthermore, the tal frequency of 215 Hz with a range of variation in duration of about 5% from cycle to cycle and the amplitude is 0.16 V peak to peak. The untrained voice is clearly less effective than the trained one and, by implication, less efficient.

The third and final speaker is an untrained female student with a touch of laryngitis saying [i] (Illustrations 287 and 288) and [ɑ] (Illustrations 289 and 290), each recorded at 5 msec/div (top tracing) and 1 msec/div (bottom tracing) with an amplitude setting of 0.1 V/div. Both [i] and [ɑ] have a fundamental frequency of 220 Hz with a mean duration of about 4.5 msec per cycle but variation in excess of 5% and, indeed, the fast tracing for [i] shows a cycle with a duration of 4.1 msec from the first peak to the second, which differs 9% from the mean. The amplitude in both cases is very small: 0.08 V peak to peak. It is obvious that the speaker, who shows signs both of breathy voice (in the lack of pronounced peaks and troughs, which is particularly well seen on the fast tracings) and of creaky voice (in the irregularity in the duration of the cycles) has the least efficient voice of the three.

2.3.4 Reading

It is suggested that the student now read the following item before proceeding with the projects below.

Shoup, J. E., and Pfeifer, L. L. 1976. Acoustic characteristics of speech sounds. In N. J. Lass (ed.), *Contemporary Issues in Experimental Phonetics,* pp. 171–224. Academic Press, Inc., New York.

Oscilloscope studies are so uncommon that the author can offer no other suggested readings on the speech wave form that would be appropriate for the beginning student.

2.3.5 Student Projects

2.3.5.1 *Replication Projects*

a. Make oscilloscope tracings of [i], [ɑ], and [u] at 0.2 and 0.002 sec/div and comment on how they differ from each other.
b. Make oscilloscope tracings at 0.2 sec/div of "two small clean pans" and segment.
c. Make oscilloscope tracings at 0.1 sec/div of "bit," "beat," "bid," and "bead" and measure the durations of the vowels.

2.3.5.2 *New Projects*

a. Record six sentences from a newspaper article and mark each syllable as having either sentence stress, primary word stress, secondary word stress, or no stress. Make durational measurements for each vowel and calculate: a) mean durations for each of the four stress types and b) mean durations for the clause final stressed as opposed to clause non-final stressed vowels.
b. Find a speaker with either a laryngeal pathology or an inefficient use of the larynx, make recordings of 10 isolated vowels, and comment on the wave forms.

2.4 THE FUNDAMENTAL FREQUENCY TRACKER

2.4.1 The Instrumentation

The sound spectrograph and the oscilloscope are such useful pieces of equipment partly because they do tasks that no other instrument can do and partly because they are so versatile, i.e., they do so many different things. The fundamental frequency tracker, which we discuss in this section, and the intensity tracker, which we discuss in section 2.5, perform only restricted tasks.

The fundamental frequency tracker, or pitch[5] meter, is used only for recording the number of vocal fold vibrations per second across time (see Illustration 291). It takes running speech as an input, subjects the voiced passages to analysis (voiceless stretches, of course, having no pitch), and provides an output that shows fundamental frequency in Hz on the vertical axis and time in msec on the horizontal axis. Data in this form look rather like a musical score in that high pitches are shown at the top of the line and low pitches at the bottom; rising pitches track to the right and upward whereas falling pitches track to the right and downward. The output is delivered either on paper or on a monitor screen (oscilloscope), the paper write-out being produced either by an ink-writing pen (stylus) on graph paper, rather like what one sees in some barometers, or by the light reflected from a galvanometer playing across light sensitive paper. The most common ink writers are the Siemens *Minograf* and *Oscillomink*; the Honeywell *Visicorder* is a common gavanometer write-out.

---

[5]Strictly speaking, the term *fundamental frequency* (usually written f_0 and spoken "f zero" or "f sub-zero") should be reserved for discussions of physical events, in our case the number of vocal fold vibrations per second, whereas the term *pitch* should be used for our perception of f_0, for example in statements such as "I shall first rank these five sounds by pitch and then find out their f_0." A third term, *tone,* refers to units in a linguistic system; a language with two tones, high and low, could be played on two differently tuned drums (i.e., "talking drums").

Furthermore, some write-outs take the form of a simple straight line which tracks up and down whereas others take the form of an up-and-down sinusoidal motion toward and away from a superior horizontal baseline where small deviations from the baseline represent high pitches and large deviations low pitches. In other words, one may draw in the fundamental frequency at the bottom of the sinusoids.

Like all instruments, the pitch meter, with its simple representation of pitch contours (i.e., fundamental frequency as it changes across time), gives a spurious impression of reality, whereas in fact much of the fine detail merely reflects the construction of the instrument. For example, an instrument cannot be made more accurate with respect to frequency without sacrificing precision in the time dimension and vice versa. It is impossible to do both things at the same time. In this sense a pitch contour says as much about the pitch meter as it does about the input signal. In addition, a pitch meter has to work on the incoming wave form and can only judge the beginning and end of a glottal cycle by estimating where the wave crosses a horizontal zero line. Sometimes the human eye and the experience of the phonetician can make better decisions than the machine.

Finally, mention should be made of computer-controlled pitch extractors, which calculate for each glottal cycle the duration of the period and present the data in the form of a pseudo-pitch contour where f_0 is the reciprocal of duration, i.e., $f_0 = 1/\text{time}$, e.g., 100 Hz:1/100 sec. Computer programs of this kind work very fast and can handle large bodies of data with great accuracy but can be fooled by sudden changes of pitch or voice quality.

Illustrations 292–295 show four types of write-out: the single line ink-writer, the single line galvanometer tracing, the single line tracing of a computer-controlled pitch extractor, and the sinusoidal galvanometer tracing.

2.4.2 Operation

The material to be analyzed is read into a microphone and passed through an amplifier before being led into the pitch meter, which in turn is connected to a paper write-out or a monitor screen or both. If material has already been recorded on tape, the tape recorder may be connected directly to the pitch meter. The amplifier level should be set high enough to activate the needle on the voltmeter of the pitch extractor but not so high that the needle runs into the red, which will distort the signal. The write-out controls should be set so that the high and low frequencies are well separated on the paper but not so spread that the tracing overlaps a second channel of data if more than one channel is being recorded at the same time.

Finally, once the settings have been made, one should take a lead from an oscillator (sine wave generator) to the pitch meter and play in a series of signals spaced out every 25 Hz between 50 Hz and 400 Hz to use as a calibration. One can later superimpose these signals and make up a ruler.

2.4.3 Demonstration Projects
2.4.3.1 *Intonation*
2.4.3.1.0.1 *The problem* There are three major functions of pitch in language: grammatical, lexical, and attitudinal. When, for example, the difference between an affirmative and a negative sentence or between a present tense and a past tense is to be seen not in segmental but only in tonal differences we may talk of the grammatical function of tone. When two lexical items (words) have identical consonants and vowels but differ in their tones we may speak of the lexical function of pitch (see topic 2.4.3.2). English does not use pitch in these ways but does make great use of the attitudinal function since one of the most important features of an intonation contour is to express something of the way a speaker feels about the situation he finds himself in at the moment of talking. This is not the only function of an intonation contour, of course, since it also helps define what we might call the phonological sentence as opposed to the grammatical sentence; an intonation contour spans the phonological sentence and marks its beginning and its end. So, for example, the grammatical sentence "If you come I'll give it to you" might be uttered as one phonological sentence on one intonation contour [‾˙‒‒↘...] or as two phonological sentences on two intonation contours [‾˙↗,‒↘...]. Differing contours define differing attitudes and the pitch meter helps us to define what these contours are.

2.4.3.1.0.2 *The data* Illustrations 296–301 show the English word "nine" spoken on six different intonation contours: 1) dispassionate [↘], 2) cheerful [↘], 3) impressed [⌢], 4) critical [↗], 5) questioning [↗], and 6) but not... [∨].

It should be particularly noted in this and subsequent sections that the fundamental frequency tracker on which these illustrations were made was set in such a way that it did not respond to the low intensity voicing during the pressure stage of an obstruent. For example, it is quite clear from the microphone tracing that the [b] of "broke" in Illustration 316 is voiced throughout but the fundamental frequency tracing registers zero.

2.4.3.1.0.3 *The interpretation* On the whole there is little interpretation to do on an intonation contour. The utterance needs first to be segmented, probably by reference to a wave form recorded on a second channel, although the voiceless stretches of the frequency contour also help. Then details that are largely redundant for defining intonation contours should be ignored, for example frequency perturbations at the transitions between consonants and vowels and the lowering of the frequency during the pressure stage of voiced plosives and during nasal consonants. A high tone syllable followed by a low tone syllable with no voicing break in between will doubtless show up as a glide from high to low and, depending on what the investigator is doing, the sequence could be treated either as "high plus low" or as a "fall."

The only serious problem in interpretation will occur when the instrument is having a bad day (and anyone who has worked in a laboratory knows that machines have personalities and moods, so beware!). The tracker may go berserk at certain frequencies or when confronted with a certain type of voice. Sometimes it is possible to extrapolate a contour through a bad section, sometimes it is not. If not, it is better either to try again or to ask the technician to make some adjustments.

Illustration 296 shows a low falling nucleus; the attitude is dispassionate and the frequencies are 105 Hz to 80 Hz.

Illustration 297 shows a high falling nucleus; the attitude is cheerful and the frequencies are 170 Hz to 80 Hz.

Illustration 298 shows a rise-fall nucleus; the attitude is impressed and the frequencies are 95 Hz to 120 Hz to 80 Hz.

Illustration 299 shows a low rising nucleus; the attitude is critical or bad-tempered and the frequencies are 100 Hz to 125 Hz.

Illustration 300 shows a high rising nucleus; the attitude is questioning and the frequencies are 125 Hz to 190 Hz.

Finally, Illustration 301 shows a fall-rise nucleus preceded by an initial upglide; the attitude leads one

to expect "No, not that one but something else" and the frequencies are 135 Hz to 165 Hz to 85 Hz to 135 Hz.

2.4.3.2 *Tone*

2.4.3.2.0.1 *The problem* Tone languages (and more than half the languages in the world *are* tone languages) are by definition languages that use fundamental frequency to distinguish between words that are otherwise (i.e., segmentally) identical. So, for example, [bà] with a low tone may mean one thing and [bá] with a high tone may mean something else. Tone is measured on the syllable center, which is usually a vowel.

The pitch meter may be used either to confirm the tones that we have heard on the syllables of lexical items or to quantify the frequency range of tonal units in the language for given speakers or to show the relationship between the base tones in a word (which one might look up in a dictionary) and the intonational contour of a sentence onto which the base tones are superimposed.

So, for example, many tone languages have an intonation contour (usually called "terraced") that falls steadily throughout the sentence such that a high tone at the end of the sentence may have a lower frequency than a low tone at the beginning. In particularly long sentences tones shift so slightly that even the best-trained ear is subject to error as the point of reference moves and memory limitations come into play. In such cases, the use of a pitch meter is recommended.

2.4.3.2.0.2 *The data* "Kòfí" [kòfí] and "Kwàdwó" [kʷàdʒʷó] (two boy's names) and "hwèhwɛ́" [çʷìçʷɛ́] (a verb meaning "to look for") are three words from Twi, a tone language spoken in Ghana, West Africa. Each has a LH sequence of base tones (a low tone followed by a high tone) such that the tone contour of each is similar to that of the first three words of a long list in English when read aloud with pauses between each, for example " 'A giggle.' 'A gaggle.' 'A goggle'... " [.-ʹ.-ʹ.-] (Illustrations 302–304).

When these three Twi lexical items are put into a sentence, however, "Kòfí hwèhwɛ́ Kwàdwó" (Kofi is looking for Kwadwo), the tonal contour is similar to that of a list of English words read aloud *without* pauses between each one, for example, "There's 'a giggle,' 'a gaggle,' 'a goggle,' and a... " [···ʹ.-ʹ._ ...] (Illustration 305).

2.4.3.2.0.3 *The interpretation* When the three English words are spoken separately (Illustrations 302–304) the three low tones are more or less the same (120 Hz, 110 Hz, and 110 Hz), as are the three high tones (148 Hz, 140 Hz, and 145 Hz).

However, when the words are part of a sentence with a terraced intonation contour (Illustration 305) the H of the first word (200 Hz) is higher than the H of the second word (185 Hz), which in turn is higher than the H of the third word (155 Hz).

Similarly, the L of the first word (180 Hz) is higher than the L of the second word (150 Hz), which in turn is higher than the L of the third word (130 Hz). The first L (180 Hz) even has a higher fundamental frequency than the third H (155 Hz).

These data would be paralleled exactly by the Twi words and sentence referred to previously; furthermore, if we were to reverse the names and say ''Kwadwo is looking for Kofi'' the same picture would hold true for the sentence as a whole but the frequencies on the names would be reversed.

2.4.3.3 *Inherent Pitch*

2.4.3.3.0.1 *The problem* Because consonants differ from each other in the articulatory configurations necessary for their production, they will set up different oral and pharyngeal pressures which press back on the vocal folds and which will in turn result in different fundamental frequencies. In the case of the plosives, frequency may be examined either during the pressure stage, immediately upon release, or some 50 msec after release before the steady state of the following vowel has set in.

The vocal folds, of course, do not vibrate during the pressure stage of voiceless plosives, but there is a delicate balance between the pressures above and below the vocal folds before the release of voiced plosives which permits voicing to take place, although only at relatively low fundamental frequencies.

Just after the release the fundamental frequency is relatively high for all plosives but higher for voiceless plosives than for voiced ones. Fifty msec later the fundamental frequency has fallen somewhat and by the time the steady state of the following vowel has set in, about 150 msec after the release, the fundamental frequency approaches the target value for the vowel. However, as a result of the pitch-raising effect of voiceless plosives as opposed to the pitch-lowering effect of voiced ones, even the steady state frequency of the following vowel is likely to be higher following, for example, [p], [t], and [k] than following [b], [d] and [g].

Similarly, the articulatory configurations necessary for the production of different vowels, for example, a relatively open vocal tract for [ɛ] and [a] as opposed to the relatively obstructed vocal tract for [i] and [u], result in different oral/pharyngeal pressures with consequent differences in fundamental frequency, i.e., the target value is never quite reached.

These frequency changes take place so rapidly during the production of plosives that it is preferable to measure them with a computer-controlled pitch extractor, whereas the vowels can be examined satisfactorily on a pitch meter.

2.4.3.3.0.2 *The data* Illustrations 306–309 show the fundamental frequency during the pressure, release, and post-release stages of four consonants [pʔ], [pʰ], [b], and [m] and Illustrations 310–312 show the fundamental frequency of the vowels [i], [a], and [u] in identical consonantal environments (after [tʰ] and before silence).

2.4.3.3.0.3 *The interpretation* Illustrations 306–309 show that only [b] and [m] have voicing before the oral release and normally, but not here, during this stage the fundamental frequency is relatively low. Upon release the fundamental frequency of all four is high, considerably so for [pʔ] (140 Hz), less so for [pʰ] (120 Hz), and less still for [b] (110 Hz) and [m] (100 Hz). One hundred msec after the release, all four contours fall somewhat (to 120 Hz, 110 Hz, 95 Hz, and 92 Hz, respectively), but the ranking by frequency is still maintained and indeed continues to be maintained during the steady state of the following vowel (100 Hz, 100 Hz, 92 Hz, and 92 Hz, respectively).

It should be borne in mind that there are so many variables involved in an investigation of this kind that one could not put any faith in results based on just a few tokens. Scores, even hundreds of measurements, are needed to give reliable average values. The values given in the present part are, however, quite typical.

Illustrations 310–312 show that vowels also have inherent pitch. In this case, once more isolated but typical values, the close vowels have higher fundamental frequencies than the open vowel: [i] 105 Hz, [a] 97 Hz, and [u] 103 Hz.

2.4.3.4 *Stress*

2.4.3.4.1 *Word Stress*

24.3.4.1.1 *The problem* We have already seen (in parts 2.2.3.3.4 and 2.2.3.3.5) that the abstract, linguistic feature we call ''stress'' is actually realized in a number of ways in English and that fundamental frequency is the most important cue for the perception of stress. The pitch meter is a simple tool for examining word and sentence stress in English.

2.4.3.4.1.2 *The data* Illustrations 313 and 314 look at the pair "bíllow"/"belów" to examine the role played by fundamental frequency in distinguishing between members of this pair.

2.4.3.4.1.3 *The interpretation* "Bíllow" carries a fundamental frequency contour of the type [⌐ ╲ .] (148 Hz to 115 Hz followed by 90 Hz), which we recognize as typical of two-syllable words with initial stress in sentence final position.

"Belów," on the other hand, carries a contour of the type [. ╲] (100 Hz followed by 130 Hz to 85 Hz), which we recognize as typical of two-syllable words with *final* stress in sentence final position.

If these words are put in sentence non-final position, as for example in the carrier sentences "Say the word 'bíllow' *again*" [⁻ · ⁻ − · · ╲] and "Say the word 'belów' *again*" [⁻ · ⁻ · − · ╲], the contrast will be realized in a rather different way.

2.4.3.4.2 *Sentence Stress*

2.4.3.4.2.1 *The problem* Sentence stress too is realized largely by fundamental frequency since the syllable with nuclear stress is the only one with a rising or falling contour, other syllables having relatively level pitch. There are, however, three problems of interpretation here.

First, it should be recalled that, although an intonation contour frequently has the same span as one grammatical sentence, it almost as often covers only a grammatical clause. In such cases the grammatical sentence comprises two phonological sentences. Indeed, an intonation contour may cover only a phrase or a word, for example, "Juice, tea, or milk?" [⌐, ⌐, − ╲].

Second, the nuclear syllable does not always have a moving pitch contour. Sometimes it may be level, for example, a threatening "Come here!" [_ −].

Finally, although we perceive non-nuclear syllables as relatively level in pitch, in fact an examination of the fundamental frequency contour will show a great amount of movement. For example, inherent pitch will pull contours up and down over short time spans, a high pitch followed by a low one may blend into a fall, and there will always be transitions between steady states, as in Illustrations 313 and 314, as long as they are not separated by voiceless consonants.

Nonetheless, in spite of these difficulties, the pitch meter gives us good data on sentence stress.

2.4.3.4.2.2 *The data* Illustrations 315–318 show fundamental frequency contours for the sentences "Joe broke the plate," "Jóe broke the plate," "Joe bróke the plate," and "Joe broke the pláte."

2.4.3.4.2.3 *The interpretation* Illustration 315 shows a low falling pitch on "plate" (125 Hz to 75 Hz), Illustration 316 a high fall on "Jóe" (135 Hz to 80 Hz), Illustration 317 a high fall on "bróke" (140 Hz to 80 Hz), and Illustration 318 a high fall on "pláte" (148 Hz to 80 Hz).

In addition, Illustration 315 might have shown (but did not) the contour falling a little to the [b] of "broke" and rising again after the release of the [b] (inherent pitch) and Illustration 317 might have shown (but again did not) "Joe" being uttered on a rising pitch in anticipation of the high tone onset for "bróke" (transition).

2.4.4 Reading

It is suggested that the student now read the following items before proceeding with the projects below.

Fry, D. B. 1958. Experiments in the perception of stress. *Language and Speech 1*: 126–152.

Lieberman, P. 1967. *Intonation, Perception, and Language*. Research monograph No. 38, pp. 67–93. The MIT Press, Cambridge, Mass.

Ohala, J. 1970. Aspects of the control and production of speech. *UCLA Working Papers in Phonetics 15*: 35–48.

2.4.5 Student Projects

2.4.5.1 *Replication Projects*

a. Record "nine" spoken three ways and measure the fundamental frequency of each syllable.

b. Record "a subject" and "to subject" and measure the fundamental frequency of each syllable.

c. Record "Jóe broke the plate" and plot the intonation contour on a calibrated piece of graph paper.

2.4.5.2 *New Projects*

a. Record the sentence "Ibrahim's got thrée wives" with a falling nucleus (cheerful), a rise-fall nucleus (amazed), and a high rise nucleus (questioning) and plot the contours on a calibrated piece of graph paper.

b. Find either a foreign student for whom English is not a mother tongue or a client in a speech clinic who uses inappropriate intonation patterns. Record three sentences and analyze the contours. What is inappropriate about them?

2.5   THE INTENSITY TRACKER AND THE SOUND LEVEL METER

2.5.1   The Instrumentation

The intensity tracker, or intensity meter, is used only for recording the amount of energy in a signal at a given moment in time or during a predetermined period of time (see Illustration 319). It takes running speech as an input, subjects it to analysis, and provides an output that shows intensity in decibels (dB) on the vertical axis and time in msec on the horizontal axis. Upward excursions of the tracing therefore indicate increases in energy, which will be perceived as louder, whereas downward excursions indicate decreases in energy, which will be perceived as softer. The output is delivered either on paper or on a monitor screen, the paper write-outs being produced either by an ink-writing stylus or by the light reflected from a galvanometer.

It is not necessary to distinguish between variations in intensity (I), which is measured in watts per square centimeter; pressure (P), which is measured in dynes per square centimeter; work, which is measured in ergs; energy, which is an expression of work done, and amplitude (see item 2.2.3.4.0.1), since for our purposes they may all be considered ways of talking about physical events that are perceived as variations in loudness.

In fact the most common way of calibrating these variations is by reference not to any absolute but to a ratio between the energy in two sounds.

If the pressure of one sound were found to be 1 dyne/cm² and that of another 100 dynes/cm², the second sound could be said to be 100 times louder than the first, which is a ratio of 100:1 or 10×10:1 or, in logarithmic terms, 10^2:1. Taking the logarithm (^{2}) and multiplying by 20 we say that the second sound is $2 \times 20 = 40$ dB louder than the first. A ratio of 10,000:1 or $10 \times 10 \times 10 \times 10$:1 or 10^4:1 gives a figure of $4 \times 20 = 80$ dB louder. Similarly, if the pressure ratio between two sounds is 1:10,000 = 1:10^4 we say that the second is 80 dB softer than the first, or -80 dB. Any two sounds may be compared in this way, although in practice we usually compare a given sound with the softest sound that most people can hear (0.0002 or 2×10^{-4} dynes/cm²).

Providing that one has a system with at least three channels it is therefore possible to obtain synchronized write-outs for the wave form (Mike), fundamental frequency (f_0 in Hz), and intensity (I in dB) for any given utterance.

It is possible, however, to take readings in dB by using a different piece of equipment—the sound level meter,[6] which does not give a write-out but merely indicates the level by the excursion of a needle round a calibrated dial (see Illustration 320). This procedure is convenient for some purposes but static, whereas the intensity meter is dynamic. The sound level meter is difficult to read when the needle is in motion and is usually set so that the latter sticks at maximum deflection, whereas the intensity meter tracks steadily up and down as the intensity changes in running speech.

The precision sound level meter can be set up in a fixed position to monitor airplanes, factory noise, or speech while the small portable sound level meter is held in the hand to do similar tasks but with less accuracy. They are particularly useful for estimating overall speech levels.

One intensity or sound level meter may differ from another with respect to the time window through which a piece of speech is examined. One should not suppose that a meter that gives a reading each 10 msec is necessarily to be preferred to one that gives a reading only every 200 msec, since in the former case one may not be able to see the wood for the trees. In fact, a time window the length of approximately one speech segment is sufficient in most cases since all we usually want to see is the peak value for each syllable center and the smaller peak values for the continuant consonants. Fine detail superimposed on these peaks would only make interpretation more difficult; a smoothed, averaged, integrated curve (let us assume for our purposes that these three terms mean the same thing) serves us better.

Both the intensity meter and the sound level meter may be used for an additional purpose, spectrographic analysis, and in this respect they function a little like the sound spectrograph. However, they perform this task at an altogether more primitive level.

The intensity meter may, for example, be set up either to read the energy throughout the whole frequency spectrum (Full scale) or to read the energy in only part of the frequency spectrum, either the bottom half of the speech range (Low pass) where vowels have most of their energy or the top half of the speech range (High pass) where many fricatives have most of their energy.

---

[6]This description refers specifically to the Brüel and Kjaer 2209 precision sound level meter.

The precision sound level meter has a built-in octave or half-octave band filter. Two tuning forks, with the second one having twice the frequency of the first, are said to be one octave apart such that the band of frequencies between 250 Hz and 500 Hz is one octave, that between 500 Hz and 1000 Hz is a second octave, that between 1000 Hz and 2000 Hz is a third, and so on. The speech range covers something like eight octaves and the meter can be set to read only the energy in a given octave. One band may respond only to the fundamental frequency, another only to close vowels, a third only to open vowels, a higher one only to [ʃ], and a still higher one only to [s].

In summary, the intensity meter is useful for obtaining data on the amount of energy in each segment of a sample of running speech, and the sound level meter enables us to monitor the overall speech level and to identify those frequency bands where most of the energy lies.

2.5.2 Operation

The material to be analyzed is read into a microphone and passed through an amplifier before being led into the intensity meter, which in turn is connected to a paper write-out or a monitor screen or both. If material has already been recorded on tape, the tape recorder may be connected directly to the intensity meter. The amplifier level should be set high enough to activate the needle on the voltmeter of the intensity meter but not so high that the needle runs into the red, which will distort the signal. The operator should be careful to set the write-out controls so that the tracing does not overlap with that of another channel of recording, such as a fundamental frequency tracing.

Finally, once the settings have been made, but before one begins to record, one should play a fixed signal (white noise will do well) through an amplifier and into a loudspeaker and adjust the gain (volume) until a sound level meter placed in front of the loudspeaker reads, let us say, 40 dB. At this point the microphone, which picks up the signal for the intensity meter, may be placed near the sound level meter and a 40-dB tracing will be obtained. Similar tracings may be obtained at 5-dB steps between 40 dB and 80 dB to use as a calibration. One can later superimpose these tracings to make up a ruler.

The sound level meter is extremely easy to operate—one merely has to screw on the microphone and turn on the unit for it to read an incoming signal. The only choices are whether or not to use the filter, whether to have the meter respond through a short or long time window (Fast/Slow), and whether or not to have the needle stick at peak values (Hold).

2.5.3 Demonstration Projects

2.5.3.1 Stress

2.5.3.1.1 Word Stress

2.5.3.1.1.1 The problem We have already had occasion to point out that the term *fundamental frequency* is used for physical measurements whereas *pitch* refers to perception and *tone* to linguistic systems. It would be all to the good if we could also say that *intensity* was used for physical measurements whereas *loudness* referred to perception and *stress* to linguistic systems. I say "would be" because the term *stress* is used so loosely and in so many different ways. It is something of a cover term and one should always ask, in the presence of this word, whether it seems to refer to intensity, fundamental frequency, duration, quality, or a combination of these. One acceptable usage is to reserve "stress" for the linguistic unit of intensity, and this is what linguists used to imagine they were doing when they stated that stress implied "greater effort" or "an increase in loudness." Unfortunately the data given by way of illustration often showed that they were really referring to what one might better call "prominence" (i.e., being made to stand out by one means or another) and prominence is the result of "accent" at the linguistic level, a term still used in poetics but largely forgotten in linguistics, where it has been replaced by "stress." One can only hope that authors at least know what they mean when they use this term in this way.

Its use in topic 2.4.3.4, for example, unambiguously refers to "accent," whereas its use here in topic 2.5.3.1 could refer either to "accent" or to the linguistic use of intensity.

We have already seen the predominant role played by fundamental frequency in making syllables prominent in English. Duration plays a smaller role and intensity a yet smaller but still not insignificant one.

2.5.3.1.1.2 The data Illustrations 321 and 322 show intensity tracings for the pair "súbject"/ "subjéct." For comparative purposes (see topic 2.5.3.3.) five channel recordings have been presented: intensity (low pass), intensity (full scale), intensity (high pass), fundamental frequency, and microphone.

2.5.3.1.1.3 The interpretation We can see from Illustrations 321 and 322 that accented syllables

do indeed have greater intensity (Full scale), although, as usual, one should always keep inherent intensity in the back of one's mind. The second syllable of "impórt," for example, will always have greater intensity than the first since it is accented, long, and an open vowel. However, the first syllable of "ímport" may well not have greater intensity than the second even though it is accented since it is also short and a close vowel.

2.5.3.1.2 *Sentence Stress*

2.5.3.1.2.1 *The problem* The problem of sentence stress has already been discussed in part 2.2.3.3.5 and it will be recalled that one of the problems is to define the intensity relationships between the syllable which bears the sentence stress, and other syllables which bear only word stress.

2.5.3.1.2.2 *The data* Illustrations 315–318 show intensity tracings for the by now familiar sentences "Joe broke the plate," "Jóe broke the plate," "Joe bróke the plate," and "Joe broke the pláte."

2.5.3.1.2.3 *The interpretation* Illustration 315 shows that in the sentence "Joe broke the plate" the first stressed syllable ("Joe") has greater intensity than the second ("broke") and the second more than the third ("plate"). Illustration 316 shows the first and nuclear syllable to have an intensity peak slightly greater than that seen in Illustration 315. When the second word has the nuclear stress (Illustration 317) we see a high peak on that syllable and when the final word has the sentence stress (Illustration 318) the greatest intensity is seen on that syllable, in marked contrast to the descending contour of the neutral pattern.

In other words, direct evidence of the accentual pattern of a sentence can be obtained from an intensity tracing.

2.5.3.2 *High Pass and Low Pass Filters*

2.5.3.2.0.1 *The problem* We sometimes need to compare the energy in a given consonant with that in a neighboring vowel. Maybe we merely need to segment an utterance a little more accurately; maybe we want to know whether a target plosive really had a pressure stage or not; maybe we have to find out whether a fricative has an appropriate amount of energy in it.

In such cases, it is useful to use the high and low pass filters and, in the case of the fricatives, it may be convenient to use the octave filter on the sound level meter.

2.5.3.2.0.2 *The data* Illustrations 323–326 show the syllables [fa], [θa], [sa], and [ʃa] recorded on three channels of the intensity meter: full scale, low pass, and high pass.

Illustration 327 shows the sentence "She saw Susan's shoes" recorded on the same three channels with the intonation contour [ˌ - - · ˎ].

2.5.3.2.0.3 *The interpretation* We see from Illustrations 323–327 that the low pass filter has a large amplitude output for the vowels whereas the high pass filter has a large amplitude output for the fricatives [s] and [ʃ] and that both sets of data are reflected in the full scale tracing. The open vowels have more energy than the close vowels and the strident fricatives [s] and [ʃ] have more energy than the nonstrident [f] and [θ]. Furthermore, the lenis [z] has less energy than the fortis [s]. It is easier to segment an utterance by using the synchronized HP and LP channels than by using only the full scale tracing.

2.5.3.3 *Synchronous Fundamental Frequency and Intensity Tracings*

2.5.3.3.0.1 *The problem* When the focus of our attention is a prosodic (suprasegmental) phenomenon, i.e., pitch, loudness, or length, we often need to be able to look at both fundamental frequency and intensity tracings across time. The question is usually: Do fundamental frequency and intensity have an orthogonal relationship? That is to say, can you change the one without changing the other?

2.5.3.3.0.2 *The data* All the illustrations mentioned in this section were recorded with both fundamental frequency and intensity tracings and Illustrations 313–318 and 321–322 help us to answer this question.

2.5.3.3.0.3 *The interpretation* It will be seen from simple visual inspection, without taking any measurements, that the answer to the question posed above is usually "No, their relationship is not orthogonal." Since both intensity and fundamental frequency are controlled a) by vocal fold tension and b) by subglottal pressure, it is not surprising that the two tracings should look very similar. This is not to say, however, that these two dimensions can never be controlled independently.

2.5.4 Reading

It is suggested that the student now read the following items before proceeding with the projects below.

Lehiste, I. 1970. *Suprasegmentals,* pp. 133–138. The MIT Press, Cambridge, Mass.

Lehiste, I., and Peterson, G.E. 1959. Vowel amplitude and phonemic stress in American English. *The Journal of the Acoustical Society of America 31:* 428–435.

Ohala, J. 1970. Aspects of the control and production of speech. *UCLA Working Papers in Phonetics 15:* 35–48.

2.5.5. Student Projects

2.5.5.1 *Replication Projects*

a. Record and measure the intensity of the vowels in the words "súbject" and "subjéct."

b. Record and measure the intensity of the consonants in the syllables [fa], [θa], [sa], and [ʃa].

c. Make both fundamental frequency and intensity tracings for the sentence "Joe bróke the plate" and compare the data from the two channels.

2.5.5.2 *New Projects*

a. Find a speaker of a language other than English and make some recordings to determine how his language handles contrasts like those in part 2.5.3.1.2. You will have to find out quickly whether the speaker's language does this kind of thing at all, since it may merely use constructions like "It was plate that he broke."

b. Find a client who misarticulates /s/. Make recordings of /s/ in various contexts and obtain intensity measurements. Are they similar to measurements obtained from recordings of yourself?

3
Physiological Instrumentation

3.1 AIR PRESSURE INSTRUMENTATION

3.1.1 The Instrumentation

Many laboratories have one large multipurpose, multichannel unit capable of handling, among other things, air pressure, airflow, and electromyographic data. The Honeywell Medical System, described here, is typical of such units (see Illustrations 328–330).

The Honeywell system has 12 separate channels, each with an amplifier, an analyzer, a write-out, and a monitor screen. A patch panel provides interconnections between channels.

The controls of the amplifier and analyzer may be adjusted to give a read-out: a) of appropriate amplitude, i.e., the tracing is large enough peak to peak to read easily but not so large that tracings on different channels overlap, and b) with an appropriate time window, i.e., there is neither too much nor too little detail on the write-out for the task in hand.

The write-out device is a visicorder, which uses a beam of light reflected up and down from a galvanometer responding to changing voltages to trace the output on a moving roll of light sensitive paper. One may choose between paper speeds of 1, 2, 4, or 8 × 0.1, 1 or 10 inches per sec, i.e., 12 choices within the range 0.1 and 80 inches per sec, although speeds of from 1 to 8 inches per sec are adequate for pho-

netic research and clinical diagnosis. One constraint that many laboratories are likely to feel is the cost of a roll of paper—about $24 for 100 feet. A 100-foot roll driven at 1 inch per sec will be enough for only 20 min worth of data, so most student practice runs will have to be at 1 or 2 inches per sec.

The visicorder can also produce vertical and horizontal calibration marks on the paper as it rolls. The time marker makes vertical lines on the write-out every 0.01, 0.1, 1, or 10 sec, depending on one's needs and the paper speed. The resultant grid makes it easy to quantify the data.

We have already seen (subsection 2.4.1) that the write-out for each channel could equally well be a stylus tracing in ink on a roll of graph paper.

The monitor screen (oscilloscope) gives a temporary visual representation of what will appear on the write-out if the latter has been activated. Each channel has an amplitude control, and the speed at which the signal sweeps across the 25 × 37 cm cathode ray tube may be adjusted to 1, 2.5, 5, or 10 cm per sec. As a result the screen may hold between 3.7 and 37 sec of speech at any one time.

The patch panel is a series of input and output points for each channel. One may plug a lead, i.e., a wire or cable, from an outside source into the amplifier/analyzer/visicorder input and take a lead from the visicorder into the monitor screen. If necessary one may switch from channel to channel and, in addition, there are inputs and outputs for the fundamental frequency, intensity, and wave form (Mike) trackers, all of which are incorporated into the unit and which can be plugged into the visicorder or oscilloscope for a write-out, which is synchronized with the physiological data. Signals for channels 1 to 7 on the Honeywell Medical System may be brought directly into the amplifiers from the rear of the unit through more closely fitting connections.

The only additional piece of equipment needed to obtain air pressure data is a pressure transducer (see Illustration 331). A transducer merely turns a signal in one physical medium into a signal in another medium (see subsection 2.1.1). In the case of a pressure transducer, the subject places one end of a small bore plastic tube (about 1 or 2 mm in diameter) into his mouth or nose and the other end into a transducer such that, when the subject blows, the positive pressure is turned into a voltage increase. Conversely, when the subject sucks, the negative pressure is turned into a voltage decrease. The transducer is connected by a lead to the input for the amplifier/analyzer/visicorder at the rear of the medical system; the visicorder gives a write-out on which an excursion upward from the zero line (which is the tracing when the subject is neither sucking nor blowing and has put the transducer onto a table) indicates a rise in pressure and a downward excursion below the zero line indicates a fall below atmospheric pressure, usually called positive and negative pressures, respectively.

3.1.2 Operation

Since a laboratory should have a set of typed instructions for the use of the medical system which includes amplifier settings appropriate for various pressure measurements using specified transducers on specified channels with specified tube lengths and diameters, all the investigator has to do is plug in the transducer, attach a clean tube, turn the power on, check the amplifier settings, connect the visicorder to the monitor screen at the patch panel and, having put the tube in his mouth, say "[pɑ], [pɑ], [pɑ]." If there is a triple up-and-down deflection on the screen and a series of right-to-left deflections of the light beam in the visicorder the investigator is ready to begin recording. The recording paper will roll merely by pressing the "drive" button. A second push on the same button will stop the paper.

The oral pressure tracing may be calibrated by connecting a cylinder of oxygen to the input of a U-tube oral manometer (see section 3.4) and the output of the manometer to the input of the pressure transducer. By turning on the tap of the oxygen cylinder it is possible to force the water round the calibrated manometer by fixed amounts measured in centimeters of water (cm H_2O), 1 cm H_2O being equal to a pressure of 1000 dynes per cm^2, although the pressure transducer registers not absolute pressure but pressure variations above and below atmospheric. The visicorder write-out should first be driven with the manometer reading 0 (atmospheric). Then the manometer should be set to read 1 cm H_2O and the paper driven again. A third reading at 2 cm H_2O should be recorded and so on up to 12 cm H_2O. These calibrations may then be superimposed to make a ruler.

3.1.3 Demonstration Projects
3.1.3.1 *Oral Pressure*
3.1.3.1.1 *Voiced and Voiceless Plosives*
3.1.3.1.1.1 *The problem* In order to produce a bilabial plosive, [p], a speaker must force air out of his lungs, raise the soft palate to prevent air from escaping through the nose, bring the two lips together, allow air pressure to build up behind the lips, and finally open the lips to allow the pressure to be released. If the open end of a pressure transducer tube is placed in the mouth a centimeter or so behind the lips, the rise and fall in pressure will be detected by the transducer and passed on to the visicorder. If the investigator is examining tip-dental or blade-alveolar rather than bilabial plosives, the open end of the tube will have to be inserted farther until it is on the glottal side of the place of articulation. To obtain measurements for palatal or velar plosives it is preferable to insert the tube not through the lips but through the nose (see topic 3.1.3.3).

It will be of interest to see whether the oral pressure measurements for voiced and voiceless plosives and for nasals differ from each other.

3.1.3.1.1.2 *The data* Illustrations 332–334 and 335–337 show oral pressure (P_0) for [pɑ], [bɑ], [mɑ] and for [tɑ], [dɑ], [nɑ].

3.1.3.1.1.3 *The interpretation* Illustrations 332–334 show that there is a greater buildup of oral pressure for the voiceless than for the voiced plosives, which in turn have more than the nasals. The low oral pressure for the nasals is easily explained since the soft palate is not raised, which allows the air to escape through the nose. The intermediate values for the voiced plosives are a necessary consequence of the fact that they are voiced. If the oral pressure for [b] and [d] got too high voicing would cease, so the speaker has to use one of several means

at his disposal to prevent this from happening, for example allowing the pharyngeal walls to expand or lowering the larynx a little. There are no such constraints on the voiceless plosives, so their pressure values are usually high. As a result we sometimes call the voiceless plosives "fortis" (i.e., strong) and the voiced ones "lenis" ['li:nɪs] (i.e., weak). Furthermore, the high pressure fortis plosives usually have a period of aspiration following the release and a delayed onset of voicing.

Small pressure variations caused by vocal fold vibrations are superimposed on the pressure curves for voiced consonants.

The oral pressure values for the plosives in these illustrations, [p] 7.5, [b] 3.4, [t] 10, and [d] 5.6 cm H_2O, are greater than but comparable with those given by Arkebauer et al., 1967, *Journal of Speech and Hearing Research 10*: 196–208: /p/ 6.69, /t/ 6.64, /b/ 3.14, and /d/ 2.29 cm H_2O and by Subtelny et al., 1966, *Journal of Speech and Hearing Research 9*: 498–518: /p/ 6.43, /t/ 6.18, /b/ 4.37, and /d/ 4.52 cm H_2O. The nasals, [m] 0.5 and [n] 0.5 cm H_2O, also have greater oral pressure values than those given by Subtelny et al.: /m/ 0.22 and /n/ 0.43 cm H_2O.

3.1.3.1.2 *Voiced and Voiceless Fricatives*
3.1.3.1.2.1 *The problem* The fricatives also need a buildup of pressure behind the place of articulation for their production, and in spite of the fact that there is always at least a narrow passage for the air to pass through, the pressure still rises to high values.

How do the oral pressures for the fricatives compare with those for the plosives and nasals?

3.1.3.1.2.2 *The data* Illustrations 338–341 and 342–345 show oral pressure for [fɑ], [θɑ], [sɑ], and [ʃɑ] and for [vɑ], [ðɑ], [zɑ], and [ʒɑ] using the same settings, the same speaker, and the same production level as were used for Illustrations 332–337.

3.1.3.1.2.3 *The interpretation* Illustrations 338–341 and 342–345 show that voiceless fricatives have oral pressures similar to those we have seen for voiceless plosives and that voiced fricatives have pressures at least equal to and often in excess of those of voiced plosives in spite of the fact that fricatives do not have a complete obstruction of the vocal tract behind which pressure may be built up. It is clear that the narrowing for a fricative is small enough to hold back pressures behind it and that high pressures are necessary to generate turbulence.

The values seen in these illustrations, [fɑ] 6.5, [θɑ] 8.2, [sɑ] 10, [ʃɑ] 11.4, [vɑ] 8.3, [ðɑ] 6.4, [zɑ] 6.6, and [ʒɑ] 6.3 cm H_2O, are once more greater than those given by Arkebauer et al., op cit.: /f/ 5.56, /θ/ 5.77, /s/ 5.74, and /ʃ/ 6.25 cm H_2O; /v/ 3.15, /ð/ 3.79, /z/ 3.57, and /ʒ/ 3.87 cm H_2O; and by Subtelny et al., op. cit.: /f/ 5.80, /s/ 5.69, /v/ 3.82, and /z/ 4.30 cm H_2O.

3.1.3.1.3 *Oral and Nasal Consonants*
3.1.3.1.3.1 *The problem* Nasal consonants might well be classified as stops since two articulators are brought together at some place in the oral cavity and form an obstruction to the passage of air from the lungs. In this respect they are identical to plosives. However, the soft palate is not raised so that air is allowed to flow through the nose. The question is whether the impedance of the nose, i.e., the degree to which the unusual shape of the nasal cavity hinders the passage of air, is great enough to allow pressure to build up in the mouth.

3.1.3.1.3.2 *The data* Illustrations 332–334 and 335–337 show oral pressure for [pɑ], [bɑ], [mɑ], and for [tɑ], [dɑ], [nɑ].

3.1.3.1.3.3 *The interpretation* We have already seen in part 3.1.3.1.1 that pressure does build up in the oral cavity during the production of nasal consonants, although much less than for either the voiced or voiceless plosives.

3.1.3.1.4 *Implosives, Ejectives, and Clicks*
3.1.3.1.4.1 *The problem* Most of the sounds produced by man are uttered on air being driven from the lungs, i.e., on a pulmonic egressive airstream, but sounds that do not use lung air are not uncommon. Three such types are the implosives, ejectives, and clicks.

The implosives and ejectives use a pharyngeal airstream, which is produced by raising the soft palate, making a stop in the oral cavity, and tightly closing the glottis, which traps a column of air within the oral and/or pharyngeal cavities. A subsequent lowering of the larynx will decrease the pressure of the air within this chamber below atmospheric so that when the oral stop is released air will flow into the mouth. Sounds produced on such a pharyngeal ingressive airstream are called implosives. On the other hand, a subsequent raising of the larynx will increase the pressure of the air within this chamber above atmospheric so that when the oral stop is released air will flow out of the mouth. Sounds produced on such a pharyngeal egressive airstream are called ejectives.

Clicks are produced on an oral ingressive airstream. Two stops are made in the oral cavity, one at the velum and another farther forward, which traps a column of air within the oral cavity only. The speaker then either retracts the velar stop or lowers the tongue in the mouth between the two stops, leaving the air in a larger chamber and at less than atmospheric pressure so that when the more forward stop is released air flows into the mouth. Since the oral cavity is independent of the pharyngeal and nasal cavities during the production of a click, these sounds may be simultaneously nasalized and/or voiced.

The production of implosives, ejectives, and clicks cannot be fully illustrated without oral pressure data.

3.1.3.1.4.2 *The data* Illustrations 346–349 show oral pressure for the bilabial plosive [bɑ], for the bilabial implosive [ɓɑ], for the bilabial ejective [p'ɑ], and for the voiceless bilabial click [Ɵɑ], whereas Illustrations 350–353 show oral pressure for a similar blade-alveolar set [dɑ], [ɗɑ], [ɟɑ], and [t'ɑ].

3.1.3.1.4.3 *The interpretation* Illustrations 346–349 clearly show that the plosive exhibits a positive oral pressure of 5.6 cm H_2O and that the ejective has a higher oral pressure still, 22 cm H_2O, whereas the implosive with -7.6 cm H_2O and the click with -44 cm H_2O have negative oral pressures. The pressures seen in Illustrations 350–353 show a similar relationship: [d] 7.6, [t'] 24, [ɗ] -12.6 and [ɟ] -36 cm H_2O. The pressures developed for the ejectives and clicks were so large that the amplitude settings had to be halved in order to get the tracings on the paper at all.

3.1.3.1.5 *Word Stress*
3.1.3.1.5.1 *The problem* We have already examined the problem of word stress from a number of points of view but it would be useful to ask whether the pressures developed for plosives and fricatives show differences as between stressed and unstressed syllables.

3.1.3.1.5.2 *The data* Illustrations 354 and 355 show oral pressure for the pair "pérvert"/"pervért."

3.1.3.1.5.3 *The interpretation* We see from Illustrations 354 and 355 that the overall greater intensity in the stressed syllable is not really reflected in the oral pressure tracings. It is true that the /p/ of "pérvert" has 9.6 cm H_2O whereas the /p/ of "pervért" has only 8 cm H_2O but, in addition, the /v/ of "pérvert" has 6.5 cm H_2O, which is greater than the 5.9 cm H_2O for the /v/ of "pervért." Both final /t/s have 5.5 cm H_2O.

3.1.3.1.6 *Sentence Stress*
3.1.3.1.6.1 *The problem* We have seen that there are a number of cues in the acoustic signal that enable us to define how the linguistic entity "sen-tence stress" is realized and we shall now see whether there are any further cues to be obtained from physiological data.

3.1.3.1.6.2 *The data* Illustrations 356 and 357 show oral pressure for the sentences "Péter broke the plate" and "Peter bróke the plate."

3.1.3.1.6.3 *The interpretation* Since both fundamental frequency and duration are better cues for sentence stress than subglottal pressure and since there is a closer relationship between oral pressure and airflow than between oral pressure and subglottal pressure, it is not clear that sentence stress need in any way be reflected in the oral pressure tracing; indeed, Illustrations 356 and 357 do not give us any particularly convincing further cues.

In Illustration 356 the oral pressure for the /p/ of the first word (9.8 cm H_2O) is not much greater than that for the /p/ of the final word (8.5 cm H_2O), although it does exceed that for the /p/ in "Peter" of Illustration 357 (7.8 cm H_2O); in Illustration 357 the /b/ of the stressed word has less oral pressure (7.3 cm H_2O) than the /p/ of the final word (8.8 cm H_2O), although it does exceed that for the /b/ in Illustration 356 (3.9 cm H_2O). Topic 3.2.3.6 reveals whether airflow correlates better with accent than does air pressure.

3.1.3.1.7 *Loudness Registers*
3.1.3.1.7.1 *The problem* It is possible to shift the loudness register of an utterance above or below what one might consider normal for stylistic effect. It is also possible to shift the register of just one word or of a phrase within a larger utterance. In such cases, does the oral pressure tracing reflect the register shift?

3.1.3.1.7.2 *The data* Illustrations 358 and 359 both show the sentence "Bill said 'Bang'" [_ _ ⌐], said once on a uniform normal loudness level throughout and once with the last word very loud.

3.1.3.1.7.3 *The interpretation* These data refer back to what was said in item 3.1.3.1.6.3 and show that the intensity is not necessarily reflected in the oral pressure tracing. The tracings for the first two words of each sentence are similar and the microphone and intensity tracings show that the last word of Illustration 359 will be perceived as louder than the last word of Illustration 358. The flow rate too is greater for "BANG" than for "Bang." However, the /b/ of "Bang" has an oral pressure of 13 cm H_2O, whereas that of "BANG" has only 11.2 cm H_2O—an inverse correlation. Once more we see that oral pressure is not a useful cue for sentence stress.

3.1.3.2 *Nasal Pressure*
3.1.3.2.1 *Nasal and Oral Consonants*
3.1.3.2.1.1 *The problem* In parts 3.1.3.1.1 and 3.1.3.1.3 we saw that the ability of a speaker to impound pressure in the oral cavity depends to a considerable degree on his being able to make a velic stop by closing the velopharyngeal port, although even nasal stops produced with a lowered soft palate exhibit an increase in oral pressure.

Since there is no airflow through the nose during the production of oral consonants, there can obviously be no buildup of nasal pressure such as we find for nasal consonants when one nostril has been blocked by inserting a ball of cotton wool and the other by inserting a so-called nasal olive. A nasal olive is a nostril-size hollow plastic or wooden sphere with an output tube 1 or 2 mm in diameter onto which one can slip a tube whose other end is attached to a pressure transducer. Since the cotton wool and the nasal olive occlude the nasal cavity there will be a pressure buildup, which will be sensed by the transducer, turned into a voltage, and fed into a channel of the medical system. A nasal pressure tracing of this kind is useful for detecting any flow of air through the nose.

The nasal cavity is rather large and air flowing from the lungs for the production of a bilabial nasal [m] will have to work on both the oral and nasal cavities, so nasal pressures are generally lower than oral pressures. As a result, a pressure transducer is used with specifications different from those used for measuring oral pressure. Also, and for the same reason, the amplifier/analyzer settings are different for the nasal pressure channel.

3.1.3.2.1.2 *The data* Illustrations 360–362 and 363–365 show nasal pressure (P_n) for [pɑ], [tɑ], [kɑ] and [mɑ], [nɑ], [ŋɑ].

3.1.3.2.1.3 *The interpretation* The oral consonants show no nasal pressure, although there is a small amount of nasal leak during the production of the vowels of Illustrations 360–362, whereas the nasals do: 1.4 cm H_2O for [m], 1.0 cm H_2O for [n], and 1.2 cm H_2O for [ŋ]. In addition, the vowels following these nasal consonants are clearly nasalized.

Attention should be drawn to one small detail in Illustrations 360–362: whereas the oral pressure rises during the pressure stage of [p] and [t] and falls immediately on release, the small oral pressure for [k] occurs only after release and is therefore a reflex of the explosion rather than of the pressure stage, the open end of the transducer tube being close to the lips.

3.1.3.2.2 *Nasalized and Oral Vowels*
3.1.3.2.2.1 *The problem* All vowels (and indeed liquids and fricatives too) may be produced with the soft palate either raised (oral) or lowered (nasalized) and it is convenient to distinguish between the terms *nasalized* for vowels and other continuants, where the nasal component is a secondary feature added to the primary configuration of the oral tract, the air escaping through both the mouth and the nose, and *nasal* for stop consonants, where the nasal component is not a secondary feature since the air escapes only through the nose.

3.1.3.2.2.2 *The data* Illustrations 366 and 367 show nasal pressure for [pi] and [pĩ].

3.1.3.2.2.3 *The interpretation* There is a firm velic closure for [i], but there is egress for the air through the nose during the production of [ĩ]. The nasal pressure value recorded for [ĩ] (1.6 cm H_2O) is, indeed, even greater than that for the nasal consonants discussed previously.

It was stated in item 3.1.3.2.1.3 that there was a small amount of nasal leak during the production of the vowels in Illustrations 360–362 and, similarly, it would appear that there is nasal leak during the production of the [i] of Illustration 366 and (see below) the [ɑ] of Illustration 368. However, given that the nasal pressure tracing as a whole never rises above the zero line but merely oscillates at low amplitude at the fundamental frequency of vibration of the vocal folds (compare the microphone tracings), the nasal pressure transducer may be responding merely to disturbances transmitted through the soft tissue of the velum, i.e., there may in fact be no nasal leak.

3.1.3.2.3 *Nasal Leak and Velopharyngeal Closure*
3.1.3.2.3.1 *The problem* It is also true that some vowels, viz., those produced with the tongue low in the mouth, have a certain amount of inherent nasalization, since the sides of the tongue have a direct muscular attachment to the soft palate, which tends to lower when the tongue is pulled down. [i] and [u] are only intentionally nasalized, but [ɑ] is often incidentally accompanied by nasal leak. For example, the vowel in [ka] (to remain) of Twi may exhibit some incidental nasalization, but not as much as the intentionally nasalized vowel in [kã] (to bite).

Needless to say, those who physically cannot make a velopharyngeal closure will always show nasal leak, as a nasal pressure tracing will demonstrate for unoperated cleft palate cases (see item 3.4.3.3.0.2).

3.1.3.2.3.2 *The data* Illustrations 368 and 369 show nasal pressure for [pɑ] and [pɑ̃].

3.1.3.2.3.3 *The interpretation* There is nasal pressure not only for the intentionally nasalized [ɑ̃] (1.5 cm H_2O) but also for the incidentally nasalized [ɑ] (0.1 cm H_2O) (although see the alternative interpretation in item 3.1.3.2.2.3). The nasal pressure tracing shows similar values for [ɑ̃] (1.5 cm H_2O) and for [ĩ] (1.6 cm H_2O) in part 3.1.3.2.2, whereas many speakers would show some incidental nasal leak for [ɑ] but not for [i].

3.1.3.2.4 *Simultaneous Oral and Nasal Pressure Tracings*

3.1.3.2.4.1 *The problem* The oral and nasal pressure data presented so far fall into greater relief when viewed as synchronous tracings on two channels of the medical system. Is there both oral and nasal pressure during a given segment or neither? Is there only oral pressure or only nasal? Are the onsets and offsets of oral and nasal pressure neatly synchronized or are there small errors of timing? Does nasalization run right through a vowel between two nasal consonants? Is there a small nasal consonant transition between a nasalized vowel and an oral plosive due to the making of the oral stop before the raising of the soft palate? Is there a short prenasalized segment before a word-initial voiced plosive due to the late raising of the soft palate? All these questions may be answered by viewing simultaneous oral and nasal pressure tracings.

3.1.3.2.4.2 *The data* Illustrations 370–372 show oral and nasal pressure for the English word "mean," for the French word "bombe" [bɔ̃b], and for the English word "bombard."

3.1.3.2.4.3 *The interpretation* The illustrations show that for this particular production of "mean" the soft palate was indeed lowered for the whole utterance and that the French word "bombe" has a brief transitional nasal consonant since the nasal pressure only falls 60 msec after the oral pressure begins to rise. The English word "bombard," however, has a very obvious nasal consonant with a duration of 140 msec before the second [b], as can be seen from the segment that has both oral and nasal pressure.

3.1.3.3 *Pharyngeal Pressure*

3.1.3.3.1 *Velar and Bilabial Plosives*

3.1.3.3.1.1 *The problem* In the case of a bilabial plosive the supraglottal pressure may be measured either in the pharynx (P_{ph}) or in the oral cavity (P_o), since either placement of the tube will give the same value. The production of a velar plosive, however, demands a stop made between the back of the tongue and the soft palate such that, although the pressure in the pharynx between the glottis and the velum rises, the pressure in the mouth does not.

In order to obtain pharyngeal pressure measurements it is more convenient to insert a rubber catheter (i.e., a pliable tube) about 20 cm long into a nostril, through the nose, over the top of the soft palate, and down into the pharynx than to use a tube inserted through the mouth, which would: a) unnecessarily interfere with articulation and b) elicit a gag reflex.

Gã children of southern Ghana know this technique as a game of "magic": they push a string through the nose only to pull it back through the mouth, and I mention this to discount the impression that it must be rather uncomfortable. In fact, very few subjects find it difficult. A small sliver of masking tape is slipped round the catheter as a marker at about 14 cm, which is an average distance from the nostrils to the pharynx in the adult male, and the tube is slipped slowly through the nose by the subject himself. The sensation is new to most people and best described as a very strong tickle. Once the catheter is well on its way, the subject should articulate a prolonged [mmm] in order to lower the soft palate so that the tube will have free access into the pharynx. At this point the investigator may shine a torch (flashlight) into the mouth of the subject in order to determine when the catheter has slipped past the velopharyngeal port and into the pharynx. Once it can be seen dangling down behind the uvula, the free end may be taped down firmly onto one cheek with masking tape and then joined to the input tube of the pressure transducer. From time to time the subject may have to snort in and out, or uncouple the catheter from the input tube and blow down the catheter to free mucus from the entry, and the investigator must keep a constant eye on the monitor screen to suggest when this is necessary.

Finally, a word of warning: since this technique is invasive, i.e., something is put inside the body of the subject, its use will be subject to federal and state laws and university regulations on the use of human subjects, and the investigator should always know what these are.

3.1.3.3.1.2 *The data* Illustrations 373 and 374 show oral and pharyngeal pressure for [pɑ] and [kɑ].

3.1.3.3.1.3 *The interpretation* The oral and pharyngeal pressure tracings for [p] are identical, even in amplitude, providing that the amplifier settings are compatible (and they are not the same here), whereas for [k] the pharyngeal pressure rises but the oral pressure does not. The post-release oral pressure rise in [kɑ] is explained in item 3.1.3.2.1.3.

3.1.3.3.2 *Labial-Velar Plosives*

3.1.3.3.2.1 *The problem* Labial-velar plosives (which are rather like bilabial clicks except for the airstream mechanism) have two primary places of articulation; that is to say the speaker makes simultaneous bilabial and velar stops. They may also be released simultaneously, although in fact the velar stop is usually released first. A pulmonic egressive labial-velar (see part 3.1.3.1.4) will obviously have a pharyngeal pressure tracing like that of a [k], while the oral pressure will rise only when the velar stop is released before the bilabial one.

However, when the airstream is pharyngeal ingressive (with or without voicing) or a combination of oral and pharyngeal ingressive (with or without voicing) there will be rather uncommon pressure variations in either the oral or pharyngeal cavities or in both.

It is clear that in these cases one needs to be able to examine both the oral and pharyngeal pressure tracings simultaneously.

3.1.3.3.2.2 *The data* Illustrations 375–380 show oral and pharyngeal pressure for three types of pulmonic egressive labial-velar [kp] and [gb], and Illustrations 381–384 show oral and pharyngeal pressure for two types of pharyngeal ingressive (i.e., implosive) labial-velar [kɓ] and [gɓ].

3.1.3.3.2.3 *The interpretation* Illustrations 375–380 show that in the production of [kp] and [gb] the velar stop is made before the bilabial one since the pharyngeal pressure rises before the oral pressure. In Illustration 378, in fact, the velar stop has an 80 msec lead. Furthermore, the airstream must be pulmonic egressive since the pharyngeal pressure rises after the velar stop is made, except for the initial 30 msec negative dip in the P_{ph} tracing for Illustration 380.

In Illustration 375 [kpa] the oral pressure falls before the pharyngeal pressure, suggesting that the tongue has been lowered between the labial and velar stops to create a lowered pressure in the oral cavity while the pharyngeal pressure continues to rise as air is forced out of the lungs. The velar release is made first, causing the oral pressure to rise again, and, as the lips are still together, the pharyngeal pressure rises still more. At the bilabial release both the oral and pharyngeal pressures fall and voicing begins almost immediately.

In Illustration 376 [gba] the oral pressure again falls before the pharyngeal pressure, but this time the lowered pressure in the oral cavity actually becomes negative and at the same time the pharyngeal pressure begins to fall off, suggesting a glottal closure followed by a lowering of the larynx, which would increase the volume of the pharyngeal cavity. Once more the velar release is made first, causing the oral pressure to rise again, although the larynx is still lowering and the pharyngeal pressure still falling off as a consequence. This laryngeal maneuver makes it possible for voicing to continue throughout the consonant and, in fact, it will be seen from the microphone tracing that voicing becomes stronger after the velar release. At the bilabial release both the oral and pharyngeal pressures fall and the amplitude of the voicing on the microphone tracing increases dramatically.

Illustrations 377–380 show essentially the same features, but in each case the timing is subtly different. One might note in particular that in Illustration 378 voicing did not begin until the larynx was lowered to reduce pharyngeal pressure and create better conditions for voicing, whereas in Illustration 376 voicing set in long before that and never ceased. In Illustration 380 we see a third type, where voicing set in early but could not continue as the pharyngeal pressure rose. Only when the larynx had begun to fall was voicing able to resume.

Illustrations 381–384, the implosive labial-velars [kɓ] and [gɓ], show more complex articulations still. Once more in Illustrations 383 and 384 the velar stop is made before the bilabial one and the pharyngeal pressure rises before the oral pressure, but in Illustrations 381 and 382 bilabial, velar, and glottal stops must have been made simultaneously because the pharyngeal pressure stays at zero for some time while the oral pressure rises for an instant, suggesting that inertia is still moving the tongue up, and then falls steeply to -13 cm H_2O as the tongue lowers between the bilabial and velar stops, creating a larger oral cavity.

The two voiced implosives then show the pharyngeal pressure falling as the larynx lowers to create a larger pharyngeal cavity. Voicing begins during this stage, but the flow of air outward from the lungs is so small that the pharyngeal pressure remains negative. In both cases the velar stop is released first and the oral pressure rises sharply from about -12 cm H_2O while the pharyngeal pressure is still falling from about -5 cm H_2O. Shortly afterward the bilabial stop is released and both pressure tracings return to zero.

The two voiceless implosives are very different both from each other and from the voiceless labial-velars discussed above. Illustration 383 shows the pharyngeal pressure continually rising from the initial velar stop to the final bilabial release as air is forced out of the lungs. During this time a negative oral pressure of -12 cm H_2O has first been built up by a lowering of the tongue and then destroyed by the velar release, with a loud "pop" as the positive pharyngeal pressure hits the negative oral pressure. In fact, this consonant is not an implosive at all in the true sense of the word but a kind of bilabial click imploded from the velar end, i.e., we have combined pulmonic egressive and oral ingressive airstream mechanisms. Illustration 381 is similar to 383 in all respects except that the pharyngeal pressure tracing barely leaves the zero line throughout.

These sounds, common enough in West Africa but not found in Europe or the United States even in the speech clinic, are discussed at length to show how we can surmise details of rather intricate articulations from simultaneous pressure tracings.

3.1.3.4 Subglottal Pressure
3.1.3.4.1 Tracheal Puncture
3.1.3.4.1.1 The problem The role of subglottal pressure (P_{sg}) in the control of fundamental frequency and intensity is now well known in its broad outlines but there is no routine procedure for measuring it since the body must be invaded in order to get a sensing device below the level of the vocal folds. Both techniques at our disposal demand the presence of a doctor. This is not to suggest that the measurement of subglottal pressure is either dangerous or painful for the subject, but there is what is called a "non-zero risk" involved, i.e., a doctor must be there just in case.

The tracheal puncture involves inserting a large bore (1.5 mm) hypodermic needle between the third and fourth rings of the trachea in the midline, and to this needle one then attaches the input tube of a pressure transducer.

The technique is accurate and simple and does not interfere with articulation. The subject is free to utter anything from sustained vowels to a running text, and, given simultaneous use of a pitch meter and an intensity meter on two other channels, it is possible to see how changes in subglottal pressure affect fundamental frequency and intensity.

3.1.3.4.1.2 The data Illustration 385 shows simultaneous records of esophageal pressure and tracheal pressure during respiration and speech.

3.1.3.4.1.3 The interpretation Illustration 385 shows that variations in tracheal pressure can be simply correlated with esophageal pressure. In other words it is not necessary to insert a hypodermic needle into the trachea to obtain measurements of subglottal pressure because the much easier and safer method of recording esophageal pressure gives the same results.

3.1.3.4.2 The Esophageal Balloon
3.1.3.4.2.1 The problem Ladefoged writes: "We are at present obtaining oesophageal pressure records from a small latex balloon 1.5 cm in diameter and 2.5 cm long, sealed to the end of a polythene catheter of 2 mm bore. The balloon is passed through the nose into the oesophagus until it is just above the bifurcation of the trachea. This is usually about 34 cm from the external nares for a subject 1.8 m tall. When the balloon is filled with 2 ml of air, an approximate sphere of air is held between the thin posterior membrane of the trachea and the vertebral column. Thus any pressure changes in the trachea are transmitted to the air in the balloon" (*Folia Phoniatrica 12(3),* 1960). The catheter, of course, is then connected to a pressure transducer. The position of the balloon is important in that it must be high enough to avoid variations brought about by heart beat yet low enough not to be affected by a lowering of the larynx.

3.1.3.4.2.2 The data Illustration 386 shows an esophageal pressure tracing (middle channel) for the sentence "Wánnyá bí â, / ǹsí fíè hà ǹnè. //" (You-not-get some if, not-sit home here today, i.e., If you don't get any, don't come home today) uttered by a speaker of Twi.

3.1.3.4.2.3 The interpretation The single grammatical sentence is uttered as two breath groups separated by a pause. The subglottal pressure rises rapidly just before each clause begins, reaches a peak shortly afterward, maintains a rather steady value of about 9 cm H_2O throughout each breath group, and falls slowly toward and after the end of the clause. Such behavior has been reported for speakers of very different languages and may be a universal phenomenon. In spite of the fact that the lungs develop a wide range of pressures depending on the volume of air in the lungs and the amount of respiratory muscle activity, and notwithstanding the fact that these conditions are continually changing from the beginning of an utterance to the end, we are able without effort to maintain a constant preselected subglottal pressure throughout a given utterance.

Such variations in subglottal pressure as we do find are rather small and tend to correlate either with the placement of sentence stress or with fundamental frequency or intensity changes. The former has been a subject of considerable debate because, although subglottal pressure contours often correlate well with fundamental frequency tracings and thus reflect sentence stress placement, it is believed that the observed increases in subglottal pressure (usually about 5 cm H_2O) are not large enough to account totally for the accompanying increases in fundamental frequency which rises, in physiological tests, only about 6 Hz with each cm H_2O.

Illustration 386 also shows that the high tones, marked with an acute accent (´) over the vowel, and the low tones, marked with a grave accent (`) over the vowel, do correlate to a degree with small variations in subglottal pressure, but the range of variation is even smaller than that discussed for sentence stress.

3.1.3.4.3 *Fundamental Frequency*

3.1.3.4.3.1 *The problem* In the last two parts we have dealt with running speech; parts 3.1.3.4.3 and 3.1.3.4 look at isolated plosives and sustained vowels.

The problem with the consonants is twofold: first, what subglottal pressures are needed to make the vocal folds vibrate at all and, second, how does the fundamental frequency immediately upon release of a plosive differ from that of the target frequency of the following vowel for a range of subglottal pressures?

The first question has been answered by van den Berg et al., who showed that subglottal pressures of 0.25 cm H_2O were sufficient to initiate phonation providing the airflow rate was high enough, the glottal width small enough, and the vocal folds not too tense. The crucial factor is that the subglottal pressure must be greater than the supraglottal pressure. Without this pressure drop (delta P, ΔP) across the glottis the vocal folds cannot vibrate.

The second question was touched on in topic 2.3.3.3, where it was seen that voiceless fortis plosives, particularly glottalized ones, have a large ΔP, which results in a high fundamental frequency immediately after the release, whereas voiced lenis plosives have a small ΔP, which results in a low post-release frequency.

The problem with the vowels is to determine, given constant airflow from the lungs, what conditions will lead to an increase in subglottal pressure and what effect this will have on the fundamental frequency.

3.1.3.4.3.2 *The data* Illustration 387 shows glottal area variations as a function of time for sustained vowels at low frequency/ low intensity, high frequency/ low intensity, low frequency/ high intensity, and high frequency/ high intensity.

3.1.3.4.3.3 *The interpretation* Illustration 387 shows that a low frequency/ low intensity sustained vowel differs from a high frequency/ low intensity one with respect to both timing and glottal area, the high frequency sound having both a smaller peak and average glottal area per cycle. The necessary consequence of this is an increase in subglottal pressure, which is correlated with the higher fundamental frequency. This is true at both high and low intensities.

3.1.3.4.4 *Intensity*

3.1.3.4.4.1 *The problem* We have seen what happens to sustained vowels at fixed intensities as the fundamental frequency is changed, but it remains for us to find out what happens when the fundamental frequency is fixed and the intensity changed.

3.1.3.4.4.2 *The data* Illustration 387 suffices for this problem too.

3.1.3.4.4.3 *The interpretation* Since the closed period of the cycle is greater for low frequency/high intensity than for low frequency/low intensity, it is assumed that subglottal pressure builds up to a greater value each cycle at high intensity given constant airflow. The two high-frequency plots, however, have similar closed periods, so the high subglottal pressure and intensity must be caused not by the glottal tension that regulates the closed period but directly by the activity of the respiratory muscles.

Wilbur Gould and Hiroshi Okamura (see subsection 3.3.4) give the following actual subglottal pressure measurements for the four classes discussed: low frequency/ low intensity 2.6 cm H_2O, low frequency/ high intensity 5.6 cm H_2O, high frequency/ low intensity 7.3 cm H_2O, and high frequency / high intensity 14.6 cm H_2O.

3.1.4 Reading

It is suggested that the student now read the following items before proceeding with the projects below.

Arkebauer, H.J., Hixon, T.J., and Hardy, J.C. 1967. Peak intra-oral air pressures during speech. *Journal of Speech and Hearing Research 10:* 196–208.

Ladefoged, P. 1964. A phonetic study of West African languages. *West African Language Monographs,* No. 1, pp. 5–13. Cambridge University Press, Cambridge, England.

Lieberman, P. 1968. *Intonation, Perception, and Language.* Research Monograph No. 38, pp. 66–95. The MIT Press, Cambridge, Mass.

Malécot, A. 1966. The effectiveness of intra-oral air-pressure-pulse parameters in distinguishing between stop cognates. *Phonetica 14:* 65–81.

3.1.5 Student Projects

3.1.5.1 *Replication Projects*

a. Record and measure oral pressure for [pɑ], [bɑ], [mɑ] and [tɑ], [dɑ], [nɑ].
b. Record and measure oral pressure for "pérvert"/ "pervért" and "súbject"/ "subjéct."
c. Record and measure simultaneous oral and nasal pressures for English "mean" and "bombard" and French "bombe."

3.1.5.2 *New Projects*

a. Find a speaker of a West African language that has some form of [kp] and [gb] (almost anything in southern Ghana and Nigeria will do and students from these countries are to be found in any large city or university town) and run simultaneous oral and pharyngeal tracings to find out the nature of these labial-velars.
b. Find a cleft palate client from the speech clinic and run tests using channels for oral and nasal pressure to determine the amount of nasal leak and the conditions under which it is found.

3.2 AIRFLOW INSTRUMENTATION

3.2.1 The Instrumentation

Another channel of the medical system may be used for airflow data, the transducer in this case being one of two kinds: the pneumotachograph (see Illustration 388), sometimes called a Fleisch tube, or the warm wire anemometer.

The pneumotachograph has a closely fitting face mask with an open-ended output tube which contains a small-mesh metal screen through which the air must pass. The screen sets up a resistance to the flow of air such that the pressure on the input side of the resistance is greater than the pressure on the output side, the difference being called a pressure drop, pressure differential, or delta P (ΔP). Two bleed tubes, one on either side of the screen, feed into the transducer, which compares the two pressures with the known resistance, calculates the airflow, and converts it into a voltage, which is then passed on to the amplifier/ analyzer/ visicorder.

The pneumotachograph is cheap, easy to use, and consistent and differentiates egressive and ingressive flow, but it does interfere to a degree with articulation, especially jaw movement, and furthermore tends to give slightly exaggerated flow values since the speech mechanism compensates for the resistance offered to the flow of air.

The anemometer is a thin wire heated by an electric current passing through it and is thus rather like a miniature electric fire (i.e., electric heating element). If one cools an electric fire by blowing on it, the electric current (flow) is altered systematically as the resistance of the wire is changed by the cooling process and the variations in flow can be converted into a voltage. This is the principle behind the anemometer: a wire, or a network of wires, is held in front of the mouth and the flow of air is converted into a voltage, which is then passed on to the amplifier/analyzer/visicorder.

The anemometer is also cheap and easy to use, and it does not interfere with articulation at all; however, it is sensitive to variations in temperature and humidity and therefore has an unstable baseline, which makes calibration difficult. In addition, it does not differentiate egressive and ingressive flow.

Brief mention should also be made of the plethysmograph or body plethysmograph. This piece of apparatus consists of an airtight chamber in which a subject can sit with his body totally enclosed except for the head, which projects through a collar around the neck that seals the chamber. In general appearance it is like a Turkish bath. As the subject breathes out his lung volume falls, the rib cage gets smaller, the air in the plethysmograph becomes rarefied, and, since there is a pneumotachograph built into the wall of the chamber, air from outside will flow inward. Conversely, as the subject breathes in, the pneumotachograph will register an outward flow of air. The technique thus gives data on both ingressive and egressive air flow, and, by extension, on lung volume and subglottal pressure changes, without interfering with articulation in any way.

It should be noted that airflow data refer to volume velocity (measured in cubic centimeters per second, cm³/sec, cc/sec) and not to particle velocity (measured in centimeters per second). Volume velocity is comparable to the number of gallons of water that flow out of a (tap) faucet each minute, whereas particle velocity is comparable to the speed at which a molecule of water flows along a stream. Particle velocity speeds up at a constriction such as the glottis but, as long as air continues to flow at all through the vocal tract, volume velocity remains fairly constant from lungs to lips. We see volume velocity variation only when the lungs fail to provide a constant flow or immediately after the release of a stop when the pressure is high.

3.2.2 Operation

Once a channel has been selected, the investigator need only connect the flow meter to the rear of the medical system, switch on the power, check the amplifier settings against the instructions for the use of the flow meter, connect the visicorder to the monitor screen at the patch panel, and, having put the face mask firmly over his mouth, taking care neither to obstruct the output tube nor to twist and therefore close either of the two pressure tubes, say [pɑ], [pɑ], [pɑ]. If there is a triple up-and-down deflection on the screen and a series of right-to-left deflections of the light beam in the visicorder, the investigator is ready to begin recording. The recording paper will roll merely by pressing the drive button. A second push on the same button will stop the paper.

3.2.3 Demonstration Projects

3.2.3.1 *Consonants and Vowels*

3.2.3.1.0.1 *The problem* Air forced from the lungs will flow through the vocal tract unless the latter is totally obstructed. The voiceless glottal fricative [h] offers little or no obstruction to the flow of air. Voiced vowels also offer little or no obstruction other than the periodic opening and closing of the glottis, which turns a direct flow (DC) into an alternating, i.e., on and off, flow (AC). Sonorants and fricatives offer more resistance, but only the plosives completely stop the flow of air. Once flow has been stopped, of course, pressure will build up, providing that the lungs are still forcing air out, and there will be a high rate of airflow during the brief period of from 1 to 5 msec after the release of a stop.

Hence, flow rates for vowels are moderately high and constant over long durations, whereas those for plosives are zero during the pressure stage and very high immediately afterward. In addition, plosives use an egressive airstream mechanism whereas implosives and clicks use an ingressive one.

Since voiceless segments have a DC flow, tracings for them will merely rise when the air begins to flow outward and fall when the air ceases to flow, as can be seen, for example, in Illustrations 338 and 339 before and during the [f]; between the first [ɑ] and the [θ], during which time the speaker takes a breath, during the [θ]; and after the second [ɑ] when he takes a second breath.

Voiced sounds, however, have an AC flow and the tracings for them will rise and fall at the fundamental frequency of vibration of the vocal folds, as can be seen, for example, in Illustrations 338 and 339 during the two vowels. Measurements are usually made (as here) along the top of these sinusoidal tracings, although for some purposes it is preferable to draw in a flow curve by hand through the center amplitude of the sine wave. A sensitive flow meter will give accurate data on fundamental frequency.

3.2.3.1.0.2 *The data* Illustrations 332–334 show airflow (volume velocity) through the mouth for [pɑ], [bɑ], and [mɑ] and Illustrations 389–391 show airflow through the mouth for [pi], [ti], and [ki].

3.2.3.1.0.3 *The interpretation* No air flows through the mouth during the pressure stage of any of the consonants, the airflow tracings reading zero in all cases, but during the articulation of the vowels the airflow rate is constant and moderately high at about 300–500 cc per sec. The flow rate immediately after the release of the plosives is usually higher than for the vowels and this is discussed in the next topic.

3.2.3.2 *Voiced and Voiceless Plosives*

3.2.3.2.0.1 *The problem* We have seen that volume velocity remains constant between lungs and lips with one exception: when flow is brought down to zero during the articulation of a plosive, pressure builds up behind the stop, which causes an excessively high flow rate of brief duration as the stop is released.

Since voiceless fortis plosives have higher oral pressures than voiced lenis plosives, and these in turn have higher pressures than nasal consonants, it will be interesting to note whether these differing pressures result in different airflow rates.

3.2.3.2.0.2 *The data* Illustrations 332–334, which we have already discussed, and Illustrations 389–391 give us answers to these questions.

3.2.3.2.0.3 *The interpretation* Illustrations 332–334 show that the airflow rate during the aspiration stage of the voiceless plosive [p] (1300 cc/sec) is much higher than that of the following vowel (500 cc/sec), whereas the flow rate immediately after the release of the voiced plosive [b] (1000 cc/sec) is less than that of the voiceless one and often (but not here) not much more than that of the following vowel (500 cc/sec). In addition, we see that the flow rate immediately following the release of the oral stop during the articulation of a nasal consonant [m] (500 cc/sec) barely exceeds that for the following nasalized vowel (350 cc/sec).

If we compare the oral pressure data for [p], [b], and [m] given in part 3.1.3.1.1, we see that the release of high pressure correlates well with a high short-term flow rate, i.e., there is more than one cue for the fortis/ lenis distinction in consonants.

Illustrations 389–391 show for a set of voiceless plosives that place of articulation has some effect on airflow after release: [p] 700 cc/sec, [t] 550 cc/sec, and [k] 450 cc/sec.

3.2.3.3 *Voiced and Voiceless Fricatives*

3.2.3.3.0.1 *The problem* We have seen that mean oral pressure measurements for plosives are higher than those for fricatives and that oral pressures for voiceless consonants are higher than those for voiced, but that voiced fricatives give higher values than voiced plosives. Is the same true for flow data on these same consonants?

3.2.3.3.0.2 *The data* Illustrations 338–341 and 342–345 show airflow through the mouth for [fɑ], [θɑ], [sɑ], [ʃɑ] and [vɑ], [ðɑ], [zɑ], [ʒɑ].

3.2.3.3.0.3 *The interpretation* Both voiced and voiceless plosives have higher flow rates immediately after release than fricatives ([p] 1300 cc/sec, [b] 1000 cc/sec, [f] 700 cc/sec, and [v] 900 cc/sec) but, whereas voiceless plosives have a higher flow rate than voiced, the voiceless and voiced fricatives differ little from each other and, indeed, as here, the latter often have higher values. However, the nonstrident labio-dental and tip-dental fricatives, which are brief in duration, low in energy, and sometimes almost plosives, have somewhat higher flow rates ([f] 700 cc/sec, [v] 900 cc/sec, [θ] 850 cc/sec, and [ð] 800 cc/sec) than the strident high-energy ones ([s] 650 cc/sec, [z] 600 cc/sec, [ʃ] 750 cc/sec, and [ʒ] 950 cc/sec).

3.2.3.4 *Implosives, Ejectives, and Clicks*

3.2.3.4.0.1 *The problem* We have already seen in topic 3.1.3.1.4 that the implosives and clicks use an ingressive airstream mechanism, which involves a negative air pressure in the vocal tract and a resultant inflow of air on release and that the ejectives build up positive oral pressures by raising the larynx after closing the glottis rather than by expelling lung air.

Are the ingressive flow rates as great as the egressive ones? Do flow rates for implosives and clicks fall within the same range? Are flow rates for ejectives similar to those for pulmonic egressive plosives? Data in this topic speak to these questions.

3.2.3.4.0.2 *The data* Illustrations 346–349 show airflow through the mouth for [bɑ], [ɓɑ], [p'ɑ], and [Θɑ].

3.2.3.4.0.3 *The interpretation* The flow rate on the release of an ejective [p'] (600 cc/sec) is lower than that for a voiced plosive [b] (850 cc/sec) and considerably less than that for a voiceless plosive [p] (1300 cc/sec). A pulmonic egressive airstream mechanism produces higher flow rates than a pharyngeal one and, in addition, there is a considerable lag (here 85 msec) between the release and the onset of voicing during the articulation of an ejective as the vocal folds lose their excessive tension.

Clicks have an inflow of air on release but at a much slower rate (here 300 cc/sec) than that for the egressive consonants. The implosives, however, often do not have an inflow of air at all in spite of their negative oral pressure and are marked as implosives merely by the absence of a high outflow. Both Illustrations, 347 [ɓɑ] and 351 [ɗɑ], give evidence of this.

One consequence of the variations in pressure and flow across time, something that may be seen on the microphone tracings, is the high fundamental frequency and intensity during the negative pressure stage of the implosives. Once again we see the multiple consequences of a simple articulatory maneuver—in this case changes in airflow, air pressure, fundamental frequency, and intensity as a result of an appropriately timed lowering of the larynx.

3.2.3.5 *Word Stress*

3.2.3.5.0.1 *The problem* Do flow rates vary as a result of stress placement? Does a given consonant type exhibit a different airflow pattern depending on whether it is in a stressed or an unstressed syllable? We have already seen in part 3.1.3.1.5 that oral pressure buildup is not necessarily greater in a prominent syllable than in an unaccented one and we also know that pressure and flow can, but do not always, correlate well. We now examine what happens when word stress changes.

3.2.3.5.0.2 *The data* Illustrations 354–355 show airflow through the mouth for the pair "pérvert"/"pervért."

3.2.3.5.0.3 *The interpretation* It is clear that flow rates do change for identical syllables in different accentual positions and, in particular, that the flow rate for plosives is much reduced in unaccented position. The [p] in "pérvert" has 1450 cc/sec but the [p] in "pervért" has only 550 cc/sec. However, the fricatives show much less change than the plosives when the stress is shifted, the [v] in "pérvert" having 1150 cc/sec and the [v] in "pervért" only 690 cc/sec, and, moreover, the flow is smaller on the [v] in the accented syllable.

3.2.3.6. *Sentence Stress*

3.2.3.6.0.1 *The problem* It will be recalled that fundamental frequency cues for word stress (see part 2.4.3.4.1) are not the same as those for sentence stress (see part 2.4.3.4.2) but that oral pressure changes for the two accentual types may be similar (see parts 3.1.3.1.5 and 3.1.3.1.6). Insofar as airflow data are useful as a cue for word and sentence stress, will it be similar in both cases?

3.2.3.6.0.2 *The data* Illustrations 356 and 357 show airflow through the mouth for the sentences "Péter broke the plate" and "Peter bróke the plate."

3.2.3.6.0.3 *The interpretation* Illustration 356 shows not only that plosives in syllables with word stress have higher flow rates than those without—the [p] in "Péter" has 1150 cc/sec and the [t] in "Péter" (pronounced voiceless in the British manner) has 400 cc/sec—but also that plosives in syllables with sentence stress have higher rates than those without—the [p] in "Péter" has 1150 cc/sec but the [p] in "plate" has 600 cc/sec.

Similarly, the [b] in "bróke" of Illustration 357, even though it is lenis, has a flow rate of 950 cc/sec whereas the [p] of "Peter" has only 900 cc/sec, and that of "plate" only 600 cc/sec. It would seem that airflow rate can be a useful cue for both word and sentence stress and that the two kinds of accent are realized in a similar manner.

3.2.3.7 Loudness Registers

3.2.3.7.0.1 *The problem* We have seen in part 3.1.3.1.7 that overall pressure levels may shift up and down in unexpected ways as part of the production of different registers for stylistic effect. The question is whether flow rates also fluctuate from register to register.

3.2.3.7.0.2 *The data* Illustrations 358 and 359 show airflow for the sentences "Bill said 'Bang'" and "Bill said 'BANG'" both using the intonation contour [＿ ＿ ﹁].

3.2.3.7.0.3 *The interpretation* The airflow on the release of the [b] of "BANG" in the higher loudness register (1350 cc/sec) is not only higher than that of the [b] in "Bill" (700 cc/sec) and that of the [b] in "Bang" in Illustration 358 (950 cc/sec) but also higher (relatively speaking) than one would expect merely as a result of sentence stress (compare with Illustration 357).

3.2.4 Reading

It is suggested that the student now read the following items before proceeding with the projects below.

Hardy, J.C. 1965. Air flow and air pressure studies. *ASHA Reports 1:*141–152.

Isshiki, N., and Ringel, R. 1964. Air flow during the production of certain consonants. *Journal of Speech and Hearing Research 7:* 233–244.

Klatt, D.H., Stevens, K.N., and Mead, J. 1968. Studies of articulatory activity and air flow during speech. In A. Bouhuys (ed.), *Sound Production in Man*, pp. 42–55. *Annals of the New York Academy of Sciences 155:* 1–381.

Subtelny, J.D., and Worth, J.H. 1966. Intraoral pressure and rate of flow during speech. *Journal of Speech and Hearing Research 9(4):* 498–518.

3.2.5 Student Projects

3.2.5.1 Replication Projects

a. Record [pɑ], [bɑ], [mɑ] and measure the airflow rate at the moment of release of the consonants.

b. Record [fɑ], [vɑ], [sɑ], [zɑ] and measure the airflow rate for the fricatives.

c. Record "pérvert"/"pervért" and measure the airflow rate for the initial and medial consonants.

3.2.5.2 New Projects

a. Find a native speaker of a language other than English and elicit a dozen or so words that include a variety of plosives and fricatives. Record and measure them and see whether the results are similar to those you have looked at for English. For example, are the voiceless plosives fortis and the voiced ones lenis?

b. Find a client in the speech clinic with velopharyngeal insufficiency and ask him to read one paragraph from a newspaper. Record and mark up your data and suggest ways in which these data differ from what one would have obtained from a normal speaker.

3.3 THE RESPIROMETER

3.3.1 The Instrumentation

It has been found convenient, when discussing the speech mechanism, to distinguish between respiration, phonation, and articulation. The study of articulation involves a knowledge of the anatomy, physiology, and neurology of the pharyngeal, oral, and nasal cavities and their associated structures, whereas the study of phonation focuses on the larynx. In sections 3.5, 3.6, 3.7, and 3.8, which deal with electromyography, radiography, palatography, and laryngoscopy, respectively, we discuss techniques for investigating articulation and phonation. Respiration, however, is largely studied by reference to air pressure, airflow, and air volume and relies ultimately on our knowledge of the lung capacity of a given speaker. It is the respirometer, often called a spirometer, that gives us our baseline data on lung capacity.

Adult males tend to have greater body surface area and a larger rib cage than adult females, who in turn are larger than children, and, since there is a direct relationship between the size of a rib cage and the volume of air that the lungs within it can hold, some people will have greater lung capacity than others, a fact that is of some relevance to their speech mechanism.

Of greater importance for speech, however, is the relationship between the percentage of total capacity in the lungs at a given moment and the subglottal pressures that can be developed by the speaker with that volume. Pressures sufficient for short utterances of normal loudness can be developed throughout the middle 20% of vital capacity merely by the use of the passive forces of gravity, elasticity, and torque on the twisted rib joints, and, since we prefer not to waste energy, we usually use only these midrange volumes. High volumes automatically produce excessive pressures which have to be restrained by the braking, checking action of the muscles of inhalation, whereas at low volumes the passive forces produce pressures that are either negative or insufficient for speech so that the muscles of exhalation have to be used. What are these volumes? How much air is breathed in and out in quiet breathing for life support? How much when we breathe in as deeply as we can? How much when we breathe out as forcibly as possible? Are the breath requirements for life support similar to those for speech? These are all questions that can be answered by the use of a respirometer (see Illustration 392).

The respirometer is composed of a light cylinder closed at the upper end which floats in the space between a second and smaller cylinder which is open at the top but attached to the base of a third and larger container closed at the lower end, the space between the second and third cylinders being full of water. A face mask for the subject is attached to two tubes whose other ends enter the center of the bottom of the cylinders by way of one-way valves, the one allowing the subject only to exhale and the other allowing him only to inhale. On exhalation the floating cylinder rises an amount proportional to the air forced out of the lungs and on inhalation it falls. One end of a chain looped over a pulley falls to the center of the top of the floating cylinder and the other end falls to a pen fixed into a counterweight so that the chain is always taut. As the cylinder rises on exhala-

tion the pen will fall proportionate to the volume of air in the lungs and as the cylinder falls on inhalation the pen will rise. The pen traces on a sheet of paper wrapped around a vertically positioned drum turned by a motor which can be set to various speeds. The paper is calibrated to show volume on the vertical axis and time on the horizontal. The tracing is called a spirogram.

3.3.2 Operation

The investigator has only to fill the intercylinder space with water, position the floating cylinder, optionally fill the latter with oxygen from a cylinder, put paper on the drum, select the motor speed, clip a cartridge of ink into the pen holder, turn on the power, and he is ready to record. The subject should be seated comfortably and the face mask attached firmly to his face, covering both the nose and mouth.

3.3.3 Demonstration Projects

3.3.3.1 *Tidal Volume*
3.3.3.1.0.1 *The problem* The volume of air breathed in and out of the lungs during quiet breathing for life support is called the "tidal volume," which in adult males averages about 750 cc, or ¾ liter, but varies from 650 to 900 cc depending on body size and physical condition and may be even lower for particularly light breathing. Adult females have a smaller tidal volume with a mean of about 350 cc. Since some commercially available recording paper gives values that have to be doubled, an initial reading of 160 cc is not necessarily a cause for concern.

Finally, each in-and-out cycle of breathing takes about 5 sec and it should be noted that half of this is the duration of an average short sentence and, not by accident, the length of a spectrogram.

3.3.3.1.0.2 *The data* Illustration 393 shows a spirogram for a subject who begins by breathing quietly in and out, then breathes in as deeply as possible and out as forcibly as possible and ends up by breathing quietly in and out again, the three sequences combined taking about 1 min. Spirograms often, as here, read from right to left in time, and when one of the valves is leaking there is a baseline shift which can be calculated merely by lowering the pen, running the drum, and observing the tracing rise as the cylinder sinks. A correction factor can then be applied to all measurements.

3.3.3.1.0.3 *The interpretation* This subject has a constant tidal volume of about 500 cc (the second cycle, for example, measuring 490 cc peak to peak "in" and 470 cc peak to peak "out," with a mean of 480 cc). Look under "Respirometer" in the laboratory filing cabinet that contains the manufacturer's operating instructions and manuals for the equipment and you will probably find a set of tables that tells you what tidal volumes to expect given the sex, height, weight, and age of the subject. What could you say about this subject?

3.3.3.2 Inspiratory Reserve Volume

3.3.3.2.0.1 *The problem* We sometimes need to take more air than usual into the lungs, for example when singing or running or preparing to utter a very long sentence. The amount of air we can inhale over and above tidal volume until the lungs are completely full is called the "inspiratory reserve volume."

3.3.3.2.0.2 *The data* Illustration 393 shows a spirogram for a subject who, after some initial quiet breathing, took two maximally deep breaths.

3.3.3.2.0.3 *The interpretation* This subject has a constant inspiratory reserve volume of about 1170 cc, which means, for example, that from the "in" peak of the tidal cycle, which is 2320 cc on the second peak from the right at 21 sec, to the first maximally deep breath, which is 3490 cc on the fourth peak from the right at 40 sec, he is breathing in 3490 cc − 2320 cc = 1170 cc of air, which is rather more than one could get into a quart carton of milk. Inspiratory reserve volumes of 1500 cc or 1½ litres are typical of adult males.

3.3.3.3 Expiratory Reserve Volume

3.3.3.3.0.1 *The problem* At other times we need to breathe out as forcibly as we can; the amount of air we can exhale over and above tidal volume until no more air can be forced out of the lungs is called the "expiratory reserve volume." Even when a subject has breathed out as much as he can there is always about 1 liter of air left in the lungs, the so-called "residual volume" which cannot be used for speech and escapes only when the rib cage is pierced and a lung collapses.

3.3.3.3.0.2 *The data* Illustration 393 shows a spirogram for a subject who, after some initial quiet breathing and a very deep breath, breathed out as forcibly as he could.

3.3.3.3.0.3 *The interpretation* This subject has a constant expiratory reserve volume of about 1820 cc, which means that from the "out" trough of the tidal cycle, which is at 1870 cc on the third trough from the right at 23 sec, to the maximally forced exhalation at 50 sec, which is 50 cc, he is breathing out 1870 cc − 50 cc = 1820 cc of air. Expiratory reserve volumes of 1500 cc or 1½ liters are typical of

adult males. The discrepancy between the inspiratory reserve of 1170 cc and the expiratory reserve of 1820 cc (with a mean of 1495 cc) suggests that the initial quiet breathing was done at above midvolume.

3.3.3.4 Vital Capacity

3.3.3.4.0.1 *The problem* The sum of the tidal volume, inspiratory reserve volume, and expiratory reserve volume gives a value that we call the "vital capacity" of a speaker. It represents the volume of air that can be forced out of the lungs from the moment when they are as full as they can be (i.e., 100% vital capacity) to the moment when no more air can be exhaled (0% vital capacity). Vital capacity does not include the residual volume.

There are two main reasons for wanting to obtain a reading for the vital capacity of a subject: first, to determine whether the respiratory mechanism is satisfactory or deficient, and second, to be able to estimate the work that the muscles of the respiratory system are doing by plotting the pressures that can be developed below the glottis or beyond the lips at different lung volumes, i.e., at different percentages of vital capacity. Once we know what a person's vital capacity is, we can ask him to inhale a controlled 100% or 50% or any percentage of his vital capacity and then either to breathe out or breathe in through a face mask or against an esophageal balloon attached to a pressure transducer. The subject may be asked to do this task either using all available muscles of respiration or using no muscles at all, i.e., by relying only on the passive forces of gravity, elasticity, and torque which work on the rib cage.

It has been found that when the lungs are 100% full (see topic 3.4.3.1 and Illustration 396) even the passive forces can develop pressures large enough for shouting, although as the lungs empty the pressure rapidly falls until it is effectively zero (atmospheric) at about 38% of lung volume. At very low volumes, of course, the lungs will want to expand, which causes air to be sucked in, thus registering a negative pressure, i.e., one that is less than atmospheric.

However, when the subject is asked to use all available muscles of expiration while breathing out, having previously filled his lungs completely, the pressure developed will be greatly in excess of anything needed in speech and even at very low lung volumes he will still be able to produce positive pressures.

Finally, the converse is true—when the subject is asked to empty his lungs as much as he can and then use all available muscles of inspiration while breathing in, the negative pressures developed by sucking will be very large and even at high lung volumes he will still be able to produce negative pressures.

Measurements of this kind can be made only after we know what a subject's vital capacity is.

3.3.3.4.0.2 *The data* Illustration 393 shows a spirogram for a subject who, after some initial quiet breathing, breathes in as deeply as he can and then out as forcibly as he can.

3.3.3.4.0.3 *The interpretation* This subject has a vital capacity of 3400 cc as measured from the first high peak at 40 sec to the second low trough at 46 sec, which is typical of an adult male. Furthermore, the sum of the figures given above for inspiratory reserve volume (1170 cc), expiratory reserve volume (1820 cc), and tidal volume (480 cc) is 3470 cc.

3.3.3.5 Breath Requirements for Life Support and Speech

3.3.3.5.0.1 *The problem* Do we breathe in and out more often during speech or during breathing for life support? Is the in-and-out breathing cycle in speech similar to that in breathing for life support? Is the volume of air breathed in and out during speech more like tidal volume or the more extended range of vital capacity? These are three of the questions we need to ask when we try to determine whether speech puts demands on the respiratory system that are different in kind from those of life support.

3.3.3.5.0.2 *The data* Illustration 394 shows a spirogram for a subject who first takes a maximally deep breath, then three shallow breaths, and then utters the sentence "Put it on the table in front of the second card from the back" [¯···ʸ·/.__.. ¯·–··ˎ //]. He then takes three shallow breaths again and utters the sentence a second time before breathing quietly once more at the end.

3.3.3.5.0.3 *The interpretation* This is a rather long sentence to be uttered on one breath group and the subject, who is the same one who made Illustration 393, prepares for the first utterance by taking in 270 cc of air to bring his lung volume up to 2840 cc, something he does again as soon as the sentence has been spoken.

The sentence itself is 4.8 sec in duration, which is in excess of the quiet breathing rate of 2.5 sec per exhalation, but then the sentence is longer than average. As a rule breath groups in speech match the breathing rate (ventilation rate) rather closely and particularly long sentences tend to be broken up into two or more breath groups.

As if to make up for this increased duration, however, the pre-sentence inhalation is rather brief (1.8 sec) and one regular difference between speech and life support is the fact that in quiet breathing the in and out parts of the cycle are of similar duration, whereas in speech the inhalation part is much shorter than the exhalation, in this case a ratio of $1.8 : 4.8 = 3 : 8$.

The lung volume used for this sentence (870 cc) is in excess of tidal volume but placed well within the midrange of the vital capacity. At the end of the pre-utterance inhalation at 24 sec the subject has about 3 liters (2840 cc) in his lungs (60% vital capacity if one assumes that the speaker's residual volume is 1 liter) and 4.8 sec later there are still about 2 liters (1970 cc) (40% vital capacity). This means that about 1 liter of air (870 cc) has been expelled in 4.8 sec, a flow rate of only 181 cc per sec, and that at no point has the respiratory system been taxed to anywhere near capacity since the work has been done within the midrange, which will have minimized the work put on the muscles of respiration and maximized reliance on the passive forces.

Similar remarks could be made about the second sentence uttered between 39 sec and 44 sec.

3.3.3.6 Volume and Time (The Flow Rate)

3.3.3.6.0.1 *The problem* Normally when we want a measure of airflow we use a flow meter. However, since the respirometer paper has volume on the vertical axis and time on the horizontal axis, it is obviously possible to calculate the volume of air inhaled or exhaled during a given period of time, which is nothing more than airflow, normally measured in cc/sec (cm^3/sec).

3.3.3.6.0.2 *The data* Illustration 394 shows a spirogram for a subject uttering the sentence "Put it on the table in front of the second card from the back."

3.3.3.6.0.3 *The interpretation* It has been noted that the subject begins this sentence with about 3 liters of air in his lungs and ends it with about 2 liters. About 1 liter of air was used up on a sentence almost 5 sec in duration, a flow rate of $1000 \text{ cc} \div 5 = 200$ cc per sec. The actual figure, as we pointed out above, was 181 cc per sec. Furthermore, the flow rate is fairly constant from the beginning of the sentence to the end.

3.3.4 Reading

It is suggested that the student now read the following items before proceeding with the projects below.

Gould, W., and Okamura, H. 1974. Interrelationships between voice and laryngeal mucosal reflexes. In B. Wyke (ed.), *Ventilatory and Phonatory Control Systems,* pp. 347–360. Oxford University Press, New York.

Hixon, T. 1973. In F.D. Minifie, T.J. Hixon, and F. Williams (eds.), *Normal Aspects of Speech, Hearing, and Language,* pp. 94–108. Prentice-Hall, Inc., Englewood Cliffs, N.J.

Proctor, D.F. 1974. Breathing mechanisms during phonation and singing. In B. Wyke (ed.), *Ventilatory and Phonatory Control Systems,* pp. 39–57. Oxford University Press, New York.

Rahn, H., Otis, A.B., Chadwick, L.E., and Fenn, W.O. 1946. The pressure-volume diagram of the thorax and lung. *American Journal of Physiology 146:* 161–178.

3.3.5 Student Projects

3.3.5.1 *Replication Projects*

a. Make recordings of quiet and deep breathing and determine the vital capacity of a subject.

b. Make recordings of the same subject saying two short sentences and one long one and calculate the volume of air used.

3.3.5.2 *New Projects*

a. Compare recordings made by one male and one female subject.

b. Compare recordings made by a subject with respiratory problems with those already made by normal subjects.

3.4 THE MANOMETER

3.4.1 The Instrumentation

The manometer is a very simple pressure measuring device (see Illustration 395). It is merely a calibrated U-shaped glass tube mounted vertically on a stand and partly filled with water. With both ends of the tube open the level of the water will be the same in both arms and read zero on the scale. When, however, one arm of the U-tube is attached to a face mask by means of a plastic connecting tube or the connecting tube is placed directly in the mouth, the column of water will rise in the open arm when one blows and fall when one sucks.

Since the tube is filled with water, the scale will usually read in centimeters of water (cm H_2O or cm aq). However many manometers use mercury (Hg) instead, like a thermometer, and in such cases the scale will read in millimeters of mercury (mm Hg). A different type of manometer uses neither water nor mercury in a U-tube but operates on the principle of the dry barometer. It consists of a capsule sealed by a thin elastic brass diaphragm which is blown out somewhat when the capsule is pressurized and sucked in when the capsule has air removed from it. The diaphragm is connected to a needle on a dial which gives pressure measurements in ounces (oz).

Hence the data in journals are presented sometimes in cm H_2O, sometimes in mm Hg, and sometimes in oz, and the phonetician often has to convert figures before he can compare results. The following equivalencies are all that are needed to be able to do this: atmospheric pressure equals 1 bar, 1 million dynes per cm^2, 1000 cm H_2O, 760 mm Hg, 224 oz, or 14 pounds per square inch (psi). One cm H_2O, therefore, equals 1000 dynes per cm^2, 0.76 mm Hg, or 0.224 oz, and 1 mm Hg equals 1333 dynes per cm^2, 1.333 cm H_2O, or 0.295 oz.

The diameter of a U-tube is of no real consequence since pressure is force exerted over a given area (force ÷ area). The weight of the water in the tube is exerted over the cross-sectional area of the tube and if the latter is doubled, the former will be doubled also, the pressure remaining constant. However, too narrow a tube gives inaccurate data because of viscous effects, i.e., the water sticks to the side of the tube.

Finally, it should be noted that, whereas the air pressure instrumentation discussed in section 3.1 is used for running speech, i.e., dynamic events, whole words or sentences, the manometer is used to measure static pressure either in respiration for life support or in isolated syllables.

3.4.2 Operation

The biggest problem with operation is to get just enough water into the U-tube to give a zero reading on both arms. To do this a little detergent has to be added to the water to reduce viscosity (see above) and a thin metal wire has to be poked round the tube to break up the air bubbles. Furthermore, water can only be added one droplet at a time—a fraction too much and one has to start again.

However, once the water level has been fixed, all the investigator has to do is attach the connecting tube and watch the scale very carefully. I add this word of caution because although it is easy enough to assign a pressure value to a static event such as breathing in as deeply as possible—the water level just falls slowly until it will not fall any more—it is much more difficult to read the peak pressure of a pseudo-static event such as an isolated syllable since the water rises and falls quite rapidly. Only with practice can one become proficient at reading pressures developed during pseudo-static events.

Finally, mention should be made of the fact that measurements can be taken either within the speech tract, outside the lips, or through the nose. The latter are made by inserting cotton wool into one nostril and a glass bulb, called a nasal olive, into the other, the latter being attached to the connecting tube (contrast the nasal olive described in item 3.1.3.2.1.1). When measuring pressure beyond the lips, it is necessary to use a tightly fitting face mask which covers the mouth but not the nose and which attaches to the connecting tube, although oral pressure can be measured merely by inserting the connecting tube into the mouth and subglottal pressure by connecting the manometer to an esophageal balloon.

3.4.3 Demonstration Projects

3.4.3.1 *Static Oral and Subglottal Pressures*
3.4.3.1.0.1 *The problem* In order to obtain data on the relationship between lung volume and pressure (see topic 3.3.3.4), it is necessary for the subject to breathe in and out with the manometer connected to an esophageal balloon (see part 3.1.3.4.2). The pressures measured are static and, although the obtained data speak to the question of respiratory control in speech, they are obtained from nonspeech gestures.

3.4.3.1.0.2 *The data* Illustration 396 shows the relationship between lung volume as a percentage of vital capacity and pulmonic (= tracheal = subglottal) pressure as derived from measurements made using a manometer connected to an esophageal balloon. It is taken from the article by Rahn et al. mentioned in subsection 3.3.4.

3.4.3.1.0.3 *The interpretation* These data have already been discussed in topic 3.3.3.4.

3.4.3.2 *Pseudo-Static Oral Pressure*
3.4.3.2.0.1 *The problem* Even in a laboratory without a medical system one can still obtain reasonable pseudo-static data on oral pressure during the production of plosives by using a manometer, and a clinician wishing to demonstrate velopharyngeal insufficiency in a subject can use the technique to show the failure to build up oral pressures sufficient for plosive consonants.

3.4.3.2.0.2 *The data* Table 3 shows estimated oral pressure measurements in cm H_2O averaged over 12 utterances for each syllable for a normal sub-

Table 3. Estimated oral pressure measurements for two consonants from two speakers

Consonants	P_o (cm H_2O)	
	A	B
pɑ	3.8	2.5
bɑ	1.7	0.7

ject (A) and for a subject with velopharyngeal insufficiency (B) saying [pɑ] and [bɑ] with the connecting tube to a manometer inserted between the lips.

3.4.3.2.0.3 *The interpretation* The normal subject builds up a mean oral pressure of 3.8 cm H_2O for the voiceless plosive and 1.7 cm H_2O for the voiced one, whereas the subject with nasal leak can only build up an oral pressure of 2.5 cm H_2O for [p] and 0.7 cm H_2O for [b]. It is this failure to build up oral pressure due to nasal leak that may cause the subject to glottalize the consonant, the net result being a [ʔm̥] substituted for [p] and a [ʔm] substituted for [b]. The figures for speaker A are rather low compared to those quoted in part 3.1.3.1.1.

3.4.3.3 *Pseudo-Static Nasal Pressure*
3.4.3.3.0.1 *The problem* A manometer attached to a nasal olive may be used for either of two purposes: a) to check on nasal emission during the production of vowels in languages with nasalized vowels or of consonants in languages with prenasalized plosives, such as [ᵐb], and b) to estimate the amount of nasal emission by subjects with velopharyngeal insufficiency.

3.4.3.3.0.2 *The data* Table 4 shows estimated nasal pressure measurements in cm H_2O averaged over 12 utterances for each syllable for a Twi speaker saying [kã] and [hũ]. There was a nasal olive in one nostril and cotton wool in the other.

Table 5 shows estimated nasal pressure measurements in cm H_2O averaged over 10 utterances for each syllable for three speakers saying "pie" [ʔm̥ãĩ], "buy" [ʔmãĩ], "my" [mãĩ], and "eye" [ãĩ]. The first speaker (A) had no velopharyngeal insuffi-

Table 4. Estimated nasal pressure measurements for two nasalized vowels

Vowel	P_n (cm H_2O)
kã	0.8
hũ	0.8

Table 5. Estimated nasal pressure measurements for four words from three speakers

Word	P_n (cm H_2O)		
	A	B	C
pie	7.5	4.9	2.7
buy	2.6	2.9	0.8
my	1.1	3.6	0.5
eye	0.7	0.0	0.4

ciency but was saying the four words with the soft palate purposely down. There was a nasal olive in one nostril and cotton wool in the other. The second speaker (B) had moderate to severe hypernasality and spoke the four words without her obturator (appliance). There was a nasal olive in one nostril and cotton wool in the other. The third speaker (C) had velopharyngeal insufficiency and said the four words with a nasal olive in one nostril but with the other one open.

3.4.3.3.0.3 *The interpretation* Table 4 shows that small nasal pressures are built up for both nasalized vowels, 0.8 cm H_2O for each, although these values are much lower than those noted earlier for consonants.

Table 5 gives us some interesting comparative data. First, the normal speaker (A) with his soft palate down produces mean nasal pressures for [ʔm̥] = /p/ (7.5 cm H_2O) that are greater than those for [ʔm] = /b/ (2.6 cm H_2O), which is consistent with the fortis/lenis nature of these two consonants; more interestingly, the mean nasal pressures for [ʔm] = /b/ are greater than those for [m] = /m/ (1.1 cm H_2O). The speaker is able to maintain the three contrasts even if only in a very idiolectal, i.e., personal, fashion. The nasal emission for the vowel in "eye" builds up a rather similar mean nasal pressure, 0.7 cm H_2O, to that for /m/.

Second, the speaker with moderate to severe hypernasality also ranks the four utterances by mean nasal pressure, but in a different way. In this case, the pressures for /m/ exceed those for /b/, presumably because it is the *intention* of the speaker to lower the soft palate for /m/, whereas she does not want it lowered for /b/.

Third, the pressures developed by the final speaker are all lower than those already discussed because, as under normal conditions, a nostril has been left open, allowing air to escape. With a nostril

open and the nasal and oral cavities connected it is, of course, possible to achieve (and measure) airflow through the nose but not possible to build up significant nasal/oral pressures.

3.4.4 Reading

It is suggested that the student review the readings for the sections on air pressure (3.1.4), airflow (3.2.4), and the respirometer (3.3.4).

3.4.5 Student Projects

3.4.5.1 *Replication Projects*

a. Obtain a series of oral pressure readings for five utterances of [p] and five of [b].
b. Obtain a series of nasal pressure readings for five utterances of the syllable [ãɪ].

3.4.5.2 *New Projects*

a. Find a client in the speech clinic who has velopharyngeal insufficiency and estimate nasal emission for the series /pi/, /bi/, /mi/; /ti/, /di/, /ni/; /tʃi/, /dʒi/.
b. Using the same client, find whether the isolated vowels /i/, /u/, and /ɑ/ have equal nasal emission.

3.5 ELECTROMYOGRAPHIC INSTRUMENTATION

3.5.1 The Instrumentation

An additional channel of the medical system, or indeed several channels simultaneously, may be devoted to electromyography (EMG) (see Illustration 397). "Myo" is the root for "muscle" and the term tells us that the technique is used for tracing the amount of electrical activity in a given muscle as it contracts.

When a command is sent from the brain to a muscle to tell it to contract for a speech event, the command is sent in the form of an electrochemical impulse which travels along a nerve pathway. Not that an impulse travels along a pathway like a letter down a chute, rather there is electrical activity from inside to outside of a nerve cell which stimulates similar activity in adjacent portions of the nerve fiber until the disturbance has propagated down to the motor end plate where a nerve inserts into a muscle. A sufficiently large impulse arriving at an end plate will stimulate electrical activity in the muscle fibers too, causing them to contract.

Most of us know that if we take a wire and attach one end to a meter and the other end to the positive terminal of a charged battery, then take another wire and attach one end to the meter and the other end to the negative terminal of the battery, current will flow and the needle on the meter will deflect. This same principle may be used to detect the electrical activity in a muscle when it contracts. Two wires are attached to a meter at one end and inserted into a muscle at the other so that when the muscle contracts the meter will register the electrical activity.

The wires do not, in fact, always have to be inserted *into* a muscle; sometimes they can be merely placed on the surface skin above a muscle. The latter procedure involves the use of what are called "surface electrodes" (see Illustrations 398 and 399): two small buttons a few millimeters in diameter which are stuck close to each other onto the skin and now, with improved glues, even onto the mucosa inside the mouth. The wires are very thin and the voltages involved very small, i.e., not in excess of 500 microvolts (millionths of a volt; μV), or 0.5 millivolts (thousandths of a volt; mV). As a result, the signals have to be amplified considerably before being passed to the visicorder write-out.

The insertion of electrodes into a muscle, the so-called hooked wire technique, involves the use of platinum-iridium or copper wire only $^2/_{1000}$ inch in diameter—thinner even than silk sewing thread—with a polyester coating to prevent the two wires from touching each other (see Illustration 400). The wires are threaded through a hypodermic needle between ½ inch and 2 inches long depending on one's needs and, to expose the wires, the polyester is burned off the ends, which are then bent over the tip of the needle to form two hooks 1 and 2 mm in length, respectively, and staggered so that they will not short circuit the system.

Since a raw EMG signal, although easy to read in general terms, is not easy to quantify, it is customary to integrate or average it. Whereas a raw signal looks rather like an oscillogram, an integrated curve looks more like those that we have examined for fundamental frequency and intensity, i.e., it rests at zero when the muscle is not contracted (or actually a little above since most muscles are always engaged in some postural activity, otherwise we would slump onto the floor) and rises up above the zero line proportional to the amount of muscle activity. As a result, the activity may be calibrated and quantified from an integrated tracing.

Since a muscle has to contract in anticipation of a speech event, there is usually a delay of 0.1 to 0.5 sec between the onset of the increase in electrical activity in the muscle and the onset of the corresponding physical event on the microphone tracing (see Illustration 402).

Finally, it should be noted that in the early 1960s, when electromyography was first widely used for speech research, it was believed that, although most instrumental techniques used in phonetic research showed that phonological features did not match up in one-to-one fashion with physical and acoustic events, nevertheless electromyography would be able to show their invariant properties. For example, spectrographic analysis had shown that the second formant locus for /g/ depended on the kind of vowel that followed it, i.e., there was no invariant locus for /g/, but electromyographic research had revealed that, at least for /f/, there was an invariant lip muscle gesture, whatever the neighboring sounds were.

In other words, the closer back one got toward the control box in the brain, the more invariant the data would be. Unfortunately, we now know that this simple view of the relationship between phonological features and muscle activity does not hold true.

3.5.2 Operation

The threaded needles are sterilized in an autoclave or even a pressure cooker and kept sterile until just before the investigation. They are then inserted into the muscle in question and immediately withdrawn, leaving the hooked wire electrodes behind. The wires are then taped down onto the cheek or neck to prevent them from being dislodged and can easily be pulled out at the end of the session.

Students tend to look aghast when first hearing about this technique, imagine the subject as a human pincushion, and seem to suspect parallels with a torture chamber. However, a comparison with receiving a tetanus injection is more apt, especially since regulations on the use of human subjects demand that a physician do the insertion.

The loose ends of the fine wires have to be plugged into a small EMG amplifier which, like the subject, is installed in a wire screen enclosure to keep out electrical hum and nearby radio stations which have stronger signals than the muscles themselves, and the EMG unit in turn is hooked up to the rear of the medical system and fed into the amplifier/ analyzer/ visicorder as discussed in subsection 3.1.1. The amplifier settings appropriate for EMG on a given channel will be found in the laboratory instruction sheets.

3.5.3 Demonstration Projects
3.5.3.1 *The Lips*
3.5.3.1.0.1 The problem "Electromyographic work done so far," said MacNeilage in 1963 (*The Journal of the Acoustical Society of America 35:* 462) "encourages the hope of a simple motor description of articulation." Indeed, in that article, which reported a study of the production of certain word final consonant clusters each having /f/ as one member, it was found that wherever /f/ occurred at the end of a word it was marked by very similar activity on the part of those muscles that draw the corners of the lips outward.

3.5.3.1.0.2 The data Illustration 401 shows integrated EMG curves obtained during four productions of the utterance /ift/ after the application of suction cup surface electrodes to a point ¼ inches from the junction of the two lips of four subjects.

Illustration 402 shows the author saying "Peter Piper picked a peck o' pickled peppers" with surface electrodes attached to the center of the inside of the bottom lip. Both raw and integrated curves are presented for what is assumed to be primarily activity of the orbicularis oris muscle, the one that encircles the mouth within and around the lips.

3.5.3.1.0.3 The interpretation Illustration 401 shows that activity begins about 200 msec before the cessation of voicing (marked by the vertical line), reaches a peak voltage of about 200 μV just before the end of /i/, and declines to near zero over the next 300 msec.

Data of a similar kind can be obtained for the orbicularis oris muscle, as can be seen from Illustration 402. For each of the eight occurrences of [p] there is activity in the lip muscle about 100 msec before the corresponding segment on the microphone tracing. Activity reaches a peak voltage of from 150 μV to 300 μV and has durations of 150 msec–200 msec, which is also the duration of the pressure stage of the plosives as seen on the microphone tracing.

3.5.3.2 *The Tongue*
3.5.3.2.0.1 The problem The four intrinsic muscles of the tongue, i.e., the ones that have both attachments purely within the tongue, are largely responsible for the fine and rapid adjustments necessary for certain consonants, whereas the extrinsic muscles, i.e., those that have only one attachment within the tongue and the other on some other structure, pull the tongue as a mass of rather unchanging shape up or down, forward or backward in the vocal tract in the production of vowels.

The genioglossus is one such extrinsic tongue muscle, its fibers running from the inside of the lower jaw at the chin backward to the root of the tongue, upward and backward to the back and front of the tongue and upward to the blade. When the fibers to the root contract, the latter is pulled toward the chin and the mass of the tongue moves upward and forward, i.e., toward that tongue position we associate with front close vowels. We shall examine the role played by this one muscle in maneuvering the tongue into different positions in the vocal tract.

3.5.3.2.0.2 The data Illustrations 403–405 show raw and integrated EMG signals for the words [æsí], [ɔsá], and [èsú] in Twi. They were obtained following the insertion of hooked wire electrodes into the posterior fibers of the genioglossus muscle, and the data for the first syllable of each word should be disregarded since genioglossus is also involved in the distinction between low tones (marked `) and high tones (marked ´). The vertical line marks the point where voicing resumes after the [s].

3.5.3.2.0.3 The interpretation Even the raw genioglossus tracings show when the muscle is doing a lot of work and when it is doing little. On the one hand, the silence before these three words is marked only by the regular contraction of a single bundle of muscle fibers, although it should be recognized that a given electrode picks up activity in a restricted part of a muscle rather than in the muscle as a whole. On the other hand, during the word-final vowels the amplitudes of the raw tracings are at their greatest and the spikes are closest together, both marks of muscle activity. Yet it is difficult and time consuming to try to quantify the work a muscle is doing merely on the evidence of a raw EMG tracing.

The averaged genioglossus tracings are much easier to handle and it will be seen that, whereas during the silence before the three words the muscle is engaged only in postural activity at 60 μV, during the syllables under examination the curve rises up over about 200 msec to a peak for the vowel and falls off afterward over a further 200 msec to its postural value. The peak measurements of averaged genioglossus activity for [i], [a], and [u] are 790 μV, 540 μV, and 770 μV, respectively, but more useful measures are average values for either the whole syllable or the whole vowel. To obtain these it is necessary to make measurements at each division (here 62.5 msec) along the curve, add up the total, and divide by the number of measurements taken. These calculations may be seen above the curves on the illustrations giving the following profiles of averaged genioglossus activity: [sí] 399 μV, [sá] 161 μV, and [sú] 409 μV; [í] 632 μV, [á] 225 μV, and [ú] 554 μV. Among other things we notice that muscle activity is predominantly on the vowel rather than spread across the whole syllable.

Further calculations would show not only that close vowels have more genioglossus activity than open vowels and front vowels more than back ones but also that high tone vowels have more activity than low tone vowels, voiceless consonants more than voiced, and fricatives more than plosives. Since [sí] contains a voiceless fricative followed by a high tone close front vowel we usually find that this syllable exhibits a maximally large amount of genioglossus activity.

3.5.3.3 The Soft Palate

3.5.3.3.0.1 *The problem* The soft palate is a bundle of muscles which, when contracted, pull the structure in different directions, one forward and down, one backward and down, and some backward and up. The muscle that is primarily responsible for pulling the soft palate backward and up to block off the nasal cavity, and that is therefore the principal means for making the distinction between oral and nasal, is the palatal levator.

3.5.3.3.0.2 *The data* Illustration 406 shows integrated EMG signals for 18 words with the structure /fVmCVp/, where the Vs are either [i], [ɑ], or [u] (but in any case identical) and the C is either [p], [t], [k], [b], [d], or [g]. The tracings were obtained following the insertion of hooked wire electrodes into the palatal levator muscle of one subject and the focus of attention is on the medial consonant cluster, in this case a bilabial nasal followed by a voiced or voiceless plosive at one of three places of articulation. The primary question is whether the palatal levator muscle exhibits different patterns of activity for nasal and oral consonants.

3.5.3.3.0.3 *The interpretation* Even before and after the utterance, the tracing never falls to the zero line, i.e., there is always some postural activity, and only during the production of the nasal consonant at about −200 msec does this muscle fail to contract at more than the postural level. In other words, the soft palate is raised for [f], /V/, /C/, and [p], the oral segments, but not raised for [m], the nasal segment.

All 18 utterances have rather similar curves, and if we look at the point where the tracings cross the vertical lines that serve as a zero time reference and that mark the moment when the soft palate is rising between [m] and the following plosive, we see that the peak of palatal levator activity at about 500 μV

occurs immediately after the nasal consonant when the nasal cavity is being closed off for the word-medial oral stop.

The second highest peaks are to be found on the word-final [p]s. All plosives need a tight velopharyngeal seal, but when they do not follow a nasal segment less palatal levator activity is required. The vowels have less still, since a vowel does not need as tight a velopharyngeal closure as a pressure consonant. The first peaks at about −500 msec and the high troughs at about +100 msec represent palatal levator activity for the vowels; it will be seen that the thick unbroken tracings for [ɑ] usually give rather lower values than those for the other two vowels because there is a muscular connection between the tongue and the soft palate, which often results in nasal leak during the production of open vowels (see item 3.1.3.2.3.1).

3.5.3.4 The Pharynx

3.5.3.4.0.1 *The problem* The pharynx is a far from immobile tube. Its cross-sectional dimensions vary from voiceless plosive to voiced and from vowel to vowel. In all languages close vowels like [i] and [u] have a rather wide pharynx, whereas open vowels like [ɑ] have a narrow pharynx. In some languages, for example those West African languages with what is called cross-height vowel harmony, smaller variations in the cross-sectional area of the pharynx are imposed on vowels in prefixes by assimilation with the vowel in the root of a word.

A narrowing of the front-back dimensions of the pharynx is accomplished largely by the pharyngeal constrictors and a widening of the front-back dimensions by the genioglossus, a muscle already discussed with reference to tongue height and position (topic 3.5.3.2). The problem is to find out to what degree it is possible to widen the pharynx without fronting and raising the tongue; it will be seen that tongue height and position and pharynx width are closely related.

3.5.3.4.0.2 *The data* Illustrations 403–405, already discussed in topic 3.5.3.2, also throw light on variations in pharyngeal width from vowel to vowel.

3.5.3.4.0.3 *The interpretation* Those vowels known to have a wide pharynx, e.g., [i] and [u], show considerable genioglossus activity (632 and 554 μV, respectively), whereas vowels with a narrow pharynx, e.g., [a], have little (225 μV).

3.5.3.5 The Larynx and Fundamental Frequency

3.5.3.5.0.1 *The problem* There are so many factors involved in the control of fundamental frequency—subglottal air pressure, airflow, longitudinal and vertical tension, and medial compression of the vocal folds—that it is difficult to put one's finger on a principal mechanism. However, it is well known that the cricothyroid muscle, which directly controls vocal fold length and hence longitudinal tension, is intimately involved with changes in fundamental frequency.

The lateral cricoarytenoid muscle, on the other hand, contracts during voiced segments but fails to contract during voiceless stretches since it is involved in bringing the vocal folds together, i.e., in medial compression. However, since increased medial compression may result in a higher fundamental frequency, the lateral cricoarytenoid is also a potential pitch control muscle.

3.5.3.5.0.2 The data Illustrations 407–410 show raw and integrated EMG curves for the cricothyroid and lateral cricoarytenoid muscles during the articulation of "Bev bómbed Bob" and "Bev bombed Bób." There are also pitch, intensity ("Audio"), and subglottal pressure ("P_s") tracings, a microphone tracing (also called "Audio"), and raw and integrated curves for the pitch-lowering sternohyoid muscle.

3.5.3.5.0.3 The interpretation Illustrations 407 and 409 show that as the fundamental frequency rises to give prominence to the second word, so does the amount of cricothyroid activity, and that, although the pitch contour on the other two words is not flat, there is no cricothyroid activity to accompany these changes. For this particular utterance the cricothyroid is being used only to implement sentence stress.

The lateral cricoarytenoid, it will be seen, performs a quite different function. Activity begins before the utterance, continues in relatively undifferentiated fashion throughout it, and ends only when the sentence is finished. Since the utterance is voiced throughout, the activity of this muscle is clearly associated with voicing, but it does not appear to be involved here with pitch changes.

Most of the activity of the sternohyoid occurs at the very end of the sentence when the pitch is falling, so this muscle is doing the very opposite of what the cricothyroid did. This is seen most clearly in Illustration 410 where, as the intonation contour falls, so the amount of sternohyoid activity rises. On the last word, however, when the contrastive sentence stress is implemented on "Bób," sternohyoid activity ceases, cricothyroid activity begins, and the pitch rises, only for cricothyroid activity to cease and sternohyoid activity to resume very shortly after-

ward as the final syllable falls rapidly from high to low at the end of the sentence.

In general, what was said about the activity of the cricothyroid and the lateral cricoarytenoid in Illustrations 407 and 409 is true also for those muscles in Illustrations 408 and 410, except that the sentence stress now falls on "Bób" rather than "bómbed."

3.5.3.6 The Rib Cage

3.5.3.6.0.1 The problem It is often stated that the diaphragm is the main agent for enlarging the rib cage on inhalation and that passive forces and the abdominal muscles are largely responsible for reducing the size of the rib cage on exhalation. At the same time, we know that many other muscles are involved in respiration, both for life support and for speech, and the external and internal intercostals (the muscles between the ribs) are prominent among these.

3.5.3.6.0.2 The data Illustration 411 shows raw EMG tracings for the external (Insp. EMG. T5.) and internal (Exp. EMG. T6.) intercostals during phonation preceded and followed by two breaths. Also shown are airflow (V L/sec) and lung volume (% V.C.).

3.5.3.6.0.3 The interpretation The external intercostals are active not only during all four inspirations, i.e., those periods when the lung volume is increasing, but also well into the phonation stage, at which time the passive forces of the well-inflated lungs would produce very high pressures were exhalation not held back by the braking action of these muscles.

The internal intercostals do just the opposite: they are active each time the subject breathes out and also during the last 10 or so sec of phonation when the lung volume is very low and the air has to be squeezed out by muscular activity.

Illustration 411 also shows very well the fact that we are able to maintain a steady airflow, and as a consequence steady subglottal pressures (see item 3.1.3.4.2.3), even across utterances as long as 20 sec, in spite of the fact that both the volume of air in the lungs and the pulmonic pressure on the pressure-volume chart (see Illustration 396) are constantly changing.

3.5.4 Reading

It is suggested that the student now read the following items before proceeding with the projects below.

Basmajian, J.V. 1967. *Muscles Alive,* Ch. 2. The Williams & Wilkins Company, Baltimore.
Cooper, F.S. 1965. Research techniques and instrumentation: EMG. In Proceedings of the conference: Com-

municative problems in cleft palate. *ASHA Reports 1:* 153–168.

MacNeilage, P.F. 1963. Electromyographic and acoustic study of the production of certain final clusters. *The Journal of the Acoustical Society of America 35(4):* 461–463.

3.5.5 Student Projects

3.5.5.1 *Replication Projects*

a. Place surface electrodes near the corner of the lips and record raw and integrated curves for six tokens of /ift/. Average the muscle activity before and after the cessation of voicing.

b. Place surface electrodes between the fourth and fifth ribs, one pair near the sternum (where there are no external intercostal fibers) and another pair near the spine (where there are no internal intercostal fibers), then replicate the data in topic 3.5.3.6.

c. If you have access to an M.D. and a client for whom such data would be useful, insert hooked wire electrodes into the palatal levator and obtain raw and integrated curves for six tokens of the utterance "fimpip" as well as for "fipmip," "fiŋkip," and "fimkip." Is the client's palatal levator doing its job properly?

3.5.5.2 *New Projects*

a. Place surface electrodes on the center of the lower lip and record raw and integrated curves for the words "bead," "bid," "barred," "bored," and "booed" and state the role played by the orbicularis oris muscle in lip rounding for this series of vowels, all of which follow a /b/.

b. If it is summer and there are a few bare midriffs in the group, place surface electrodes on the abdomen near the belly button and have the subject phonate for as long as he can to obtain EMG curves for the abdominal muscles as a whole. Make a microphone tracing at the same time and note the point on the time scale at which these muscles become active.

3.6 RADIOGRAPHIC INSTRUMENTATION

3.6.1 The Instrumentation

Radiographic techniques involve the use of x-rays to study organs of speech which cannot otherwise be viewed or which can only be viewed by inserting something into the vocal tract.

X-rays are a form of electromagnetic radiation characterized by a very short wavelength—about $\frac{1}{250,000,000}$ inch, which is much shorter than that for visible light, *or* radio waves at the other end of the spectrum, whose wavelengths are longer still. Rays in the x-ray range pass through body structures and can be captured either on special film or on a fluoroscopic screen.

A typical piece of radiographic equipment is shown in Illustration 412.

Note that the subject is to be seated in a chair (although some units have a bed with straps which can be swung from horizontal to vertical as needed) with his head firmly positioned by a neck rest (the two dark circles) and, directly above this, two guides (the two vertical black bars), which fit onto the ears to keep the profile parallel to the film and unmoving. On the photographer's left is an x-ray emitter (A and B) and on his right an image intensifier (C), which improves the picture without increasing the radiation, a fluoroscopic screen (D), and a 16 mm (or sometimes 35 mm) camera (E) which photographs the screen.

This particular unit is set up to take movie x-rays on film (hence the term *cineradiógraphy*), but other possibilities are: videofluoróscopy, laminágraphy, and stills. *Radiógraphy* and *fluoróscopy* are interchangeable terms but the prefixes "cine-" and "video-" are not, the former being used when the image is captured on film and the latter when it is recorded on tape, rather like a tape recorder in principle. Cine has the advantage of being quite clear when played back frame by frame, whereas video suffers from being played back on a TV screen, which means that at any moment in time not all the lines are present on the screen and the image is therefore blurred when viewed as a still. However, video is just as good as cine when played back as a motion picture and has the advantage of requiring a smaller radiation dosage. One should also note that the soft tissues of the vocal tract stand out much more clearly on an x-ray if the subject has previously drunk a glass of barium mixture.

Laminagraphy involves the rotation of the emitter and film around the subject. The structure to be examined is kept at focal length and is therefore always in focus, whereas the intervening structures are blurred out as the apparatus rotates.

A motion picture, of course, does not really move—it is merely a series of stills; but since cineradiography captures either 24 or 45 frames per sec the exposure rate for each picture is quite short, with a resultant lack of clarity for the image. A true still x-ray, such as is taken when one breaks a bone, may use longer exposure times and is used for static rather than dynamic events, for example prolonged vowels or even nonspeech. Still x-rays are, as a result, the easiest of all to read and, when the structure is photographed using a more recently available technique called xeroradiography, can be of exceptional clarity.

Because the use of x-rays involves a potential radiation hazard to the subject, their use is strictly controlled by federal, state, and institutional regulations on the use of human subjects. Still x-rays use about 0.1 roentgens per exposure, and cine at 24 frames per sec gives a dosage of about 0.5 roentgens per min, but these levels are well below the normal safety limits. On the whole a well-rehearsed minute of speech from the subject will give plenty of data and an acceptably low dosage.

All students of phonetics are familiar with the typical mid-sagittal view of the vocal tract presented in introductory textbooks, i.e., a view down the middle of the head with a cut from front to back: a profile. This is the most satisfactory angle for x-ray studies, and indeed views from the front are very difficult to interpret because so many structures intervene between the surface skin and the object under investigation. In addition, even x-rays in profile are only two-dimensional images of three-dimensional structures. What we usually need is a cross-sectional *area* of the vocal tract; what we get is merely width and depth or length and depth.

Finally, analysis of x-ray films, particularly cine with about 1500 frames per min, is excruciatingly slow and needs great patience on the part of the investigator, although computer tracking of lead pellets stuck on an articulator has already become a possibility.

3.6.2 Operation

What follows is a nonsection because both student and teacher alike are passive observers as a trained radiologist in a hospital makes the x-rays that have been requested. Sometimes there is a specially screened enclosure in the hospital x-ray room which makes it possible for the investigator to see the data being collected, but few phonetics laboratories have their own radiographic unit, the rare exceptions being dental and cranio-facial research units and clinics.

3.6.3 Demonstration Projects
3.6.3.1 *Stills*
3.6.3.1.0.1 *The problem* Once a still x-ray has been developed, placed on an opaque glass slide viewer, and the light under the glass turned on, the investigator is confronted with the question of what meaningful measurements can be made and it is soon seen that, since the skull is so complex, measurements have to be made from reference points, which are always easy to pick out.

The principal structures of interest to the phonetician are the lips, the hard and soft palates, the tongue, the front and back walls of the pharynx, the hyoid bone and larynx, and the cutting edge of the upper and lower teeth. The outlines of these structures should be traced on transparent paper placed over the x-ray and then the first two reference points should be sought, two highlighted points at either end of the hard palate—the anterior nasal spine (ans), which is above the front upper teeth and behind the nostrils, and the posterior nasal spine (pns), which is a little above and behind the back upper teeth. A line drawn through these points provides a convenient reference plane called the "nasal line," which can be extended backward as far as the back wall of the pharynx.

A number of other planes are used in dental and cleft palate research, but for all practical purposes the necessary measurements can be made merely by dropping one plane at right angles to the "nasal line" from the anterior nasal spine through the front teeth and lower jaw, another from the posterior nasal spine through the back of the tongue, a third from the nasal line to the highest point of the tongue in the mouth, and a fourth from the nasal line to the highest point of the soft palate.

Finally, a number of planes may be drawn parallel to the nasal line, one through the highest point of the tongue in the mouth, a second through the narrowest point across the pharynx above the epiglottis, and a third through the widest point across the epiglottal ventricle. A further plane may be drawn at the narrowest point across the velopharyngeal gap, which usually, of course, equals zero.

Reports based on measurements made in this way are called cephalometric studies and the reference lines are called cephalometric planes.

3.6.3.1.0.2 *The data* Illustration 413 shows a still mid-saggital x-ray of the vocal tract from lips to larynx. Illustration 414 shows a tracing of a mid-sagittal x-ray with reference points superimposed.

3.6.3.1.0.3 *The interpretation* The mid-sagittal x-ray of a 16-year-old girl shown in Illustration 413 is useful for identifying most of the structures that are of interest to the phonetician. The lips are to the right, the spinal column to the left, and the base of the cranium at the top, with the frontal sinus showing clearly as a black oval just above the forward and downward projecting nasal bone at the bridge of the nose. The soft tissue of the nose, lips, chin, and throat are to be seen faintly on the right-hand side. The upper and lower teeth (which are without fillings and include an unerupted upper wisdom tooth) are easily seen at the right almost halfway up the picture, as are the top six neck bones (cervical vertebrae) in the bottom half of the picture, center left. The edge of the lower jaw (mandible), or rather *edges,* since both sides can be seen as almost parallel lines, is seen rising backward from the chin (near the bottom right-hand corner) toward the second vertebra from the top. At this point it makes a sharp turn upward (crossing the rear wall of the dark pharynx exactly at the angle) to make a joint with the skull just above and forward of the first (topmost) vertebra and in front of the faint white circle which is the ear canal.

The body of the hyoid bone is seen very clearly as a small bright oval just above and behind the angle between the chin and the neck, below the center of the lower jaw. The large horn of the hyoid bone projects as white lines upward and backward from the body into the dark area which is the pharynx. The vocal folds are immediately below the horizontal black oval, beneath and a little behind the body of the hyoid at the level of the fifth vertebra. The false vocal folds are immediately above this same black oval. The dark tube below the larynx is the trachea and the dark area sloping upward and backward from the vocal folds is the entry into the larynx (the vestibule) at the bottom end of the pharynx.

The pharynx proper is even darker in tone and its back wall runs from the entry to the esophagus at the level of the fourth vertebra directly upward, through the horns of the hyoid bone, past the angle of the lower jaw, over the soft palate (which is the hanging white mass at the level of the teeth), and turns gently upward and forward into the rear of the nasal cavity at the level of the first vertebra, crossing the vertical double white line, which is the pterygoid plates of the sphenoid bone just behind the upper wisdom tooth.

The sella turcica of the sphenoid bone is the highlighted white bowl-shaped structure a little above and behind the pterygoid plates. The nasal cavity is the fairly dark area intersected by numerous white lines to the front of the pterygoid plates. Between the upper wisdom tooth and the roots of the upper cutting teeth, and immediately beneath the nasal cavity, are two bright horizontal lines, the top one straight and the bottom one somewhat curved. This is the hard palate, at the front end of which is a sharp bright point near the nostrils (the anterior nasal

spine). The rear end of the hard palate (the posterior nasal spine, normally seen as a bright spot) is obscured by the wisdom tooth. The sharp curve just below and behind the anterior nasal spine is the alveolar ridge.

Hanging downward and backward (since the x-ray was taken during breathing for life support, not speech) is the light-colored soft palate, bounded above by the dark-toned naso-pharynx and below by a thin black line which runs from the uvula to the upper wisdom tooth. This line is a continuation of the one that starts as the front wall of the laryngeal entry, curls upward and downward behind the horn of the hyoid bone as the epiglottis, crosses the lower jaw just forward of the angle as the root of the tongue, and then turns upward and forward below the soft palate as the back of the tongue. The front, blade, and tip of the tongue are hidden behind the teeth.

Having identified these landmarks on the x-ray, students will find it useful to place a piece of transparent material on top of Illustration 143 and trace the structures that have been described. On one's first examination of an x-ray of the vocal tract, structures tend to be much less obvious than they seem to be to the teacher, but all that is needed is practice.

The profile in Illustration 414 is taken with the lips to the right and the pharynx to the left and only the essential structures have been traced, these being only those mentioned in item 3.6.3.1.0.1 minus the lips, hyoid bone, and larynx but including the angle of the lower jaw. The following measurements can be made: 1) B-I, tongue height (open/ close); 2) H-I, tongue position (front/ back); 3) D-E, velar height; 4) G-F, velopharyngeal gap; 5) J-K, jaw opening; 6) L-M, upper tongue root position; 7) O-P, lower tongue root position; 8) M-N, upper pharyngeal width; 9) P-S, lower pharyngeal width a; 10) R-S, lower pharyngeal width b; and 11) P-Q, epiglottal ventricle width.

In addition, larynx height could be measured by reference to the plane S-O and lip protrusion from the plane A-O. Finally, it is customary to take one sequence of film with a metal ruler against the subject's cheek, a special ruler with holes drilled in it 1 cm apart so that one can be sure that 1 cm really is 1 cm. It will be obvious that when a cineradiographic film is projected onto a wall all measurements will be enlarged by a certain amount. The frames with the ruler will tell us by how much.

3.6.3.2 *Laminagraphy*

3.6.3.2.0.1 *The problem* It has already been noted that, whereas x-rays taken in profile are usually fairly easy to read, those taken from other angles are not since several structures may intervene between the surface skin and the object under investigation, causing their images to get superimposed on each other.

Attempts to examine the vocal folds from the front of the neck in order to make an estimation of vocal fold mass run into this problem because the muscular vocal folds are screened by the more dense tissue of the laryngeal cartilages and, similarly, x-rays of the pharynx taken from the front below the chin in order to measure side-to-side pharyngeal width are difficult to interpret because of the unwanted images of intervening structures.

This problem can sometimes be solved by the use of laminagraphy.

3.6.3.2.0.2 *The data* Illustration 415 shows a frontal laminagram of a male larynx taken during sustained phonation in chest voice.

3.6.3.2.0.3 *The interpretation* Data of this kind are taken using an x-ray unit which travels about 20 inches (or 15°) through a plane 13–17 cm from the vocal folds, the exposure time being 1.5 sec. The trachea is seen as a light tube in the center at the bottom of Illustration 415, the vocal folds are the dark wedge-shaped masses projecting over the trachea almost to the center line about half-way up the picture, the laryngeal ventricles are the two light patches immediately above the vocal folds with the false vocal folds marking the upper surfaces of the ventricles, and the entry to the larynx is seen less clearly as a light grey tube around the center line at the top of the picture.

Students are urged to lay the illustration on a tabletop and to view it from close up, from a middle distance, and from long range while standing up, in order to determine for their eyes the distance at which the structures stand out most clearly.

It is easily seen that the vocal folds are quite substantial muscular masses and not at all like cords, and it is from such data that we know that the folds become less massive and thinner as the fundamental frequency is raised.

3.6.3.3 Cineradiography
3.6.3.3.1 Tongue Height
3.6.3.3.1.1 *The problem* The great advantage of motion picture x-rays is that they enable us to capture some dynamic aspects of speech. The sustained vowels used for stills represent rather unnatural articulations and it is even more unnatural to hold the pressure stage of a plosive, but by using cineradiographic techniques one can plot frame-by-frame the movement of individual articulators, especially when one has stuck little lead pellets onto them. By looking from frame to frame in this way one can make best estimates of steady state positions or state the absence of them when they are not to be found.

At 24 frames per sec (i.e., one frame each 42 msec) one may still miss the actual stop of a plosive, but not by much, and the ever-changing configurations of the tongue, pharynx, and soft palate for both consonants and vowels are made real for us in a way that no other technique can really rival. These talking skeletons may look like the dance of death, but every student should try to see a film such as *Physiological Aspects of Speech—Velopharyngeal Function of Normal Speakers* (number HSC-751 in the Indiana University (Bloomington) Audio-Visual Center catalog of 16 mm educational motion pictures).

3.6.3.3.1.2 *The data* Illustrations 416 and 417 are tracings made from a cineradiographic film of a Twi speaker reading a list of words with different vowels. The frames have been chosen to show steady state tongue positions for [i] and [ɔ]. The measurements are in "projected millimeters" (p mm), which are 1.6 times greater than natural. The tracings were made by the use of a special projector which enables the film to be stopped frame by frame. A sheet of paper is taped onto a wall, the film is projected against it, and the tracings made by hand. Care must be taken to keep the distance between the projector and the wall constant for all tracings.

3.6.3.3.1.3 *The interpretation* Illustrations 416 and 417 show that the highest point of the tongue in the mouth (measurement B-I of Illustration 414) is a mere 7 p mm from the nasal line for [i] but 22 p mm for [ɔ]. Since measurements for [e] and [o] were between these two figures and those for [a] were greater than 22 p mm, the traditional classification of vowels on a close/open continuum is seen to have some validity.

3.6.3.3.2 Tongue Position
3.6.3.3.2.1 *The problem* The traditional description of vowels also classifies them on a front/back continuum and, although it is now known from acoustic studies (see item 2.2.3.1.0.1) that a value for the cross-sectional area of the vocal tract at the point of maximum constriction is more valuable than a reading for the highest point of the tongue in the mouth, it is nonetheless of some interest to ask whether the former can be deduced from the latter.

3.6.3.3.2.2 *The data* Illustration 418, which is taken from the same film as Illustrations 416 and 417, shows a steady state tongue position for [ʋ].

3.6.3.3.2.3 *The interpretation* The highest point of the tongue in the mouth for [ʊ] is approximately beneath the posterior nasal spine, 75 p mm behind the anterior nasal spine, whereas the position for [i] in Illustration 416 is 41 p mm. Since [e] and [ɛ] have values rather like [i] and since [ɔ] in Illustration 417 is 80 p mm, it is clear again that the traditional classification has some validity, particularly since only the open vowels, and especially the back open vowels, have points of maximum constriction that are not also the highest point of the tongue in the mouth (see part 3.6.3.3.3 below).

3.6.3.3.3 Pharynx Width

3.6.3.3.3.1 *The problem* Other things being equal, a muscular contraction to move the tongue upward and forward will also enlarge the pharynx in the front-back dimension so that one would expect [i] to have a wider pharynx than [u] or [ɛ] and [u] to have a wider pharynx than [ɔ].

Furthermore, it is only by comparing the measurements for the highest point of the tongue in the mouth and for pharynx width that one is able to determine whether the point of maximum constriction is in the pharynx or in the mouth.

3.6.3.3.3.2 *The data* Illustrations 416–418 show steady state tongue positions for [i], [ɔ], and [ʊ].

3.6.3.3.3.3 *The interpretation* [i] has a particularly wide pharynx, 42.5 p mm, whereas [ʊ] has only 13.5 p mm, and [ɔ] a very narrow 9 p mm. The tongue height for [ʊ], however, shows that the constriction in the mouth (12 p mm) is even smaller than that in the pharynx (13.5 p mm), whereas [ɔ] has a much narrower constriction in the pharynx (9 p mm) than in the mouth (22 p mm).

The pharynx widths for [e], [ɛ], [u], and [o] are of a fairly high value, although less than that for [i], and with the exception of [ɔ] only the fully open vowels have a narrower constriction in the pharynx than in the mouth.

On the whole, pharynx width can be predicted from the highest point of the tongue in the mouth even though it may not make acoustic sense to want to do it that way.

3.6.3.3.4 Soft Palate Position

3.6.3.3.4.1 *The problem* Speakers of languages with nasalized vowels and clients with velopharyngeal insufficiency can be examined by x-ray techniques for an estimate of soft palate position.

3.6.3.3.4.2 *The data* Illustration 419, which is taken from the same film as Illustrations 416–418, shows a steady state tongue and soft palate position for [ũ].

3.6.3.3.4.3 *The interpretation* Whereas the vowels so far examined have had a completely raised soft palate, [ũ] has the soft palate so low that its highest point is below the nasal line and the velopharyngeal port is open to a value of 17.5 p mm—a larger opening than that in the mouth, 13.5 p mm. This vowel is truly nasalized and the hump above the nasal line, which marks the point where the palatal levator muscle enters the soft palate and which can so easily be seen in the other vowels, is quite absent. Not shown here is a case like [a], where there is a small nasal leak but, nonetheless, a pronounced hump showing that the nasalization is not intended but rather a necessary consequence of the muscular connection between the tongue and the soft palate. Open vowels usually have some nasal leak.

3.6.3.3.5 Larynx Height

3.6.3.3.5.1 *The problem* We have not so far shown how it is possible to represent graphically those dynamic aspects of speech that cineradiography handles so well, and this topic looks at how the hyoid bone and the larynx move up and down during the course of a whole word. The technique is simple if slow to implement. For a word that takes rather more than ½ sec to utter, and given a film with 45 frames per sec, the investigator has to make measurements of hyoid bone and larynx height for each of almost 30 frames and then plot the values on a piece of graph paper with increasing height on the vertical axis and time on the horizontal axis. If the same procedure is adopted for pharynx width, soft palate position, tongue height and position, jaw opening, and lip protrusion, a graphic picture of a dynamic speech event is obtained.

3.6.3.3.5.2 *The data* Illustration 420 shows hyoid bone height and larynx height for the three words [hə'tɑ], [hə'tɛ], and [hə'tu].

3.6.3.3.5.3 *The interpretation* The plots are segmented for reference and a vertical zero time line is inserted at the moment of release of the [t], which is preceded by [hə] and followed by aspiration, one of three vowels, and a final voiceless offglide ([h]).

The three traces are low and fairly identical for both plots almost up to the moment of release of the plosive. During the pressure stage of the consonant both hyoid and larynx begin to rise, reaching a peak near the beginning of the stressed vowel and falling slowly through the vowel toward their starting positions. Only during the stressed vowels do the plots differ appreciably, both the hyoid and larynx rising considerably for [ɑ] and [ɛ] but not for [u]. They stay high for [ɑ], yet fall again quite quickly for [ɛ]. The plot for [u] shows the larynx rising very little and falling again soon after. The hyoid bone even falls ½ cm below its neutral position at the end of [u]—obviously the vocal tract is being lengthened both at the lip and at the glottal end, which is necessary to bring the first two formants down for this lip-rounded back vowel (see Illustration 24).

3.6.4 Reading

It is suggested that the student now read the following items before proceeding with the projects below.

Moll, K.L. 1965. Photographic and radiographic procedures in speech research. Proceedings of the conference: Communicative problems in cleft palate. *ASHA Reports 1:* 129–139.

Painter, C. 1973. Cineradiographic data on the feature 'covered' in Twi vowel harmony. *Phonetica 28:*97–120.

Perkell, J. 1969. *Physiology of Speech Production,* pp 3–12, 76–77, 84–85, 96–97. Research Monograph No. 3. The MIT Press, Cambridge, Mass.

3.6.5 Student Projects

3.6.5.1 *Replication Projects*

a. If state regulations permit it, have a cineradiographic film made of one subject reading the English words "beat," "bit," "bet," "bat," "but," "bart," "bought," "boot," and "Bert." Make measurements of tongue height for each vowel.

b. Using the same film, make measurements of the tongue position for each vowel.

c. Using the same film, make measurements of pharynx width for each vowel.

3.6.5.2 *New Projects*

a. If you have a client in the clinic for whom a radiographic diagnosis is appropriate, have stills made of the subject uttering the prolonged vowels [i], [u], and [ɑ]. Estimate his velopharyngeal function by measuring soft palate height and length and degree of closure.

3.7 PALATOGRAPHIC INSTRUMENTATION

3.7.1 The Instrumentation

Palatography is a very simple and inexpensive technique for obtaining fairly precise data on those points where the tongue makes contact with the palate or upper teeth during the articulation of certain sounds. That is to say that dental, alveolar, post-alveolar, and palatal consonants can be usefully examined in this way, although bilabial consonants cannot be and

velar and uvular consonants usually cannot be, depending on the subject's susceptibility to the gag reflex. Of the vowels, only those with a front close tongue position exhibit contact between the tongue and the hard palate.

There are three types of palatographic technique, two static and one dynamic, the former two suffering from a serious limitation—their use is restricted to examining words during the articulation of which the tongue touches the palate or upper teeth only once. The dynamic technique has no such limitation and can handle running speech of any length.

The static techniques are either direct or indirect. Direct palatography involves spraying a black powder on the upper teeth and hard and soft palates. This done, the subject says the word to be examined and wherever the tongue touches the areas that have been sprayed the powder is wiped off. This area, called a "wipe-off," can be viewed by the subject himself or photographed in the following manner. A mirror is mounted at a 45° angle on a table with the reflecting surface upward. The subject places his mouth over the mirror until the upper end almost touches the uvula. A second mirror with an electric light bulb in front of it is placed a little in front of the subject's head in such a way that he can see the reflection of his palate and upper teeth thrown out from the mouth mirror. A round hole in the center of the second mirror can house a camera to take a permanent record of the wipe-off. A less satisfactory way of doing direct palatography is to spray or paint the tongue and have the wipe-off on the palate.

Indirect palatography involves the use of a custom-made artificial palate (see Illustration 421), rather like the palate that holds false teeth, but much thinner and much lighter.

The artificial palate is made by a dentist who first asks the subject to bite hard onto a mouthful of malleable material and then makes a cast of the "bite" or "impression" from plaster of Paris. Finally, either an acrylic plate is warmed up, rolled out as thin as 0.3 mm, pressed into the plaster cast, and allowed to cool and harden, or a quick-drying liquid acrylic is painted onto the cast. The artificial palate may cover the soft palate, but usually does not, and may cover the inner surfaces of the upper teeth, but often does not.

The artificial palate can then be smeared with olive oil, inserted by the subject, and covered with a fine powder blown out of an atomizer bulb. Some investigators use powdered French chalk, others a mixture of cocoa and charcoal or flour and gum arabic. The powder, of course, should contrast with the color of the artificial palate. The subject then says the word to be examined and afterward, taking care not to smudge it, removes the palate, which can either be photographed directly for a permanent record or placed at the bottom of a palatogram projector. The latter is a box with a sheet of plain glass at the top on which tracing paper can be laid. The box contains illumination and a lens so that the tracing paper acts as a screen for the image of the projected palatogram, which can be traced easily, accurately, and cheaply.

Once a palatogram has been obtained, it is useful to draw reference lines from left to right across the frontmost point of each pair of teeth, which divides the palate into seven zones: dental in front of the frontal incisor line; denti-alveolar in front of the lateral incisor line; alveolar in front of the canine line; post-alveolar in front of the first molar line; and pre-palatal, mid-palatal, and post-palatal in front of the lines for the remaining molars. In addition, three front-back reference lines can be drawn between and to the sides of the frontal incisors to give left, right, and central zones. The wipe-off can then be referred to the conventional places of articulation.

A palatogram is, however, a two-dimensional representation, whereas the palate is dome-shaped. This problem may be solved, when necessary, by making horizontal cuts through the plaster of Paris cast from which the artificial palate was originally made to obtain a number of sections, each 0.2 inches thick, from which one may construct a kind of contour map which can be superimposed on the palatogram.

The dynamic technique is not so simple or cheap but does use an artificial palate of the kind already described. Sixty-four pairs of small silver electrodes, each 1 mm in diameter, are implanted into the artificial palate in four rows, each running from the back teeth to the front teeth and around again to the back teeth (see Illustration 428). The first row is placed close to the teeth and the fourth row much closer to the center line, so that whereas the first row has 19 electrodes the fourth has only 13. When the tongue contacts an electrode an electrical circuit is bridged and the contact is recorded for that electrode at that moment in time. Since each electrode is assigned to a different frequency and activates a sine wave generator when contacted, the ensemble may be recorded on magnetic tape and played back to a write-out either of 64 lines divided into four groups (as in Illustrations 428–430 where the tape has been played back into a sound spectrograph) or on a palate-shaped panel with bulbs that light up when contact is made.

3.7.2 Operation

Once the apparatus has been set up, all the investigator has to do is powder the palate of the subject and take a photograph in the case of the direct technique, or smear the artificial palate with oil, powder it once it has been inserted, take care that the subject does not smudge it on removal, and photograph or trace it when it is out. The dynamic technique involves inserting the artificial palate, recording the output signals on tape, and playing them back at half-speed into a sound spectrograph.

3.7.3 Demonstration Projects
3.7.3.1 *Consonants*
3.7.3.1.0.1 *The problem* Radiographic data tell us something about place of articulation, but only in two dimensions on the sagittal plane. Palatography supplies the missing dimension, but it does so at the expense of information from the sagittal plane. The principal value of palatography, perhaps, is that it takes us away from those mid-sagittal views of the vocal tract that so dominate our literature (and perhaps our thinking too) and shows us, for example, that an alveolar stop is made not only by contact between the tongue and the alveolar ridge but also by contact between the tongue and the side teeth. Were this not the case air would be able to escape through the gaps between the teeth and pressure could not be built up. Palatograms also show us that the tongue does not contact the hard palate down the center line behind the alveolar ridge during the articulation of [t] and [d] and constantly remind us that the palate is domed in both directions.

3.7.3.1.0.2 *The data* Illustrations 422–425 show palatograms traced on a projector from an artificial palate without velum or teeth. The subject spoke four words of Gonja, a language spoken in northern Ghana: [tù] (to meet), [dʑì] (to eat), [ásí] (mounds), and [ɲɔ́] (to dye).

3.7.3.1.0.3 *The interpretation* The white sections of the palatograms (where the grid can be seen) mark the regions where there was a wipe-off; Illustration 422 shows us that [t] preceeding [u] is a dental, since the wipe-off extends right up to the teeth in zone 1, and a stop, since there is firm contact of the tongue not only with the front teeth but also with the side teeth almost all the way around. The stop is a very firm one, and the plosive as a consequence is probably fortis in nature, as can be seen from the fact that the place of articulation extends from the dental through to the post-alveolar zones. Palatograms for [d] in the same data set showed a much less extensive place of articulation. The palatal zones show no wipe-off around the center line.

Illustration 423 shows the wipe-off for the affricate [dʑ]. The place of articulation is post-palatal at the center line, but contact is firm down the side teeth from post-palatal to post-alveolar. Some of this side wipe-off might be attributed to the vowel [i] were it not for the fact that [dʑàgà] gives a similar palatogram. Clearly [dʑ] has a very high tongue position overall.

Illustration 424 is a palatogram for [ásí], and it will be seen that there is a totally unobstructed channel down the center line but firm contact between the tongue and side teeth extending as far forward as the denti-alveolar zone. The place of maximum constriction appears to be a little post-alveolar.

Illustration 425 shows that the palatal nasals do not have exactly the same tongue position as the palatal affricates even though the palatograms are broadly similar. Whereas the affricate had a post-palatal place of articulation with a suggestion of a post-alveolar constriction on the other side of the dome, the nasal has a post-alveolar place of articulation with a suggestion of a post-palatal constriction and such a narrow central passage that the tongue is seen to be very high in the mouth, which contrasts with the palatograms for [n] in the same data set.

3.7.3.2 Vowels

3.7.3.2.0.1 *The problem* It is often said that a principal difference between consonants and vowels is that for most consonants the tongue makes contact with the palate or some other structure, which enables us to learn and control our articulatory behavior by internal feedback, i.e., by the use of sensory nerves, whereas for vowels the tongue does not make contact so that we have to rely on auditory feedback. However, this is just not true and it has long been known that it is not true. Our sagittal views have fooled us.

During the articulation of front close vowels the tongue makes extensive contact with the sides of the hard palate and even more open vowels show contact between the tongue and the upper side teeth, as may back close vowels. It has yet to be shown what contact the tongue makes with the lower teeth for back open vowels.

3.7.3.2.0.2 *The data* Illustrations 426 and 427·show palatograms for the same Gonja speaker saying [épé] (home) and [àbòjù] (corn), the latter

illustrating a sound [j], which is a vocoid in form even if a consonant in function.

3.7.3.2.0.3 *The interpretation* Illustration 426 shows that for [e] the tongue makes extensive contact with the side teeth all the way back from the post-alveolar zone. Comparison with palatograms for [i] shows that contact for the closer vowel extends farther forward into the alveolar zone and much farther inward toward the center line, both being consequences of the closer and more advanced tongue position of [i].

The wipe-off for [i] is in fact more extensive in this language than that for [j], which is shown in Illustration 427. The side contact for [j] is about as extensive as that for [e] but extends somewhat farther in toward the center line. The vowel quality for this particular [j] is obviously [ɪ].

3.7.3.3 Dynamic Palatography

3.7.3.3.0.1 *The problem* Static palatograms do not tell us when certain articulatory events took place but only that they *have* occurred. For example, the tongue may have touched the alveolar ridge and side teeth but did it touch the back teeth first and the alveolar ridge only later? Is there a moment when there is contact at all points around the wipe-off or is a palatogram merely a composite that lumps together contact over a certain period of time? Is contact at a certain place of articulation of brief or long duration? Is a plosive released initially at the center line and only later around the teeth? Questions of this kind can be answered by dynamic palatography.

3.7.3.3.0.2 *The data* Illustrations 428–430 show 64-electrode dynamic palatograms.

Illustration 428 shows the arrangement of the four rows of electrodes on the artificial palate and the frequency that has been assigned to each one as seen on a spectrogram print-out at the right-hand side of the photograph. The 19 electrodes of the outermost row (Group 1) occupy the frequency band from 1700 Hz to 3500 Hz; the 17 in the second row (Group 2) occupy the band from 3600 Hz to 5200 Hz; the 15 in the third row (Group 3) are seen between 5300 Hz and 6700 Hz, and the final 13 of the innermost row (Group 4) are recorded in the band of frequencies from 6800 Hz to 8000 Hz.

Illustration 429 shows a dynamic palatogram for [ada] and Illustration 430 one for [ata]. The bottom frequency band from 0 to 1600 Hz has been reserved for a conventional spectrogram but the top four bands from 1700 Hz to 8000 Hz have been assigned to the four groups of electrodes as described previously.

3.7.3.3.0.3 *The interpretation* Illustration 430 shows that even before the first vowel has finished in [ata] the tongue has already made contact with the rear upper teeth at the outer electrodes. About 20 msec later (the time marker at the bottom appears to be set at 10 msec per division) the second row of electrodes shows contact at the rear upper teeth, by which time the outer electrode contact has moved forward. Yet another 20 msec elapse before the stop is completely made down the center line at the outer electrodes and only after this does the second row also show contact down the center line. A third of the way into the pressure period there is contact at the third row of electrodes, but only down the center line, the third row never registering throughout the word at the side teeth. No electrode from the innermost row ever registers contact during this utterance. The release of the [t] is an almost identical mirror image of what we have just described, the actual moment of release coming when the center electrodes of the outer row finally fail to show contact.

A comparison of Illustrations 429 and 430 shows that complete closure is much longer for [t] than for [d] (see the outer row, center front electrodes) and, in addition, the density of contact for rows 2 and 3 is much greater for [t] than for [d].

This highlights one aspect of palatography that is not obvious at first sight—the moment of contact need not be the end of the gesture, since tongues and palates are not incompressible nor immovable. In fact, from these data [t] is seen to be a fortis consonant and [d] to be lenis. The strong consonant has greater tongue pressure, which results in a longer period of contact and a wider area of electrical wipe-off.

3.7.4. Reading

It is suggested that the student now read the following items before proceeding with the projects below.

Jones, D. 1960. *An Outline of English Phonetics.* Heffer (W.) & Sons Ltd., Cambridge, England. This has many palatograms scattered throughout pp. 65–72 and 143–210.

Kydd, W., and Belt, D. 1964. Continuous palatography. *Journal of Speech and Hearing Disorders* 29(4):489–492.

Ladefoged, P. 1957. Use of palatography. *Journal of Speech and Hearing Disorders* 22(5):764–774.

Shibata, S. 1968. A study of dynamic palatography. *Annual Bulletin of the Research Institute of Logopedics and Phoniatrics (University of Tokyo)* 2:28–36.

3.7.5 Student Projects

3.7.5.1 *Replication Projects*

a. Using only powder blown from an atomizer and a torch (flashlight) for illumination, do some direct palatography on four subjects saying "bee," "bib," and "yob" and compare the wipe-offs.

b. Using the same direct technique, obtain palatographic data from three subjects saying "tore," "jaw," "saw," and "new" [ɲu:] and compare the wipe-offs.

3.7.5.2 *New Projects*

a. Find a student from the Indian subcontinent and elicit words containing dental and retroflex plosives and palatal affricates making sure, of course, that the tongue touches the palate and upper teeth only once during each word. Use direct palatographic techniques to obtain data on place of articulation.

b. Find a client in the speech clinic who misarticulates his /s/. Using direct palatographic techniques elicit /s/ before a series of different vowels to obtain data on place of articulation. Is it place that is at fault?

3.8   LARYNGOSCOPIC INSTRUMENTATION

3.8.1   The Instrumentation

Many of the techniques described for obtaining physiological data are invasive, i.e., some object has to be put into the subject's speech tract. To obtain air pressure data a tube has to be placed in the mouth or inserted through the nose into the pharynx or esophagus. Electromyography may involve the insertion of electrodes into muscles. Radiography involves rays that pass through the body, and even in palatography an acrylic plate may have to be put into the mouth. Laryngóscopy, the viewing of the larynx, is even more invasive since rather larger objects than have hitherto been described have to be placed far down into the vocal tract and all but one of these procedures (the one that involves the use of the fiber optic laryngoscope) place severe constraints on articulation if not on phonation itself.

There are three major problems that have to be overcome if one is to be able to view the larynx: a) the larynx is out of sight around a corner, i.e., the oral cavity and the pharyngeal cavity are almost at right angles to each other in the adult and of almost equal length, b) the larynx is dark and has to be very well illuminated if one is to see the vocal folds, and c) the frequencies of vibration of the vocal folds are too high for the human eye to be able to resolve them, i.e., all we see is a blur. The history of laryngoscopy shows how these problems have been solved one by one.

To be able to see round the corner it is necessary to use a laryngeal mirror, which is a small round mirror attached to a bent stem. The mirror has to be small enough to fit between the faucial pillars near the uvula where the vocal tract makes its right-angled turn, yet large enough to show the whole vocal fold area. The hinge and stem have to be small enough to leave the oral cavity relatively unobstructed.

Since laryngoscopy is invasive, some states have regulations against the use of the laryngeal mirror by other than ear, nose, and throat (ENT) doctors, although even in areas where the practice is permitted the investigator should be careful to avoid eliciting a gag reflex from the subject; he may find that all that is necessary to prevent this is to get the subject to gargle with a strong anaesthetic mouthwash beforehand.

Even with a satisfactory laryngeal mirror it is still necessary to observe the vocal folds with the tongue tip stuck out beyond the lips (see Illustration 431) and in a position that produces an [ε]-like vowel. Vowels like [i] and [u] obstruct the view through the oral cavity and vowels like [ɑ] and [ɔ] constrict the pharynx too much to allow us to see the vocal folds. The larynx has often been observed with a laryngeal mirror for changes in fundamental frequency, intensity, and phonation type, but only for the vowel [ε] until recently.

Second, satisfactory illumination was not really possible until the age of the electric light bulb and it is now customary to concentrate and direct a light source by the use of an ophthalmoscope mirror, the one a doctor puts on his forehead. Very strong light sources (e.g., a 5000 watt lamp) have to be passed through a water tank for cooling to avoid damaging the tissue of the larynx.

It goes without saying that, when the vocal folds are not moving, an appropriate tongue position, a laryngeal mirror, adequate illumination, and a camera are all that are needed to take still photographs of the vocal folds.

Finally, although it is not possible to separate the movements of the vocal folds with the unaided eye, the use of the stróboscope or of high speed cinematography enables us to isolate various stages of each opening and closing of the glottal cycle.

The stroboscope is an instrument that enables us to view certain moving objects, such as the vocal folds, and gain the impression that they are either not moving or only moving very slowly compared to their real speed. Imagine the vocal folds vibrating 100 times per sec with each glottal cycle taking $1/100$ sec. If the vocal folds are illuminated very briefly exactly every $1/100$ sec, and it is possible to deliver a flash as short as 5μ sec, i.e., 5 millionths of a second, the vocal folds will be seen at each flash in the same part of the glottal cycle, e.g., closed, half open, or fully open, and will as a result appear not to be moving at all. If the flashes are delivered slightly slower than the rate of vibration of the vocal folds, e.g., every $1/99$ sec, the viewer will appear to see one whole glottal cycle after 100 flashes. In other words, phonation seems to have been slowed down 100 times. If the flashes are delivered slightly faster than the fundamental frequency, e.g., every $1/101$ sec, phonation will likewise seem to have been slowed down, but the viewer will be seeing the event backward. With the vocal fold vibrations apparently slowed down in this way, their movement can be either viewed by the unaided eye or photographed.

However, our present knowledge of the way the vocal folds vibrate at high and low frequency, in loud and soft speech, with normal or unusual voicing is based largely on the examination of high speed photographic film.

As early as 1940 a technique was developed for the use of a high speed motion picture camera with an exposure rate of 4000 frames per sec, i.e., 40 frames per glottal cycle at 100 cycles per sec (see Illustration 431), and it is now possible to film at twice that rate. However, high speed cinematography requires very strong illumination, so the light has to be passed through a water tank to remove the heat. In addition, the camera is very noisy and, since a laryngeal mirror is used, dynamic speech events cannot be filmed, data for consonants are unobtainable, and the vowel can only be [ε]. Finally, there are very few units of this kind in the world so the student is unlikely to see one in action.

Fortunately, this need not worry us because the age of fiber optics has now arrived. The fiber optic bundle of a fiber optic laryngoscope or laryngeal fiberscope is composed of about 10,000 parallel glass fiber strands with a lens at one end and a camera and light source at the other; it conducts light in one direction and light images in the other.

The bundle is about as thick as a pencil and can easily be inserted by a doctor through the nose after desensitizing the mucosa of the nasal passage with an anaesthetic spray or a cotton-tipped stick dipped in anaesthetic. The bundle is inserted until it enters the pharynx and is then positioned above the vocal folds. Once again, cold light is necessary, but in this case there is no interference with articulation so the subject can utter both running speech and consonants, and the whole range of vowels can be examined.

In Illustration 432 we see the fiber optic bundle curling over to the right at the top of the laryngoscope, the viewing lens at the bottom left of the instrument, and the cold light source input and camera output just above the coiled leads.

The laryngeal fiberscope plus a motion film unit is too expensive for most phonetics laboratories, but hospitals usually have a direct viewing unit.

3.8.2 Operation

Many departments of speech pathology have a so-called manikin—a synthetic head with a vocal tract and a holder for slides of the vocal folds positioned at the larynx—which enables the student to practice using a laryngeal mirror to view the glottis. Once he has familiarized himself with the use of the mirror he may practice on a fellow student if state laws allow this. He will want to learn how to insert the mirror without eliciting a gag reflex, how to position the mirror to see the vocal folds, and how to adjust the light source to illuminate the larynx. A bright torchlight will be quite satisfactory.

It has already been pointed out that the fiberscope has to be inserted by a physician.

3.8.3 Demonstration Projects

3.8.3.1 *States of the Glottis*

3.8.3.1.0.1 *The problem* Linguists have long known that some sounds are voiced and some are voiceless, i.e., some are accompanied by vocal fold vibrations and some are not, but only more recently has it been realized that there are more than two states of the glottis and that there is, in fact, a whole continuum of states. At one end of the continuum the arytenoid cartilages may be completely abducted, held far apart, so that the vocal folds are positioned well away from each other, as in forced inhalation. At the other end, the arytenoid cartilages and vocal folds may be strongly adducted, forced together, so

that even a high subglottal pressure cannot blow them apart, as in a glottal stop. Breathy voice is produced with a glottal configuration lying somewhere between voiceless and voiced. Whereas in the voiceless state both the arytenoid cartilages and the vocal folds are held just far enough apart to prevent the folds from vibrating when air passes through from the lungs, for breathy voice the arytenoid cartilages are toed in somewhat at the front end so that, although the gap between them is almost as large as that for the voiceless state, the vocal folds are close enough together to flap in the breeze as air flows through from the lungs but never close enough to shut off the airflow completely. In the voiced state, on the contrary, both the arytenoid cartilages and the vocal folds are positioned close enough together both to vibrate as the air passes through and to shut off the airflow once each glottal cycle. A final state of the glottis, creaky voice, falls between non-breathy voicing and the glottal stop on the continuum and is characterized by the fact that the arytenoid cartilages are tightly approximated along their whole length, leaving only the muscular part of the vocal folds to vibrate. This is possible only because the folds are short and slack.

The very use of the word *continuum* cautions us that it is not really possible to isolate six states of the glottis as has been done here; Ladefoged has written in terms of a continuum of "glottal stricture" with nine values (called "phonation types"), not counting forced inspiration, adding however that the procedure is to some degree arbitrary; adjacent pairs can be collapsed and new terms can be added.

Finally, it should be noted that, although a given language may employ many states of the glottis overall, no language has been reported that uses more than three of them contrastively. However, be it three or six or nine, only by viewing or photographing the larynx have we been able to obtain data to discuss the problem satisfactorily.

3.8.3.1.0.2 *The data* Illustration 433 shows photographs of four states of the glottis: voiced, voiceless, breathy voice (murmur), and creaky voice.

3.8.3.1.0.3 *The interpretation* The larynx is viewed from above and the front end of the vocal folds is at the top of the picture. The apexes of the arytenoid cartilages are the circular white highlights at the bottom left and bottom right, but these are only seen well in the photograph of "voice." The glottal chink is the black central strip and the folds them-

selves are the white shining central masses. Often, but not here, the epiglottis is seen as a crescent-shaped enclosure around the glottis from middle left to top center to middle right (see Illustration 434).

The vocal folds are longest in the voiceless state and shortest in the creaky voice state, but it is not easy to see that the distance between the apexes of the arytenoid cartilages is greatest in the voiceless state, somewhat narrower for breathy voice, narrower still for voice, and smallest of all for creaky voice. We also know that the vocal folds are near maximum length in the fully abducted position on forced inhalation.

3.8.3.2 *Vowels*
3.8.3.2.1 *The Glottal Cycle*

3.8.3.2.1.1 *The problem* Each cycle of vibration of the vocal folds may be divided into three stages: the opening stage, when the vocal folds are moving away from each other; the closing stage, when the vocal folds are moving toward each other; and the closed stage, when both the arytenoid cartilages and the vocal folds are adducted, the latter stage not always being present.

Because of the limited resolving power of the human eye it is only possible to make statements about a glottal cycle from data obtained by stroboscopy or by high speed cinematography.

3.8.3.2.1.2 *The data* Illustration 434 shows one cycle of normal vocal fold vibration as revealed by high speed cinematography at 4000 frames per sec. At this rate one frame is taken each quarter of a thousandth of a second (0.25 msec), so the 32 frames in the cycle cover 8 msec, i.e., a fundamental frequency of 1000 msec ÷ 8 = 125 Hz. The arytenoid cartilages are obscured by a dark shadow at the bottom of each frame.

3.8.3.2.1.3 *The interpretation* The vocal folds begin to open at the front end in frame 1 and the glottal chink gets progressively wider and longer until the glottal area is at its greatest in frame 11. The opening phase covers 11 frames out of 32, which is 34% of the whole cycle. The folds begin to close from the back end starting at frame 12 and by frame 24 only a tiny chink can be seen at the front end. The closing phase covers 13 frames out of 32 (41% of the whole cycle). From frame 25 to frame 32 both the arytenoid cartilages and the vocal folds are adducted so the closed phase covers 8 frames out of 32 (25%). These data may be plotted with glottal area in square millimeters (mm^2) on the vertical axis and time (or frames) on the horizontal axis.

It may be said among other things that strong, healthy phonation is characterized by a long closed period, whereas breathy voice, a phonation type that wastes resources, is characterized by a zero closed period.

3.8.3.2.2 *Fundamental Frequency Change*

3.8.3.2.2.1 *The problem* As fundamental frequency is raised on a sustained vowel a number of things happen. Each glottal cycle becomes shorter, of course, so we have fewer frames to work with per cycle. The closed phase, during which subglottal pressure builds up, may become shorter in duration, although it may not change as a percentage of the whole cycle. The glottal area at maximum opening of the vocal folds will probably get smaller because the folds are tenser at high frequencies and will therefore not be blown apart so easily. In addition, the vocal folds get longer and thinner at high frequencies.

It is possible to observe these events by means of high speed laryngeal cinematography.

3.8.3.2.2.2 *The data* Illustration 435 shows a plot with vocal fold length, given as a percentage of the maximum recorded length on abduction, on the vertical axis and pitch, given as a percentage of the subject's total pitch range including falsetto, on the horizontal axis. The data are taken from high speed cinematographic film at 4000 frames per sec.

Illustration 436 shows a photograph of the author's vocal folds phonating at low frequency during the steady state of the second vowel of [ɪts ə pʰi] and Illustration 437 phonating at high frequency during the steady state of the third vowel of the same utterance. The former was taken about 200 msec before the release of the [p] and the latter about 250 msec after release.

3.8.3.2.2.3 *The interpretation* Illustration 435 shows that as the subjects raise their fundamental frequency the vocal folds become longer. This is true for all six subjects (marked with black or white squares, circles, and triangles, respectively). To take one example in order to show how to read this plot, the top right white triangle tells us that, if the maximum length on abduction of this subject's vocal folds were 20 mm, then 88% on the vertical axis would equal $0.88 \times 20 = 17.6$ mm; if the same subject had a pitch range of from 65 Hz to 665 Hz, i.e., 600 Hz, then 46% on the horizontal axis would equal $0.46 \times 600 = 276$ Hz; i.e., at 276 Hz this subject's vocal folds would be 17.6 mm long.

Hence, unlike long violin strings, which have a relatively low pitch, long vocal folds produce what is perceived as a high pitch. This is because a lengthening of the vocal folds makes them tenser and thinner.

Illustration 415 (see item 3.6.3.2.0.2) shows vocal fold mass as viewed from the front, and it is from this perspective that one can make estimates of vocal fold thickness.

Illustrations 436 and 437 exemplify what was said about the relationship between vocal fold length and fundamental frequency. The epiglottis is the lighter colored mass at the top of the picture, the arytenoid cartilages are the circular white highlights at the lower center, and the glottis is the vertical dark center line between the lighter colored vocal folds. It is quite obvious that the vocal folds are much longer for the high-frequency phonation.

3.8.3.3 Consonants

3.8.3.3.0.1 *The problem* We have already pointed out that neither stroboscopy nor high speed cinematography can help us with consonants, although fiber optics can, since the laryngeal fiberscope is inserted through the nose and therefore does not interfere with articulation.

Vowels differ from each other in phonation type with respect to the length of the vocal folds, which may or may not also imply a difference in longitudinal tension and stiffness, and the width of the glottis, i.e., the distance between the folds at their most abducted point at the moment in the cycle when the glottal area is smallest, and we would like to know whether voiced and voiceless, breathy and creaky plosives differ from each other in similar ways.

3.8.3.3.0.2 *The data* Illustrations 438–441 show frames from a film of the author's vocal folds taken with a camera attached to a laryngeal fiberscope for an aspirated voiceless bilabial plosive [p^h], a voiced bilabial plosive [b], a breathy voiced bilabial plosive [b^h], and a laryngealized, i.e., creaky voiced, bilabial plosive [ʔb]. Each frame was selected to show the state of the glottis about 50 msec before release, i.e., during the pressure stage.

3.8.3.3.0.3 *The interpretation* [p^h] has long vocal folds and a static glottal width rather like that for a voiceless vowel. [b] has somewhat shorter vocal folds and adduction of both the arytenoid cartilages and the vocal folds, the former being closer together than for [p^h]. The breathy voice [b^h] is very similar to the [b], although the vocal folds are rather longer, so the mechanism for breathy voice must set in closer to the moment of release or even after release. Finally, the creaky voiced [ʔb] has tightly approximated arytenoid cartilages and the epiglottis

has been pulled backward against the aryepiglottic folds, which are the white masses to the front of the arytenoid cartilages. The net result is that the short, slack vocal folds, such as we noted for the creaky voiced vowel, are barely visible 50 msec before release through the severely constricted laryngeal entry.

The need to build up pressure in the pharyngeal and oral cavities for a bilabial plosive results in different relationships between the subglottal and supraglottal pressures for consonants and for vowels, so it should not be expected that the glottal states for these consonants should be identical to those for the corresponding vowels until after the moment of release. Yet, in spite of this, there is great similarity between the two groups.

3.8.4 Reading

It is suggested that the student now read the following items before proceeding with the projects below.

Hollien, H., and Moore, P. 1960. Measurements of the vocal folds during changes in pitch. *Journal of Speech and Hearing Research 3*:157–165.

Ladefoged, P. 1974. Respiration, laryngeal activity and linguistics. In B. Wyke (ed.), *Ventilatory and Phonatory Control Systems,* pp. 299–307. Oxford University Press, New York.

Lindqvist, J. 1969. Laryngeal mechanisms in speech. *Speech Transmission Laboratory, Quarterly Progress and Status Report,* October 15, pp. 26–32. Royal Institute of Technology (KTH), Stockholm.

Ward, P.H., Berci, G., and Calcaterra, T.C. 1974. Advances in endoscopic examination of the respiratory system. *The Annals of Otology, Rhinology and Laryngology 83(6)*part 1:754–760.

3.8.5 Student Projects

3.8.5.1 *Replication Projects*

a. Using a laryngeal mirror, examine the vocal folds of a fellow student breathing in, breathing out, and holding his breath.

b. Ask the same student to try to simulate states of the glottis appropriate for breathy voice, voice, and creaky voice. He may well not be able to do this, but the viewer will nevertheless note changes in glottal configuration.

3.8.5.2 *New Projects*

Ask your university speech clinic to allow you to be present at a laryngoscopic examination of a client with a laryngeal pathology.

3.9 AN END AND A NEW BEGINNING—COMPUTERS

3.9.1 Introduction

In one respect at least instrumental phonetics is certain to change a great deal in the none too distant future. Small computers are becoming, relatively speaking, ever cheaper and it is to be expected that many laboratories will soon have computer control and processing in their inventory of available techniques. There will remain, however, many laboratories, even in the United States, without this facility and third world universities will still regard it as a luxury for the foreseeable future. Furthermore, even the privileged computer user will need the basic knowledge presented in this book if he is to work with understanding.

Yet it would be wrong to end this book without giving some idea of existing computer applications in phonetic research. The computer is a machine that accepts an *input* in the form of a string of symbols and then processes them according to a set of instructions called a *program* to give an *output* in the form of a second string of symbols. Hence a computer may be programmed to process acoustic and physiological data. It is the preparation of the program that is the most laborious part of the task because, although the computer is hard-working, reliable, and fast, it is also of itself unintelligent and has to be told how to do things in very simple steps. In this sense the preparation of a program to enable the computer to carry out some linguistic task will tell us what the human brain has to do, although not necessarily how it does it.

There are essentially four kinds of people who work with computers. First, those who know how to build and repair them or at least know how they work. These are the hardware specialists. Second, those who know how to write programs, i.e., work out instructions that will enable the computer to carry out a task. These are the software specialists. The phonetician does not have to be able to do either of these things since there are technicians to handle the hardware, and standard programs are available at the large laboratories which can be borrowed and fed into compatible computers at other institutions. Third, there are those who use computers, i.e., feed prepackaged programs into well-maintained computers and become sophisticated button-pushers. Finally, there are those who know what the computer can do for us in phonetic research and have assistants available or colleagues willing to actually do it. The phonetician, if he has the facilities, will profit from being in one of the last two categories, preferably as a user.

There is, however, a certain danger in having these remarkable technological advances at one's disposal. If it takes only half a dozen afternoon sessions under supervision for students with no knowledge of computers to turn themselves into what I called "sophisticated button-pushers," then students of electrical engineering or computer science are particularly vulnerable since they find it easy to do what looks like rather advanced work without necessarily having any more real understanding of speech events than, for example, an anthropological linguist who has taken some phonetics in a field methods course. This danger, of course lies not with the computer itself but with the way it is used and the precaution, surely, is to cover at some stage the ground this book has covered.

On the whole the computer helps us by doing tedious jobs with accuracy and speed and is able to handle bodies of data so large that, although many of them *could* be done without a computer, they would in fact not be because of lack of time. Time considerations apart, however, there are relatively few tasks that cannot be done at all without a computer, a statement that is not true of most of the electronic instrumentation discussed previously.

3.9.2 Speech Synthesis

The most creative use of the computer is in speech synthesis rather than in the analysis of speech, but since this book is not concerned with talking machines, little is said about them here. As the latter are of particular interest to the psycholinguist working on problems in speech perception, this might be considered regrettable, but it is the author's opinion that the psycholinguist, like the student of electrical engineering or computer science, needs to understand the nature of speech events before embarking on the synthesis of speech samples for experiments in perception.

Most speech synthesis can be carried out on electrical circuits without the use of a computer and ranges in kind from perfect copies of individual voices to very unnatural sounding speech, which has as its aim only that the message be understood, the former showing how far the technology has advanced and the latter addressing problems in telecommunications and perception. The computer is used primarily for storing instructions on syntax and phonology. One of the most notable recent advances of this kind is a reading machine for the blind, a piece of equipment that can accept a printed page as an input and produce quite natural sounding speech as an output, a procedure that would be quite impossible without computer access to a programmed syntax and phonology.

Speech synthesizers are essentially of three kinds, all of which may or may not be computer controlled. The terminal analog (or formant) synthesizer generates speech through electrical circuits connected either in series (i.e., the output of one circuit is the input into the next) or in parallel (i.e., the various circuits are independent of each other but their outputs are combined). However, it does so in a manner that does not model speech production. Its users are interested in ends (i.e., the speech output) rather than means (i.e., the speech production process).

Second, there is the vocal tract analog, which generates speech by using what we know about the acoustic consequences of different vocal tract *configurations* and their electrical equivalents. The vocal tract is represented by a series of sections, let us say 35 in number, one for each ½ cm from the glottis to the lips, each of which models the cross-sectional area of the vocal tract at that point. Since the cross-sectional area affects air pressure and airflow within the vocal tract, and since these determine the nature of the sound being produced, each section may be represented by a circuit with electrical equivalents for pressure (i.e., voltage) and flow (i.e., current).

Finally, there is the articulatory model, which is of interest for what it says about the acoustic consequences of physiological behavior and which synthesizes speech by modeling the movements of articulators. The *gestures* are converted into changing cross-sectional areas along the vocal tract and the latter are represented by electrical circuits, as described previously. Its users are more interested in means (i.e., speech production) than ends (i.e., the speech output).

3.9.3 Acoustic Analysis

Those techniques discussed in sections 2.2 to 2.5 can all be handled alternatively by computer in ways that make it possible to process large bodies of data accurately in a short time. Programs are available for formant frequency, wave form, fundamental frequency, and intensity display and analysis. A corpus

of data can be read into the computer and the wave form can be displayed almost immediately at any point in time by scanning with fast forward and fast reverse controls. Formant frequency analysis has been made faster and more accurate by the development of a number of new mathematical procedures, such as the cepstrum and linear prediction techniques, which can be built into the program, and fundamental frequency and intensity analysis can be handled more easily than before, partly because the analyzer can be manipulated on the spot to handle the characteristics of an individual speaker's voice, partly because average measurements can be made of large bodies of data, and partly because of the fast recall capability which aids comparison of chosen utterances.

It is now possible to calculate average values for data extending over long periods of time, such as intensity as a function of frequency for a symphony orchestra playing a work lasting ½ hr, and to compute a vocal tract area function given only acoustic data as an input, i.e., if we have the right program all we have to do is play in a steady state sound to get out a display in the form of a sagittal view of a vocal tract configuration that could have produced the sound in question.

In addition to the availability of computer-controlled scanners with fast forward and backward recall and the associated visual display units, permanent print-outs can be made of interesting features, programs may be temporarily altered merely by typing in new instructions, and displays may be altered and played back in changed form by "dynamic modeling," i.e., simply changing a parameter by drawing on a screen with a light pen or on a table with a tablet pen.

3.9.4 Physiological Analysis

The use of the computer in physiological analysis is almost entirely restricted at present to its easy control of parameters and its great speed in calculation; such use is made possible largely by the use of the FM tape recorder, which usually has four or more channels and can store information on a number of independent parameters for later display or analysis, which may or may not be computer controlled.

For example, several channels of EMG data can be recorded simultaneously on FM tape for subsequent analysis, and for any one muscle on one channel the unit can average out data for, let us say, 20 repetitions of the same word. This summation of muscle activity for a large body of data is more reliable and easier to obtain than measurements by hand from only a few samples.

If radiographic work is done on a subject with lead pellets stuck to known points in his vocal tract, it is possible to project the film onto the bottom of a computer screen and to "write in" the pellet positions by the use of a light pen. The pellet positions become the input data and average or dynamic values can be calculated with speed and accuracy.

An identical technique can be used in laryngoscopy. The film is projected onto the bottom of the computer screen and the investigator merely takes a light pen and draws in the outlines of the glottis or two points representing glottal length or width. The computer then calculates, let us say, the average glottal width for all breathy voiced as opposed to normally voiced vowels in the data.

In addition, rapid calculations of place of articulation can be made from dynamic palatography data to show us, for example, how the tongue configuration for a /t/ differs before a variety of vowels, and a large corpus of air pressure and airflow data can be scanned to give average values for different consonants.

The computer can handle large bodies of data; can make rapid calculations on any desired parameter; can search for, retrieve, and display any desired item in the corpus; and can be programmed to do certain tasks that could otherwise not be done at all. In the technologically advanced countries more and more investigators will have the opportunity to use these techniques as the years go by, but even those who are not so fortunate should be aware of what it is possible to do with the aid of these new facilities.

4
A Classified Bibliography

4.1 INTRODUCTION

This chapter is divided into four sections: a bibliography by topic, i.e., by subdiscipline within the field of phonetics; one by phonetic feature; one by instrument, which refers back to those subsections entitled "Reading"; and a list of journals of interest to the phonetician. The last three sections are self-explanatory and enable the student to put his hands quickly onto source material of a particular nature and follow up from there. The first section, however, needs a few introductory remarks.

The bibliography by topic includes items that range from the most introductory to the most advanced and the author would like to avoid that most common of faults in course bibliographies—the long list of books that takes no account of the student's previous experience.

The term *introductory* is to be strictly interpreted—the student either knows no phonetics at all or has done a little introductory work in one aspect of the field but none in the topic under review. In this sense Denes ['dɛnɛʃ] and Pinson's *The Speech Chain* is a well-tried introduction to all aspects of communication science and Abercrombie's *Elements of General Phonetics* is a most readable introduction to general phonetics, as also is the book by O'Connor. Ladefoged's ['lædɪˌfoʊɡɪd] *A Course in Phonetics* is an introductory course book and a

very fine one, and Daniel Jones' *Pronunciation of English,* old as it is, is still sound from a pedagogical point of view. An introduction to communication science, one to general phonetics, and another to the phonetics of English, this surely should be the starting point for all those who are interested in the discipline.

The term *intermediate* is taken to refer to readings for those who desire to pursue in more detail those topics already discussed and to embark on a study of speech production, speech acoustics, and speech perception without getting into deep water. At this level Minifie et al.'s *Normal Aspects of Speech, Hearing, and Language,* which the introductory level student tends to find rather intimidating, is a fine comprehensive text on communication science. Zemlin's *Speech and Hearing Science,* which would also overwhelm the beginner, is a thorough intermediate level treatment of speech production, audiology, and neurology. Ladefoged's *Elements of Acoustic Phonetics* is a simple introduction to a topic which the student should enter into only at the intermediate level; exactly the same could be said of Stevens and House's "Speech perception" in the volume edited by Tobias. Gimson's ['ɡɪmsən] *An Introduction to the Pronunciation of English* contains such a wealth of detail that it should follow an introduction such as that by Jones unless the student is an English language specialist.

Those items considered *advanced* do demand a solid background from the student if he is not to feel bewildered. The *Manual of Phonetics,* edited by Malmberg, is a standard handbook which contains many chapters that are formidable for the beginner. Pike's *Phonetics,* which could be read at the intermediate level, is a milestone in the history of phonetics where "i"'s were dotted and "t"'s crossed. Two books of readings in acoustic phonetics, those edited by Lehiste ['lɛhistɛ] and by Fry, are good collections for the advanced student, while Ladefoged's *Preliminaries to Linguistic Phonetics* is a slim but weighty volume for the student with some experience in linguistics. This book is sometimes listed as an introductory text in spite of what its author has to say in the introduction, and although the linguist might tackle it at the intermediate level, others might want to leave it until later.

All entries for books and journals (but not articles) in this section end with their call number from the Library of Congress Catalog. These numbers will probably, but not necessarily, be used by the student's home library and have been included because the literature on instrumental phonetics is not concentrated in one section of the stacks.

4.2 BIBLIOGRAPHY BY TOPIC

4.2.1 General

Introductory

1. Denes, P., and Pinson, E. 1973. *The Speech Chain*, 217 pp. Anchor Press/Doubleday Books, Garden City, New York. QP 306. D 45.
2. Dew, D., and Jensen, P.J. 1977. *Phonetic Processing*, 268 pp. Charles E. Merrill Publishing Company, Columbus. P 221. D 4.

Intermediate

3. Minifie, F.D., Hixon, T.J., and Williams, F. (eds.). 1973. *Normal Aspects of Speech, Hearing, and Language*, 509 pp. Prentice-Hall, Inc., Englewood Cliffs, N.J. QP 306. M 617.

Advanced

4. Lass, N.J. (ed.). 1976. *Contemporary Issues in Experimental Phonetics*, 498 pp. Academic Press, Inc., New York. QP 306. L 754.
5. Malmberg, B. (ed.). 1970. *Manual of Phonetics*, 568 pp. North-Holland Publishing Company, Amsterdam. QP 306. M 25.
6. Sawashima, M., and Cooper, F. (eds.). 1977. *Dynamic Aspects of Speech Production*, 417 pp. University of Tokyo Press, Tokyo.

4.2.2 General Phonetics

7. Abercrombie, D. 1967. *Elements of General Phonetics*, 203 pp. Aldine Publishing Company, Chicago. P 221. A 23.
8. Catford, J.C. 1977. *Fundamental Problems in Phonetics*, 278 pp. Indiana University Press, Bloomington. P 221. C 3.
9. Ladefoged, P. 1971. *Preliminaries to Linguistic Phonetics*, 122 pp. The University of Chicago Press, Chicago. P 221. L 154.
10. Ladefoged, P. 1975. *A Course in Phonetics*, 296 pp. Harcourt Brace Jovanovich, Inc., New York. P 221. L 2.
11. O'Connor, J.D. 1973. *Phonetics*. Penguin Books Ltd., Harmondsworth, Middlesex, England. P 221. O 25.
12. Pike, K. 1943/1961. *Phonetics*, 156 pp. University of Michigan Press, Ann Arbor. P 221. P 54.

4.2.3 The Phonetics of English

13. Gimson, A.C. 1962. *An Introduction to the Pronunciation of English*, 294 pp. Edward Arnold (Publishers) Ltd., London. PE 1135. G 5.
14. Jones, D. 1909/1963. *The Pronunciation of English*, 223 pp. Cambridge University Press, New York. PE 1137. J 56.
15. Jones, D. 1969. *An Outline of English Phonetics*, 378 pp. Heffer (W.) & Sons Ltd., Cambridge, England. PE 1135. J 76.
16. Kenyon, J.S. 1945. *American Pronunciation*, 265 pp. George Wahr Publishing Company, Ann Arbor, Mich. PE 1135. K 4.

4.2.4 The Anatomy and Physiology of Speech

17. Hardcastle, W.J. 1976. *Physiology of Speech Production*, 157 pp. Academic Press, Inc., New York. QP 306. H 29.
18. Zemlin, W. 1968. *Speech and Hearing Science: Anatomy and Physiology*, 589 pp. Prentice-Hall, Englewood Cliffs, N.J. QP 306. Z 4.

4.2.5 Acoustic Phonetics

19. Fry, D.B. (ed.). 1976. *Acoustic Phonetics*, 469 pp. Cambridge University Press, New York. QP 306. A 26.
20. Ladefoged, P. 1962. *Elements of Acoustic Phonetics*, 120 pp. The University of Chicago Press, Chicago. QP 306. L 33.
21. Lehiste, I. (ed.). 1970. *Readings in Acoustic Phonetics*, 358 pp. The MIT Press, Cambridge, Mass. QP 306. L 38.

4.2.6 Nonspeech Perception

22. Harris, J.D. 1974. *Psychoacoustics*, 99 pp. Bobbs-Merrill Company, Inc., Indianapolis. BF 251. H 33.

4.2.7 Speech Perception

23. Cohen, A., and Nooteboom, S.G. (eds.). *Structure and Process in Speech Perception*, 353 pp. See pp. 16–35 especially. Springer-Verlag, Berlin. BF 251. S 95.
24. Sebeok, T.A. (ed.). 1974. *Current Trends in Linguistics*, Vol. 12, tome 3, part 10. See pp. 2349–2386 especially. Mouton, The Hague. P 25. S 4.
25. Tobias, J.V. (ed.). *Foundations of Modern Auditory Theory*, Vol. 2, 508 pp. See pp. 3–62 especially. Academic Press, Inc., New York. QP 461. T 6. v2.

4.2.8 Statistical Procedures

26. Williams, F. 1968. *Reasoning with Statistics: Simplified Examples in Communications Research*, 182 pp. Holt, Rinehart & Winston, Inc., New York. HA 29. W 525.

4.2.9 Other

27. Lieberman, P. 1977. *Speech Physiology and Acoustic Phonetics: An Introduction*, 206 pp. Macmillan Publishing Co., Inc., New York. QP 306. L 52.

4.3 BIBLIOGRAPHY BY PHONETIC FEATURE

4.3.1 Vowels

1. Potter, R.K., Kopp, G.A., and Green, H.C. 1947. *Visible Speech*, 441 pp. D. Van Nostrand Company, New York. TK 6500. P 868.
2. Fant, G. 1968. Analysis and synthesis of speech processes. In B. Malmberg (ed.), *Manual of Phonetics*, pp. 243–253. North-Holland Publishing Company, Amsterdam. QP 306. M 25.
3. Painter, C. 1970. *Gonja: A Phonological and Grammatical Study*, 525 pp. See especially pp. 55–64

and 103–122. Indiana University Press, Bloomington. The Hague, Mouton. PL 8215. P 148.

4. Peterson, G.E., and Barney, H.L. 1952. Control methods used in a study of the vowels. *The Journal of the Acoustical Society of America 24:* 175–184.

5. Painter, C. 1973. Cineradiographic data on the feature 'covered' in Twi vowel harmony. *Phonetica 28:* 97–120.

4.3.2 Plosives and Fricatives

6. See Potter, Kopp, and Green in subsection 4.3.1.
7. See Fant in subsection 4.3.1, pp. 243–253.
8. See Painter in subsection 4.3.1., pp. 23–54 and 103–136.
9. Halle, M., Hughes, G.W., and Radley, J-P.A. 1957. Acoustic properties of stop consonants. *The Journal of the Acoustical Society of America 29:* 107–116.
10. Strevens, P. 1960. Spectra of fricative noise in human speech. *Language and Speech 3:*32–49.
11. Arkebauer, H.J., Hixon, T.J., and Hardy, J.C. 1967. Peak intra-oral air pressures during speech. *Journal of Speech and Hearing Research 10:* 196–208.
12. Isshiki, N., and Ringel, R.L. 1964. Air flow during the production of selected consonants. *Journal of Speech and Hearing Research 7:*151–164.
13. Perkell, J.S. 1969. *Physiology of Speech Production.* Research Monograph No. 53. The MIT Press, Cambridge, Mass. QP 306. P 4.

4.3.3 Nasality

14. Hattori, S., Yamamoto, K., and Fujimura, O. 1958. Nasalization of vowels in relation to nasals. *The Journal of the Acoustical Society of America 30:* 267–274.
15. Fujimura, O. 1962. Analysis of nasal consonants. *The Journal of the Acoustical Society of America 34:*1865–1875.
16. Nakata, K. 1959. Synthesis and perception of nasal consonants. *The Journal of the Acoustical Society of America 31:*661–666.

4.3.4 Liquids and Nonsyllabic Vocoids

17. O'Connor, J.D., Gerstman, L.J., Liberman, A.M., Delattre, P.C., and Cooper, F.S. 1957. Acoustic cues for the perception of initial /w,j,r,l/ in English. *Word 13:*24–43.
18. Lisker, L. 1957. Minimal cues for separating /w,r,l,y/ in intervocalic position. *Word 13:*256–267.

4.3.5 Transitions and Glides

19. Delattre, P.C., Liberman, A.M., and Cooper, F.S. 1955. Acoustic loci and transitional cues for consonants. *The Journal of the Acoustical Society of America 27:*769–773.
20. Lehiste, I., and Peterson, G.E. 1961. Transitions, glides and diphthongs. *The Journal of the Acoustical Society of America 33:*268–277.

4.3.6 Duration and Length

21. House, A. 1961. On vowel duration in English. *The Journal of the Acoustical Society of America 33:*1174–1178.
22. Lehiste, I. 1970. *Suprasegmentals,* 194 pp. See especially pp. 6–53. The MIT Press, Cambridge, Mass. P 217. L 37.
23. Peterson, G.E., and Lehiste, I. 1960. Duration of syllable nuclei in English. *The Journal of the Acoustical Society of America 32:*693–703.

4.3.7 Frequency and Pitch

24. Lieberman, P. 1965. On the acoustic basis of the perception of intonation by linguists. *Word 21:*40–54.
25. O'Connor, J.D., and Arnold, G.F. 1961. *Intonation of Colloquial English,* 270 pp. See especially pp. 1–31. Longmans Green & Company Ltd., London. PE 1135. O 37.
26. See Lehiste under subsection 4.3.6, pp. 54–105.

4.3.8 Intensity, Loudness, and Stress

27. Fry, D.B. 1955. Duration and intensity as physical correlates of linguistic stress. *The Journal of the Acoustical Society of America 27:*765–768.
28. Fry, D.B. 1958. Experiments in the perception of stress. *Language and Speech 1:*126–152.
29. Lehiste, I., and Peterson, G.E. 1959. Vowel amplitude and phonemic stress in American English. *The Journal of the Acoustical Society of America 31(4):*428–435.
30. See Lehiste under subsection 4.3.6, pp. 106–153.

4.3.9 Voicing

31. Lisker, L., and Abramson, A.S. 1964. A cross-language study of voicing in initial stops: Acoustical measurements. *Word 20:*384–422.
32. Lisker, L., and Abramson, A.S. 1970. The voicing dimension: Some experiments in comparative phonetics. In B. Hála, M. Romportl, and P. Janota (eds.), *Proceedings of the Sixth International Congress of Phonetic Sciences,* pp. 536–567. Academia, Prague. P 215. I 61.

4.4 BIBLIOGRAPHY BY INSTRUMENT

See subsection 4 at the end of each of sections 2.2 to 3.8.

4.5 JOURNALS

The following journals are of interest to the phonetician and most of the articles which he will consult are in these publications.

1. *Acta Radiologica* (and supplements). QC. A 189.
2. *The Cleft Palate Journal.* RD 252. F 64.

3. *Folia Phoniatrica.* RC 423. F 6.
4. *Haskins Laboratories—Status Report on Speech Research.* P 121. H 351.
5. *International Congress of Phonetic Sciences, Proceedings of,* 1932, 1935, 1938, 1961, 1964, 1971, and 1975. P 215. I 61.
6. *Journal of Phonetics.* P. J 874.
7. *The Journal of the Acoustical Society of America (JASA).* QC 1. A 18.
8. *Journal of Speech and Hearing Disorders (JSHD).* RC. J 8662.
9. *Journal of Speech and Hearing Research (JSHR).* RC 423. J 86.
10. *Language.* P 25. L 287.
11. *Language and Speech.* P 1. L 288.
12. *Le Maître Phonétique* (now *Journal of the International Phonetic Association*). P 215. M 23.
13. *Lingua.* P 9. L 75.
14. *Phonetica.* P 215. P 574.
15. *RLE, QPR* (Speech Communication Group, Research Laboratory of Electronics, Massachusetts Institute of Technology, Quarterly Progress Report). TK 7855. M 41. R 432.
16. *STL, QPSR* (Speech Transmission Laboratory, Quarterly Progress and Status Report of the Royal Institute of Technology (KTH), Stockholm). QC 246. S 864.
17. *Studia Linguistica.* P 7. S 93.
18. University of California Los Angeles, Phonetics Laboratory, *Working Papers in Phonetics.* P 222. T 66.
19. *Word.* P 1. W 919.
20. *Zeitschrift für Phonetik und allgemeine Sprachwissenschaft* (now *Zeitschrift für Phonetik, Sprachwissenschaft und Kommunikationsforschung*). P 215. Z 48.

Appendix
The Illustrations

I would like to express my thanks to Harriet Grossman, Rick Taplin, and Bob Samson of the Abbot Memorial Library and Media Center, Emerson College, Boston, and to Philip Kimball for having photographed my illustrations.

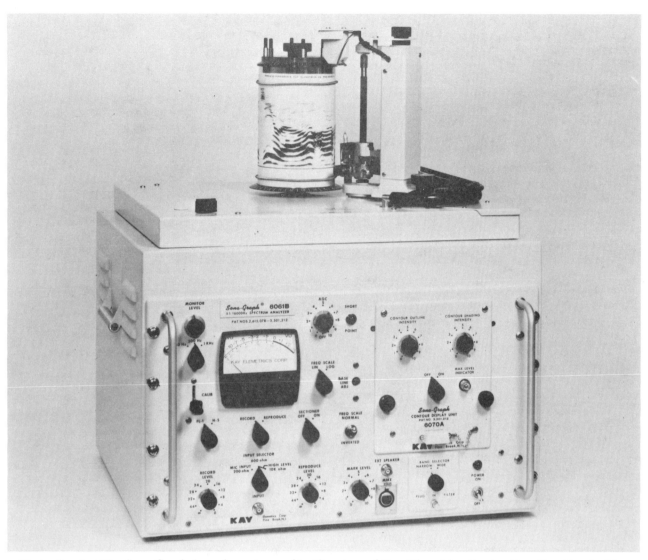

Illustration 1. The Sona-Graph (sound spectrograph). (Courtesy of Kay Elemetrics Corporation, Pine Brook, New Jersey.)

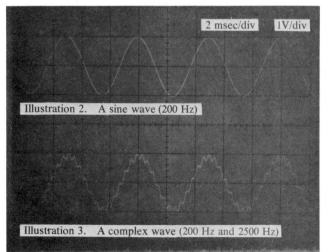

Illustration 2. A sine wave (200 Hz)

Illustration 3. A complex wave (200 Hz and 2500 Hz)

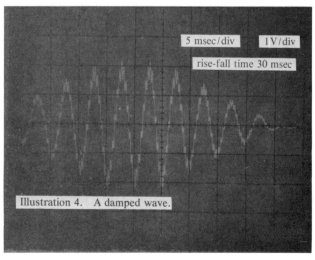

Illustration 4. A damped wave.

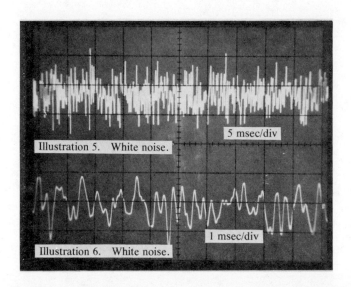

Illustration 5.   White noise.

5 msec/div

Illustration 6.   White noise.

1 msec/div

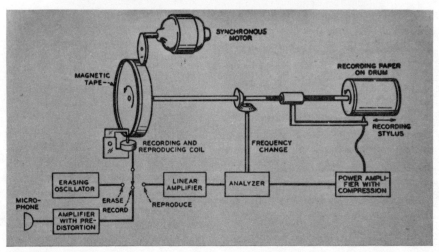

Illustration 7.   Schematic representation of the basic method of the sound spectrograph. The sound is recorded on the loop of magnetic tape, and analyzed while repeatedly reproduced. The fluctuating analyzer output builds up a pattern of light and dark areas on the electrically sensitive paper. (Reprinted from Koenig, W., Dunn, H. K., and Lacey, L. Y. 1946. The sound spectrograph. *The Journal of the Acoustical Society of America 17:*19–49. By permission of the publisher.)

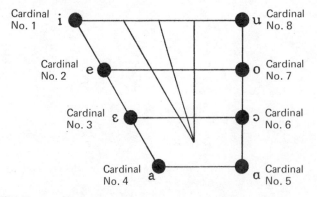

Illustration 8.   The primary cardinal vowels. (From Jones, D. 1956. *The Pronunciation of English.* Cambridge University Press, New York. By permission.)

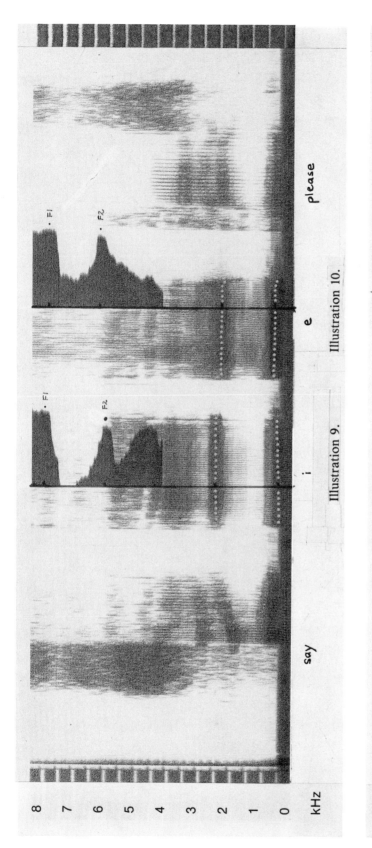

Illustration 9.

Illustration 10.

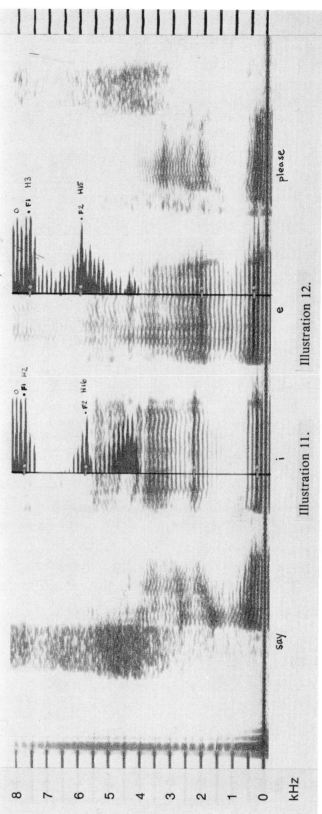

Illustration 11.

Illustration 12.

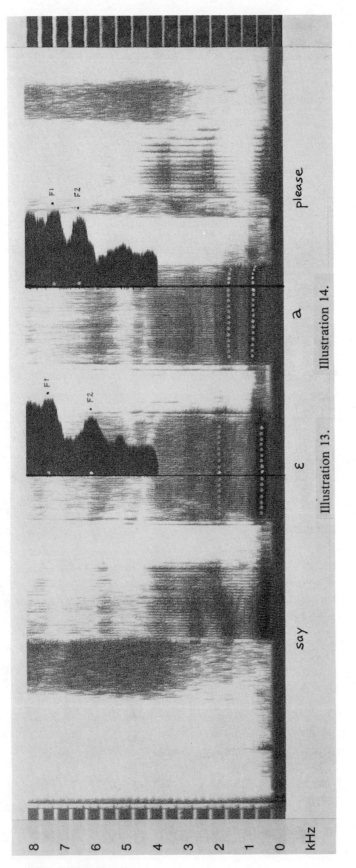

Illustration 13.   Illustration 14.

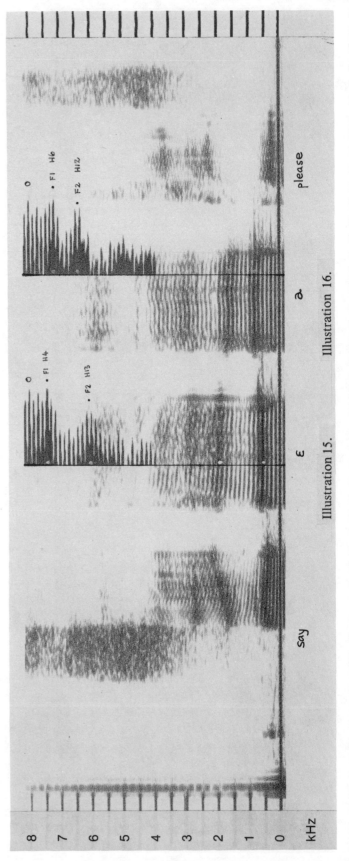

Illustration 15.   Illustration 16.

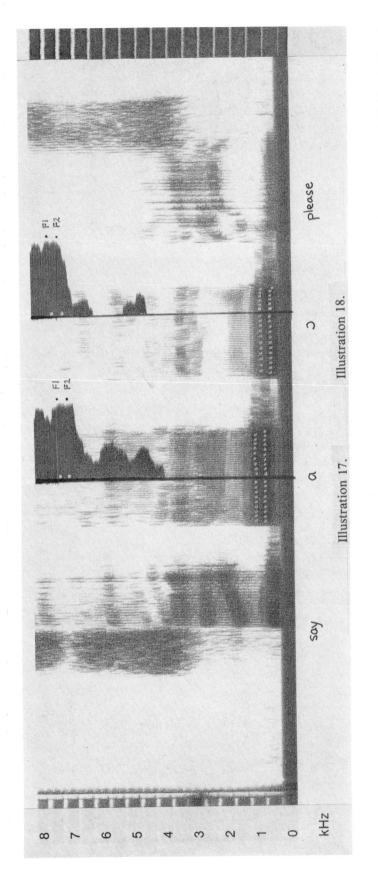

Illustration 17.

Illustration 18.

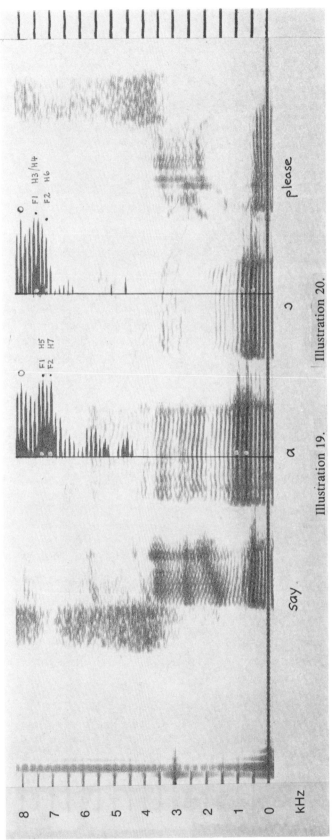

Illustration 19.

Illustration 20.

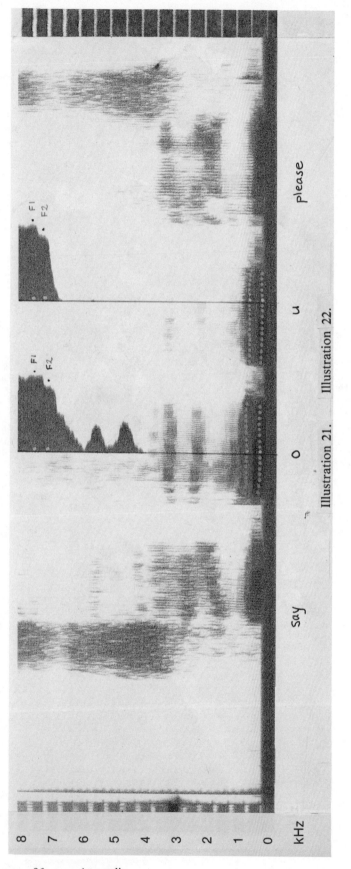

Illustration 21.   Illustration 22.

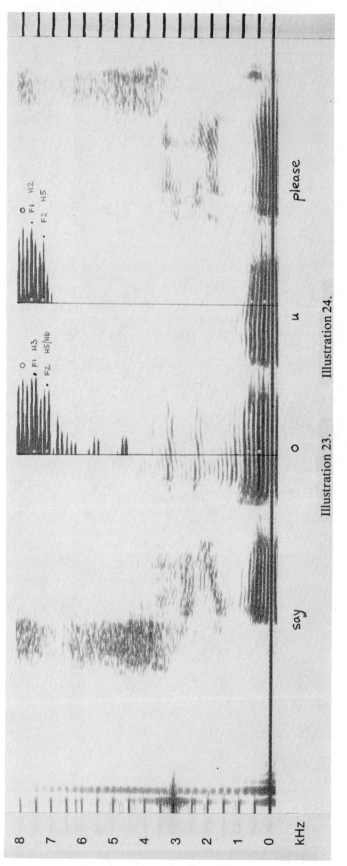

Illustration 23.   Illustration 24.

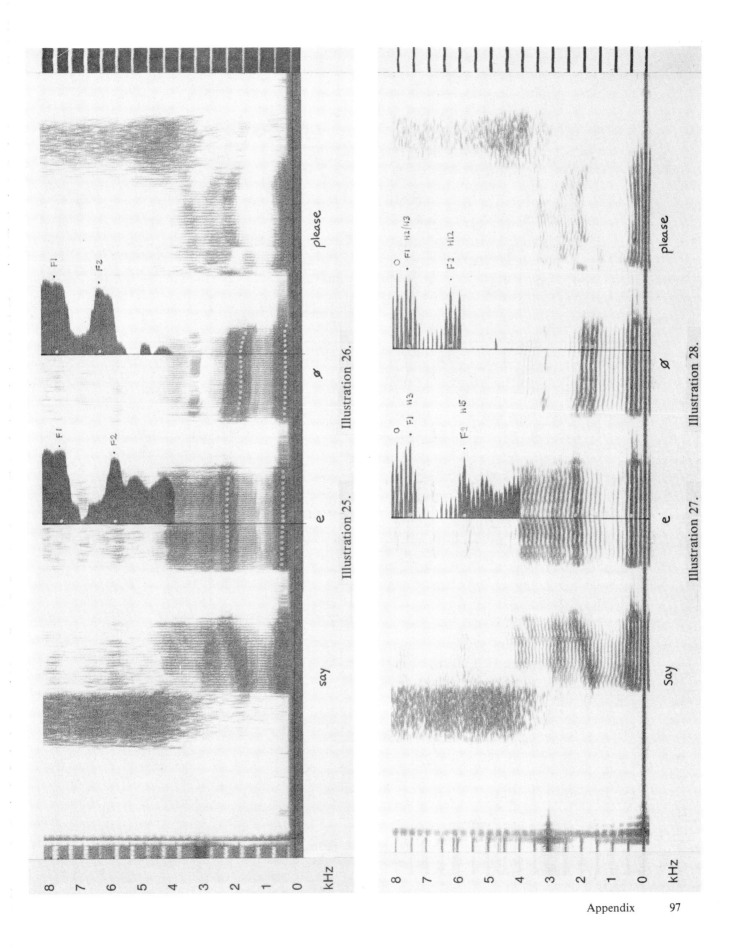

Illustration 25.

Illustration 26.

Illustration 27.

Illustration 28.

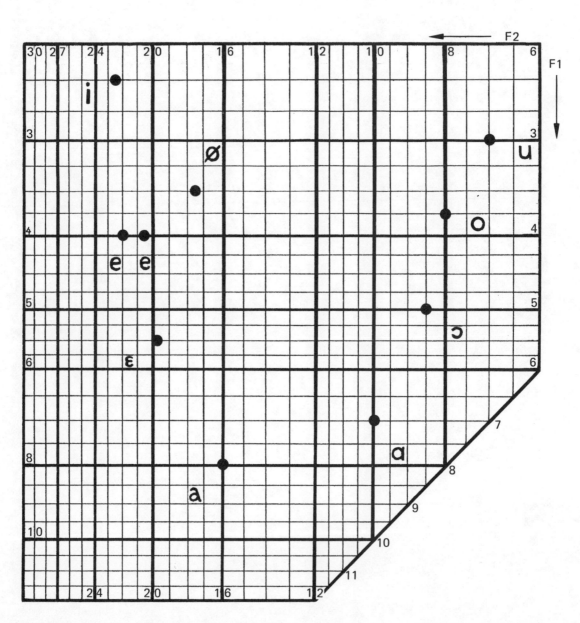

Illustration 29. Formant chart, calibrated in hundreds of cycles per second. Placing a single point on this chart is an assertion that formants have been observed at two frequencies: one formant at the frequency named along the right or left edge, the other formant at the frequency named along the top or bottom edge. (From Joos, M., 1948. Acoustic phonetics, *Language* 23:51. With permission of the Linguistic Society of America.)

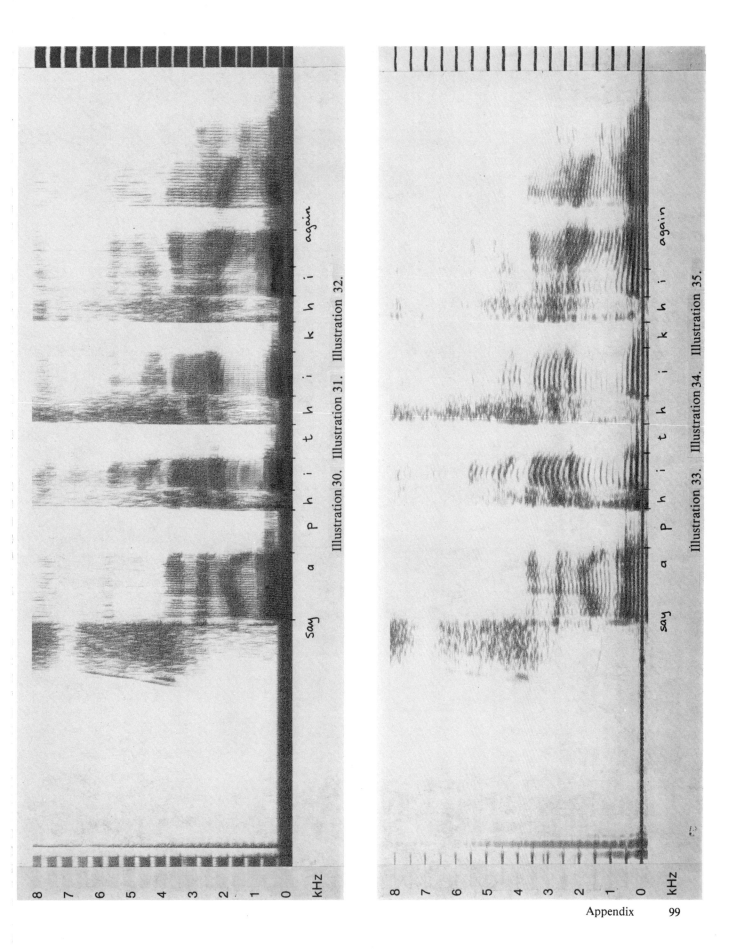

Illustration 30. Illustration 31. Illustration 32.

Illustration 33. Illustration 34. Illustration 35.

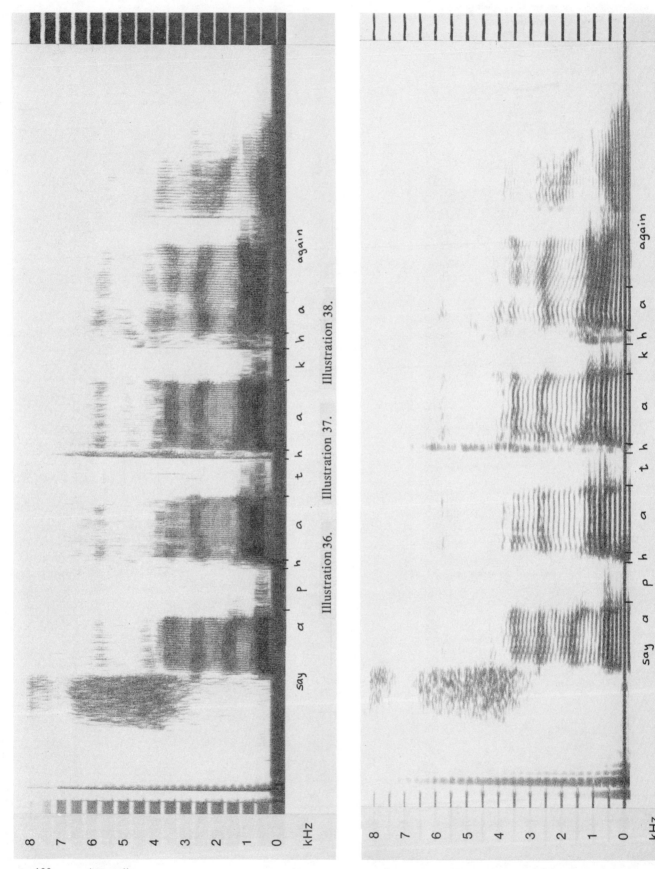

Illustration 36. Illustration 37. Illustration 38.

Illustration 39. Illustration 40. Illustration 41.

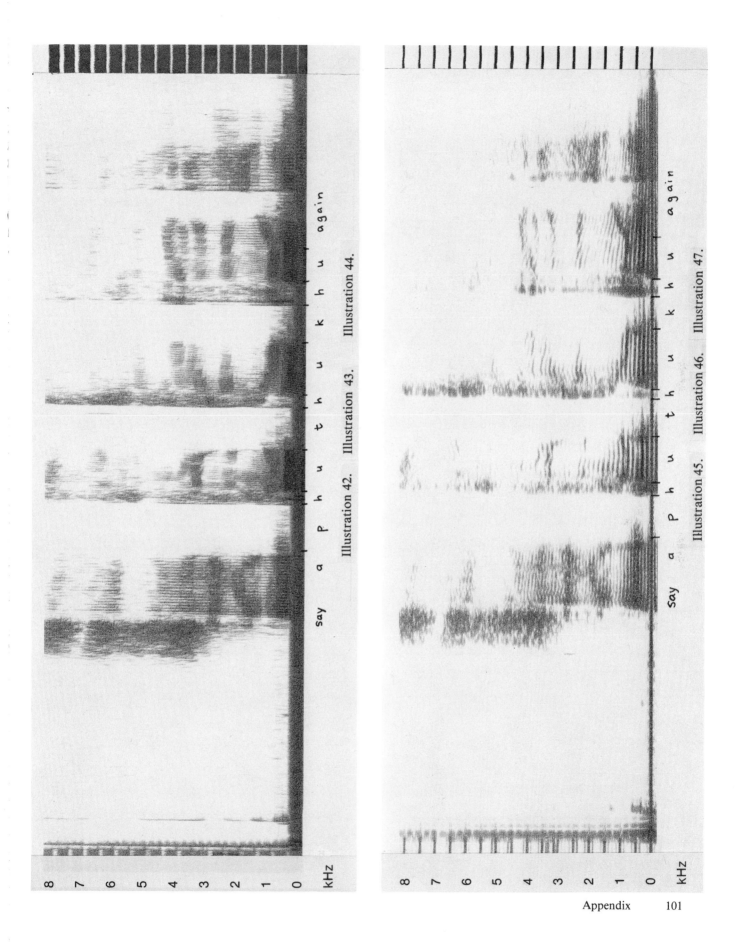

Say a P h u th u kh u again   Illustration 42.   Illustration 43.   Illustration 44.

Say a P h u th u kh u again   Illustration 45.   Illustration 46.   Illustration 47.

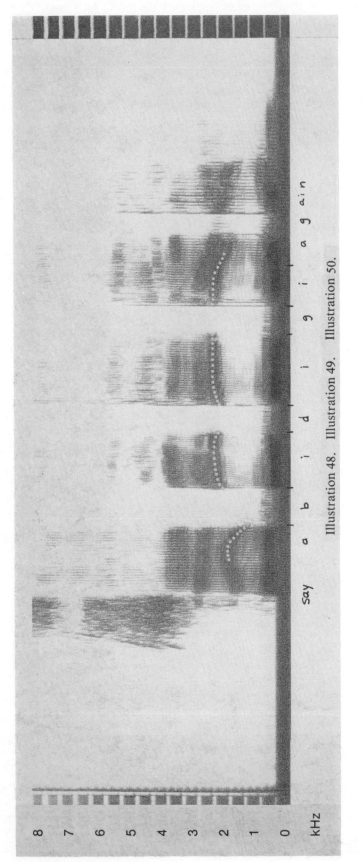

Illustration 48.   Illustration 49.   Illustration 50.

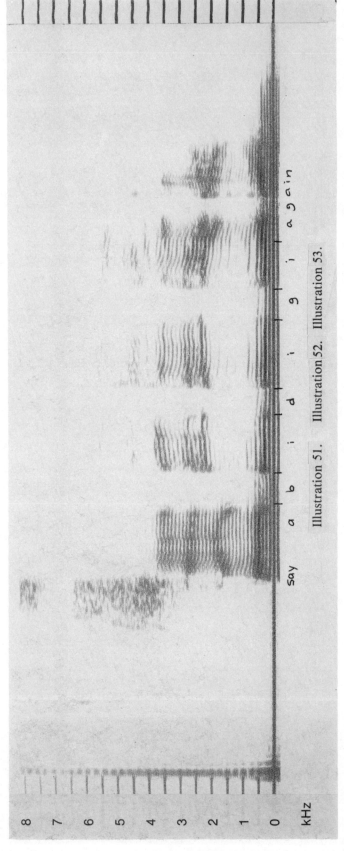

Illustration 51.   Illustration 52.   Illustration 53.

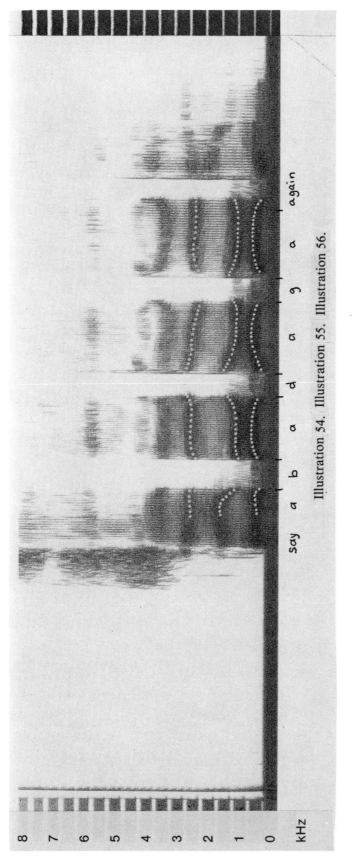

say a b a d a g a again

Illustration 54. Illustration 55. Illustration 56.

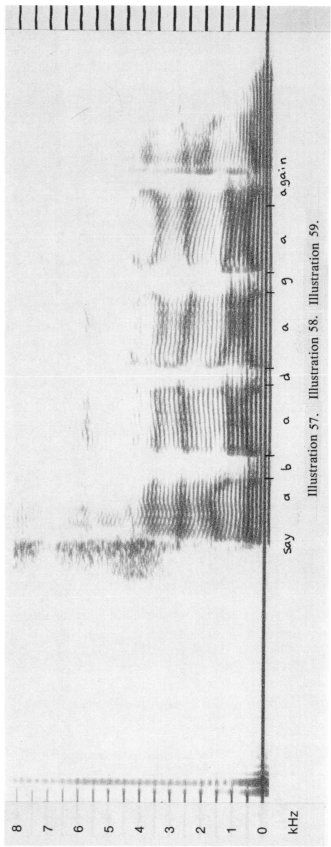

say a b a d a g a again

Illustration 57. Illustration 58. Illustration 59.

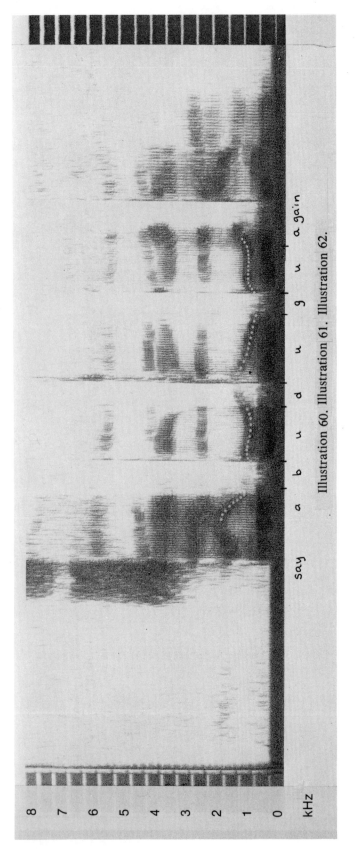

Illustration 60. Illustration 61. Illustration 62.

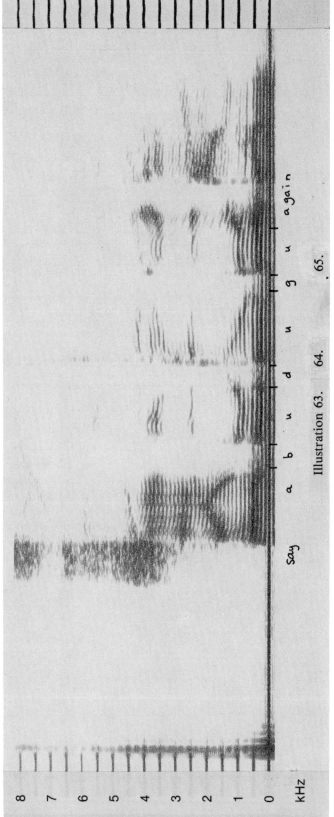

Illustration 63. Illustration 64.

65.

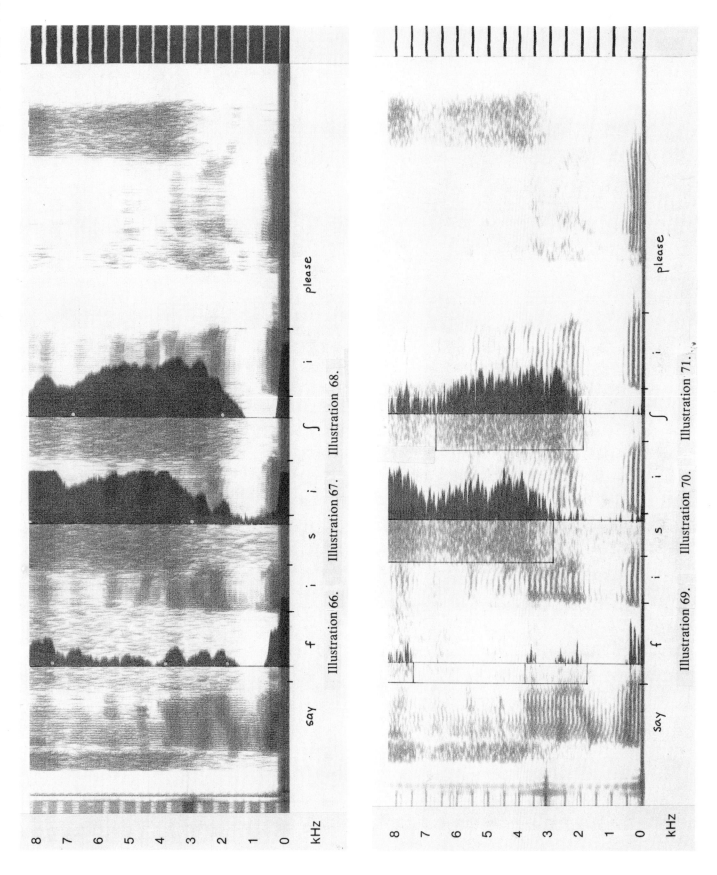

Illustration 66.   Illustration 67.   Illustration 68.

Illustration 69.   Illustration 70.   Illustration 71.

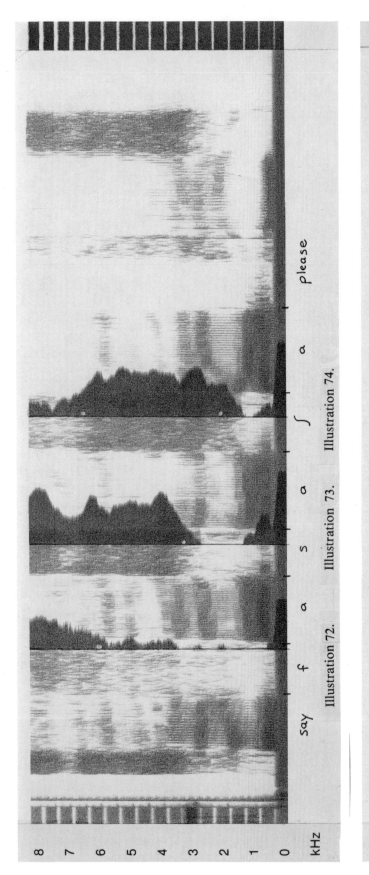

Illustration 72.   Illustration 73.   Illustration 74.

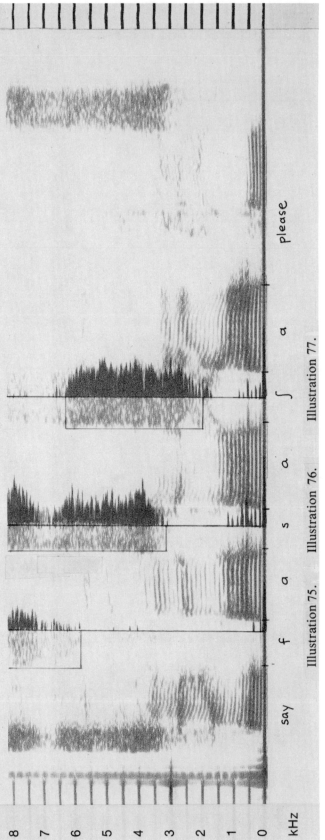

Illustration 75.   Illustration 76.   Illustration 77.

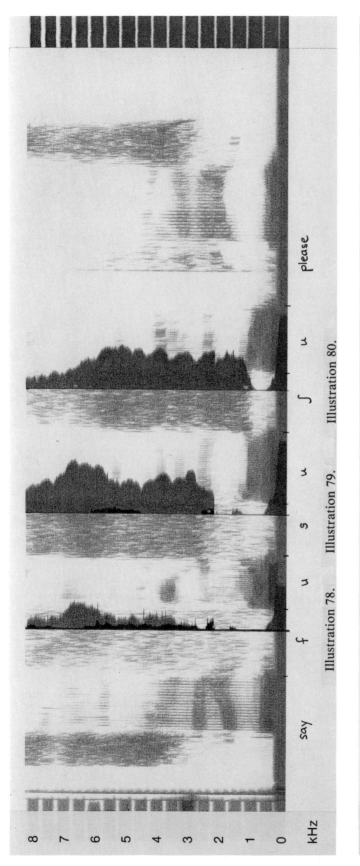

Illustration 78. Illustration 79. Illustration 80.

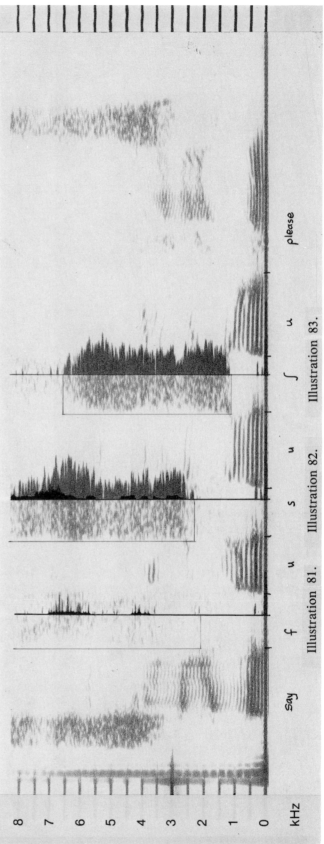

Illustration 81. Illustration 82. Illustration 83.

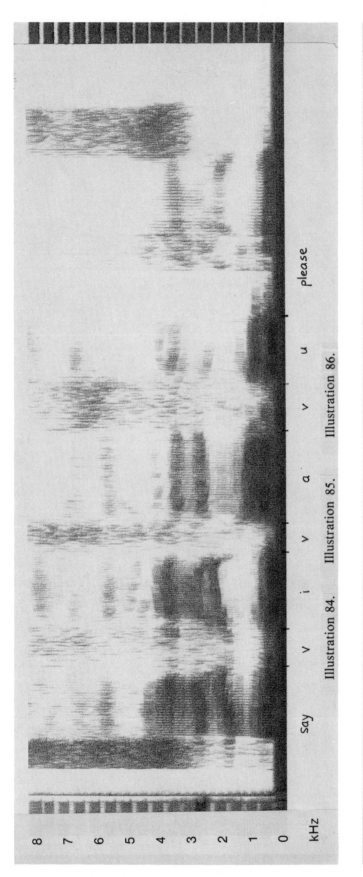

Say v i v a v u please

Illustration 84.   Illustration 85.   Illustration 86.

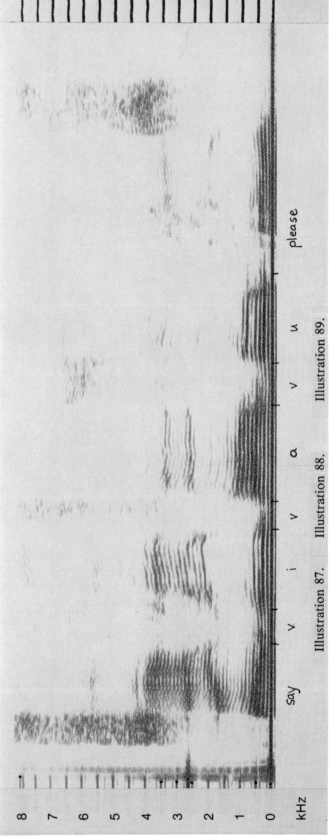

Say v i v a v u please

Illustration 87.   Illustration 88.   Illustration 89.

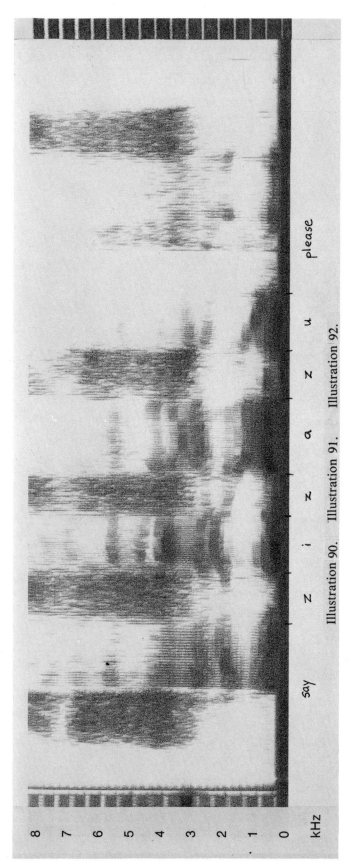

Illustration 90.   Illustration 91.   Illustration 92.

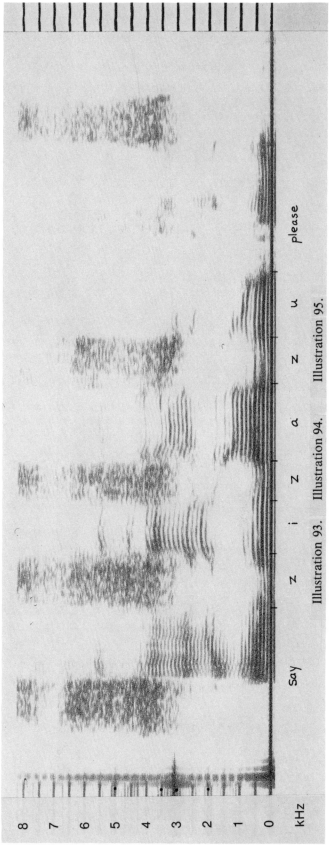

Illustration 93.   Illustration 94.   Illustration 95.

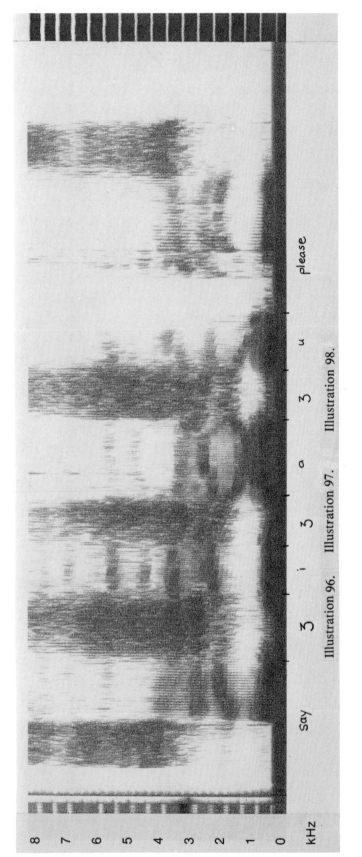

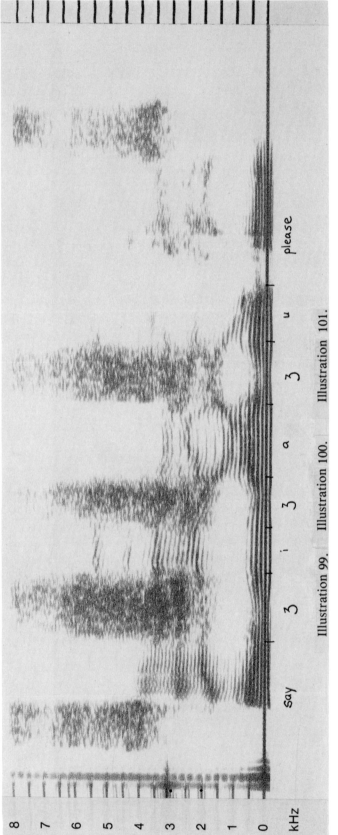

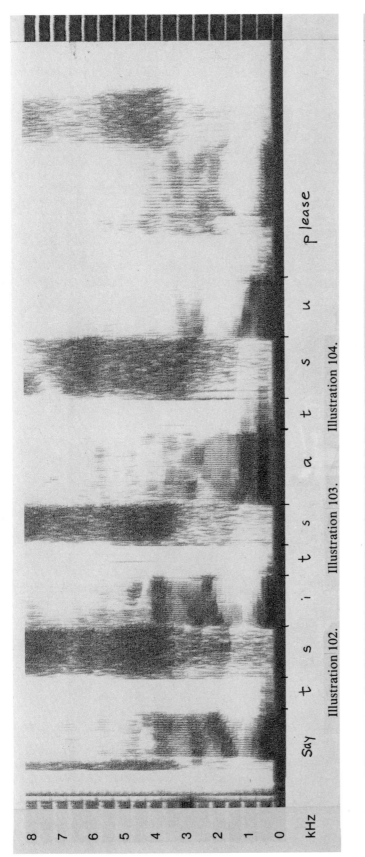

Say   t s i t s a t s u please

Illustration 102.   Illustration 103.   Illustration 104.

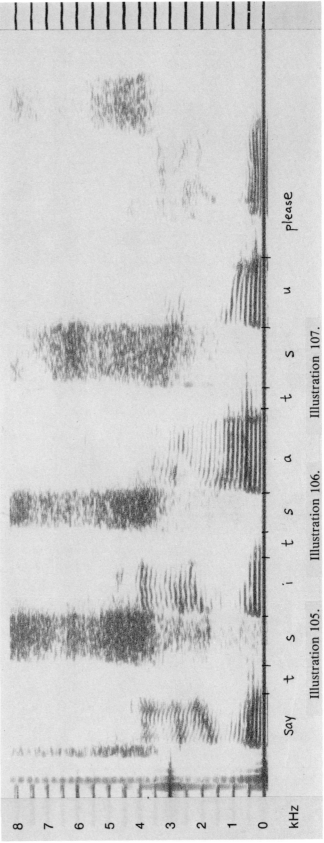

Say   t s i t s a t s u please

Illustration 105.   Illustration 106.   Illustration 107.

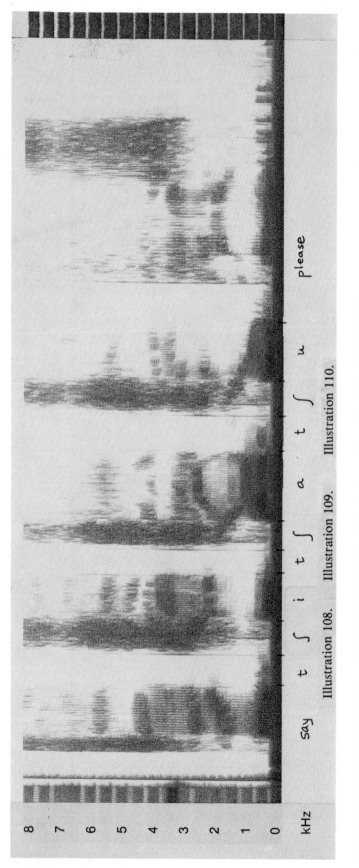

Illustration 108.   Illustration 109.   Illustration 110.

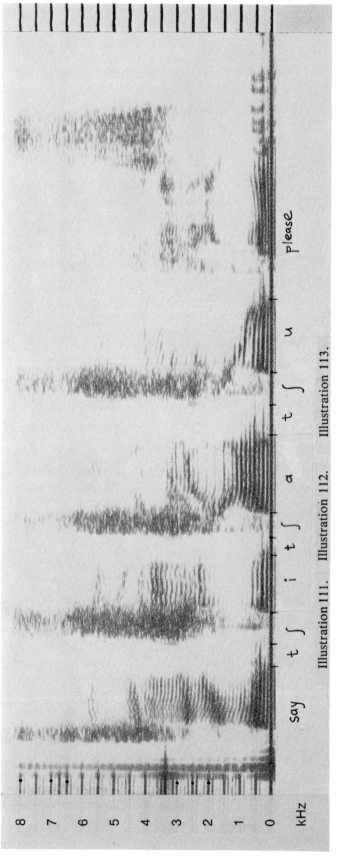

Illustration 111.   Illustration 112.   Illustration 113.

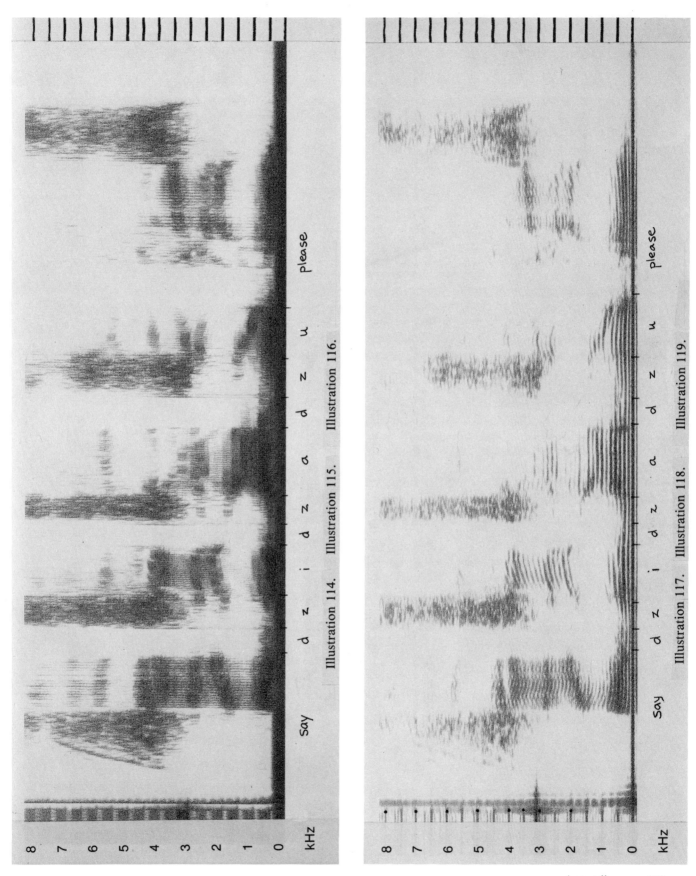

Illustration 114. Illustration 115. Illustration 116.

Illustration 117. Illustration 118. Illustration 119.

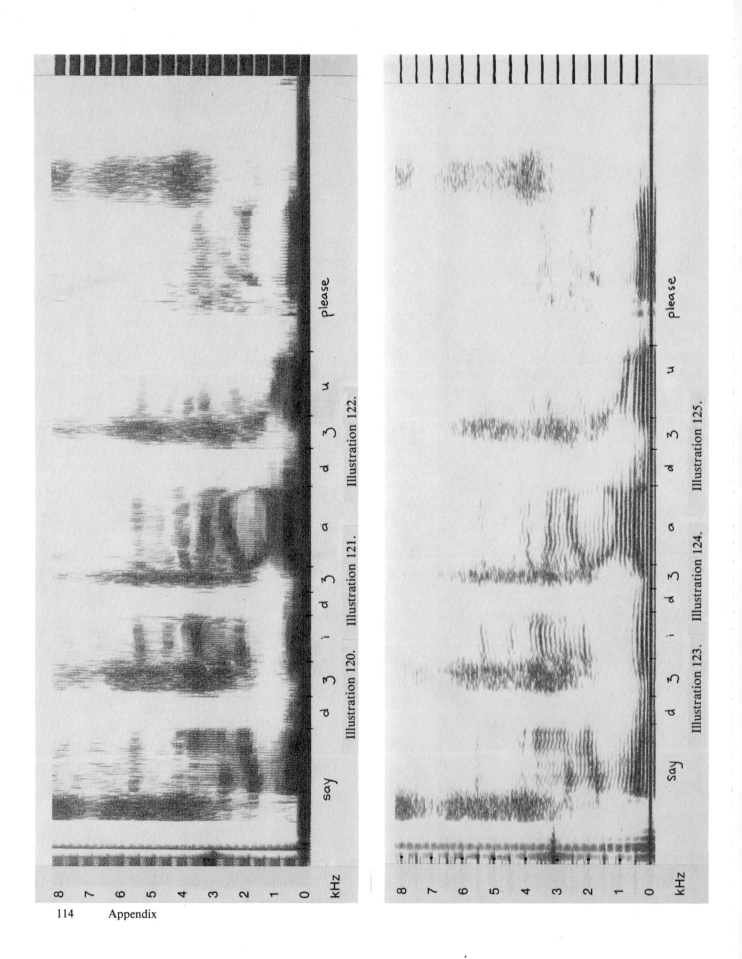

say   d ʒ   d ʒ   i   d ʒ   ʒ   a   d   ʒ   u   please

Illustration 120.   Illustration 121.   Illustration 122.

Say   d ʒ   i   d ʒ   ʒ   a   d   ʒ   u   please

Illustration 123.   Illustration 124.   Illustration 125.

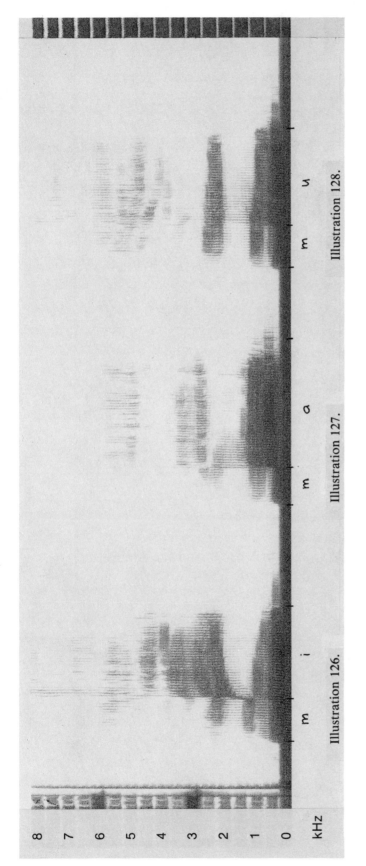

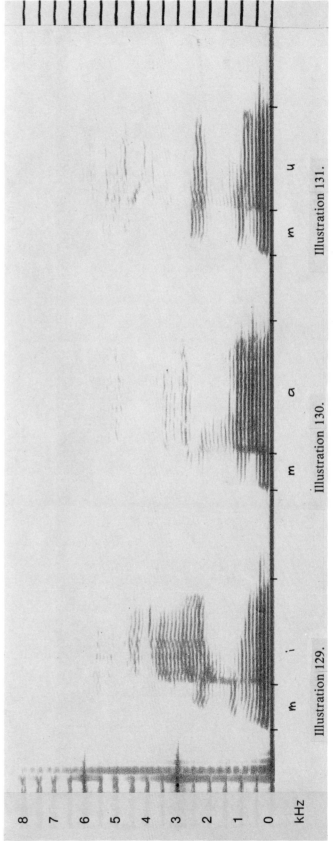

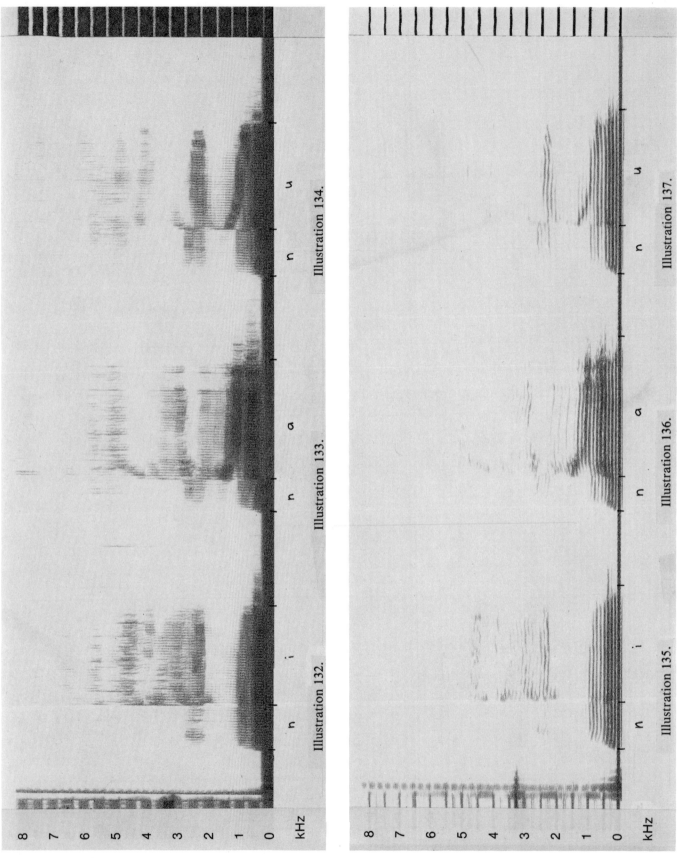

Illustration 132.

Illustration 133.

Illustration 134.

Illustration 135.

Illustration 136.

Illustration 137.

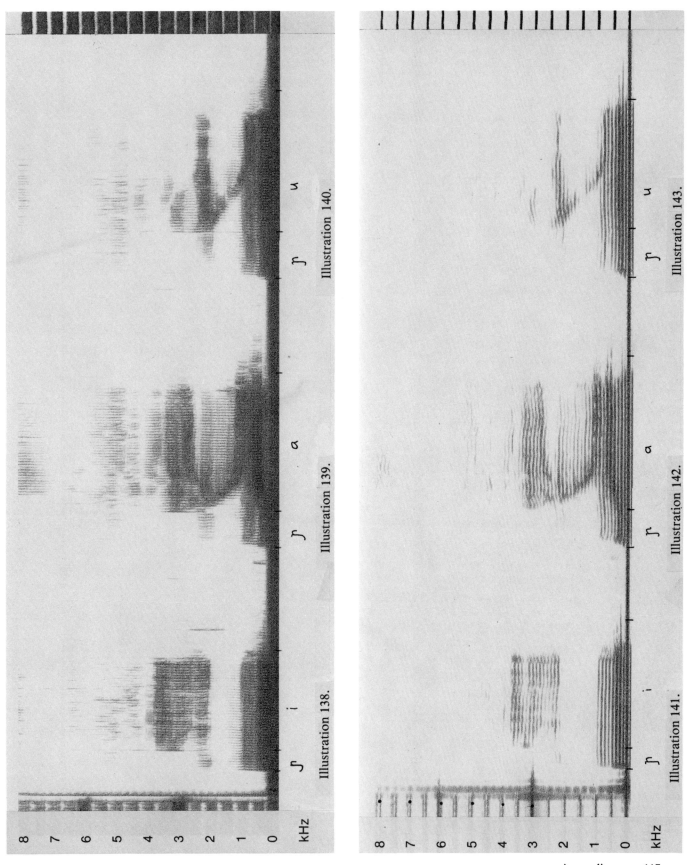

Illustration 138.

Illustration 139.

Illustration 140.

Illustration 141.

Illustration 142.

Illustration 143.

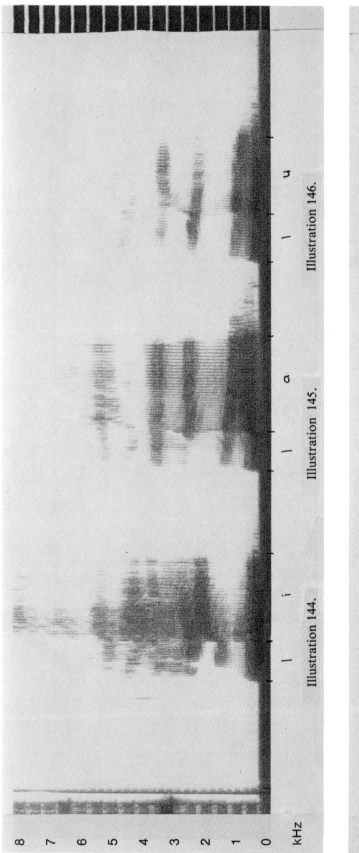

Illustration 146.

Illustration 145.

Illustration 144.

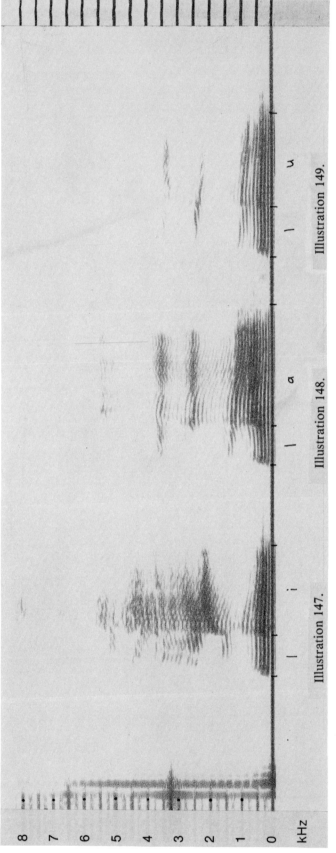

Illustration 149.

Illustration 148.

Illustration 147.

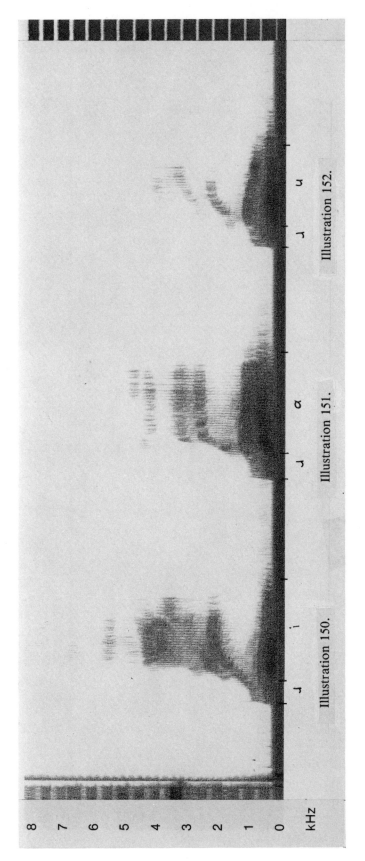

Illustration 152.

Illustration 151.

Illustration 150.

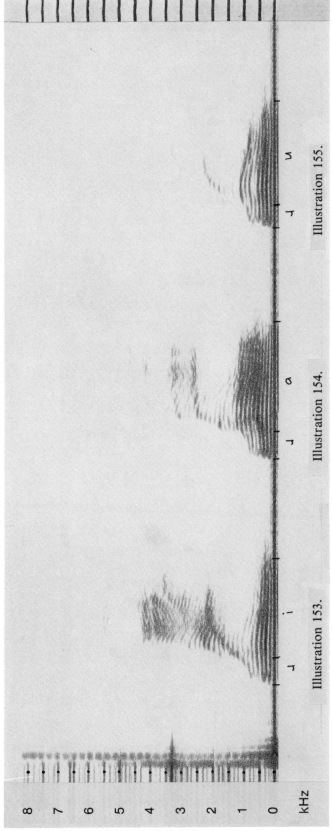

Illustration 155.

Illustration 154.

Illustration 153.

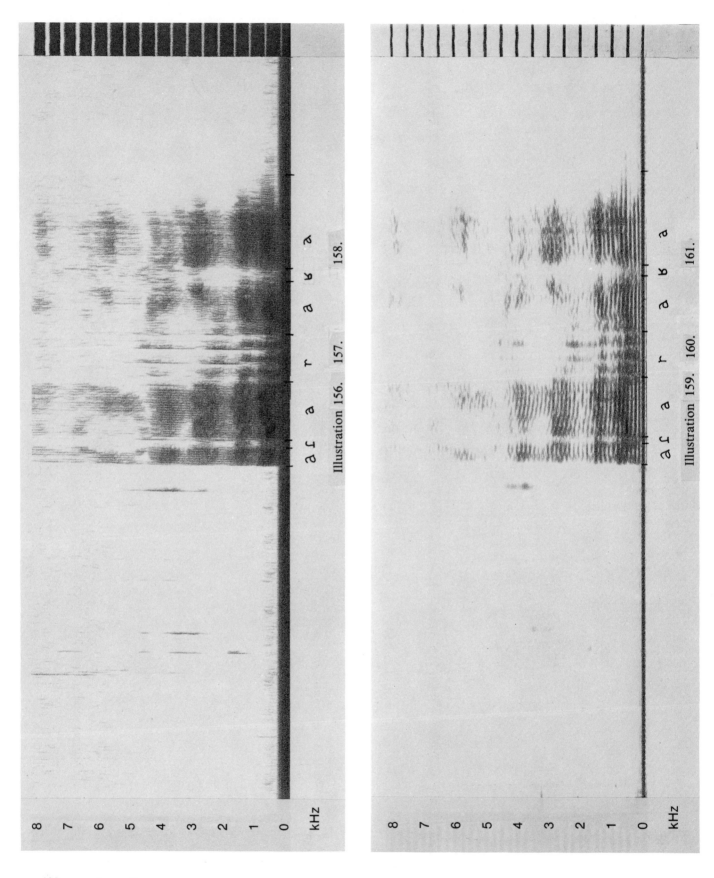

a a r a ʀ a

Illustration 156. 157. 158.

a a r a ʀ a

Illustration 159. 160. 161.

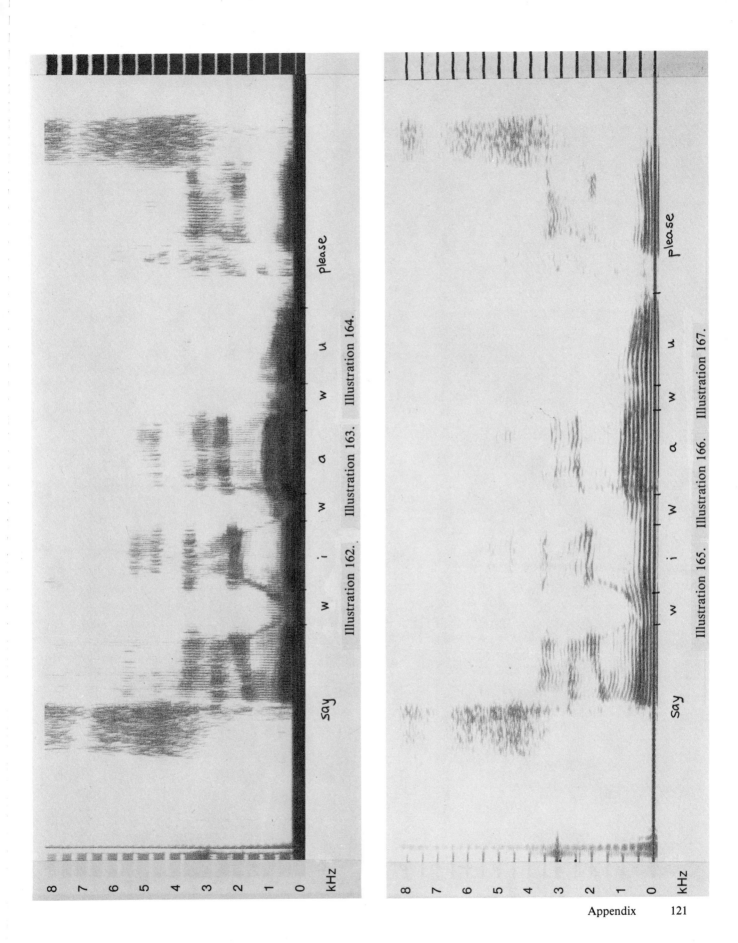

say w i w a w u please

Illustration 162. Illustration 163. Illustration 164.

say w i w a w u please

Illustration 165. Illustration 166. Illustration 167.

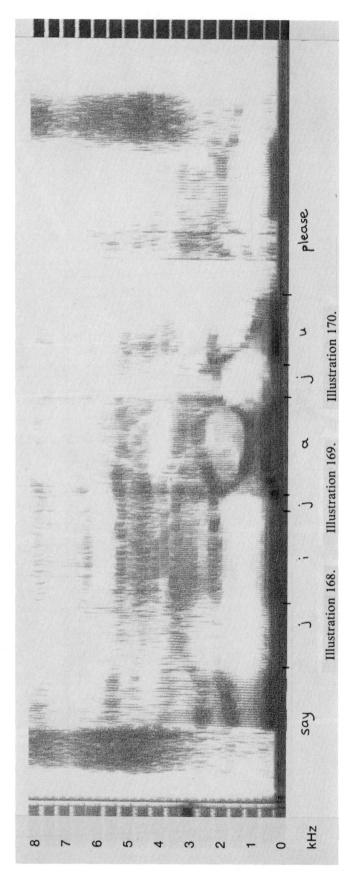

Illustration 168. Illustration 169. Illustration 170.

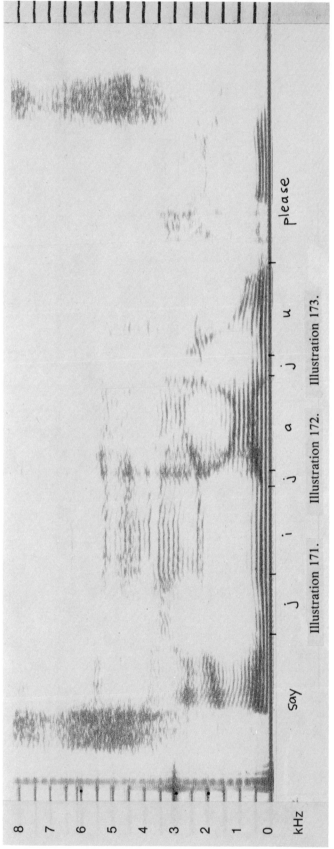

Illustration 171. Illustration 172. Illustration 173.

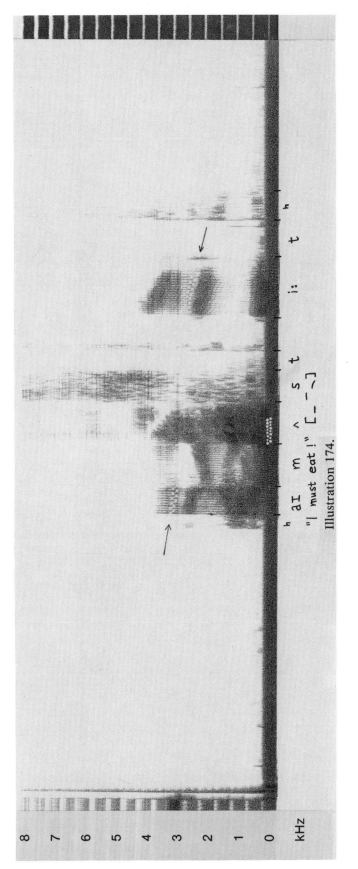

ʰ aɪ m ʌ s t   iː t   ʰ
"I must eat!" [_ - ˅]

Illustration 174.

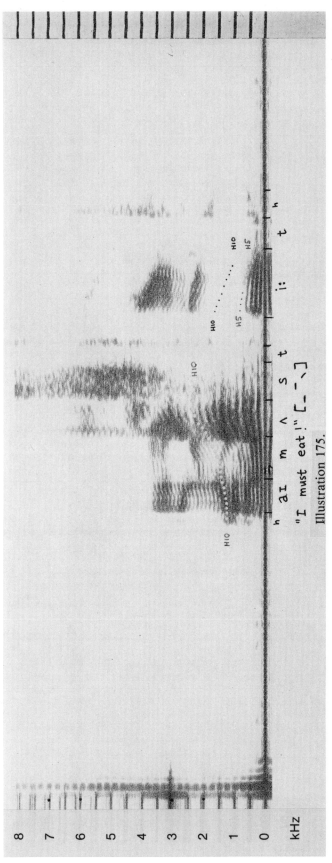

ʰ aɪ m ʌ s t   iː t   ʰ
"I must eat!" [_ - ˅]

Illustration 175.

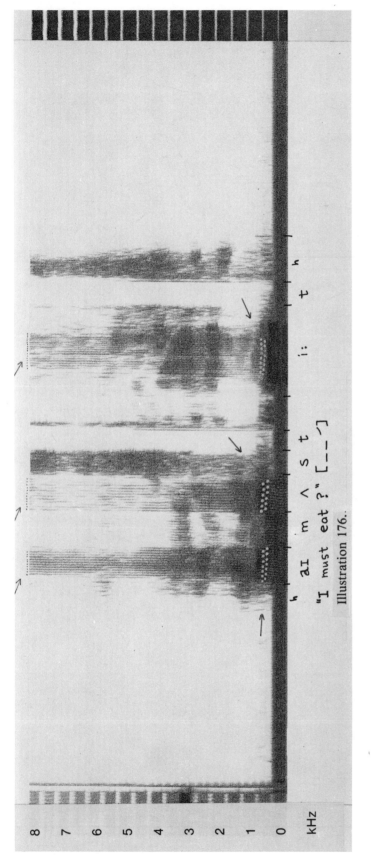

"I must eat?" [___↗]

Illustration 176.

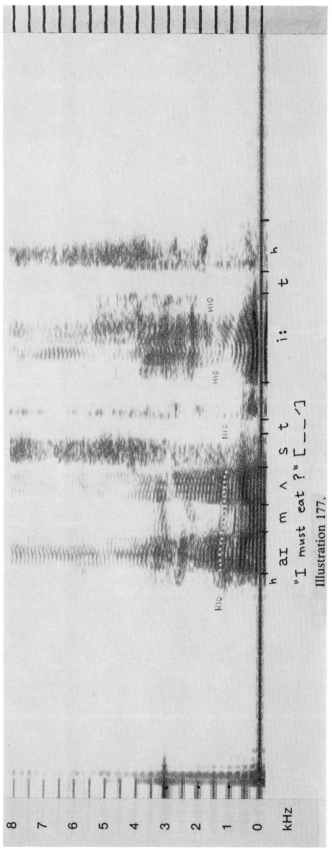

"I must eat?" [___↗]

Illustration 177.

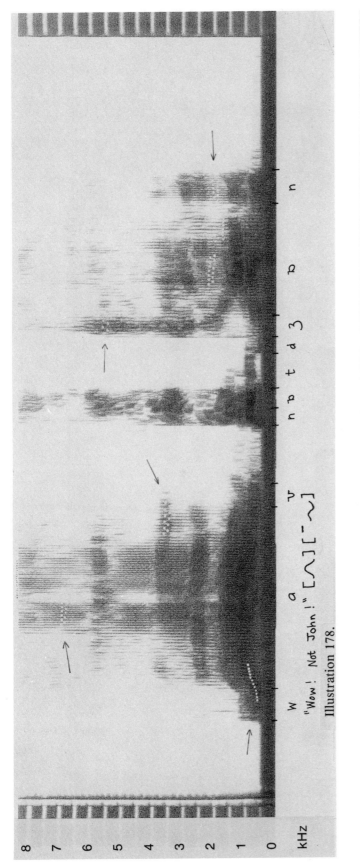

"Wow! Not John!" [ʌʌˈ] [ˈ~]

Illustration 178.

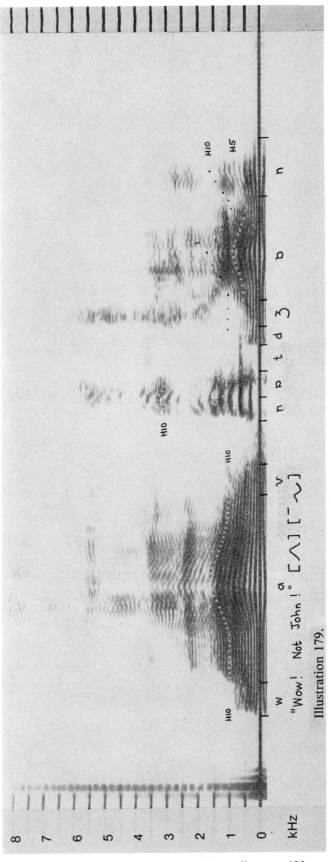

"Wow! Not John!" [ʌʌˈ] [ˈ~]

Illustration 179.

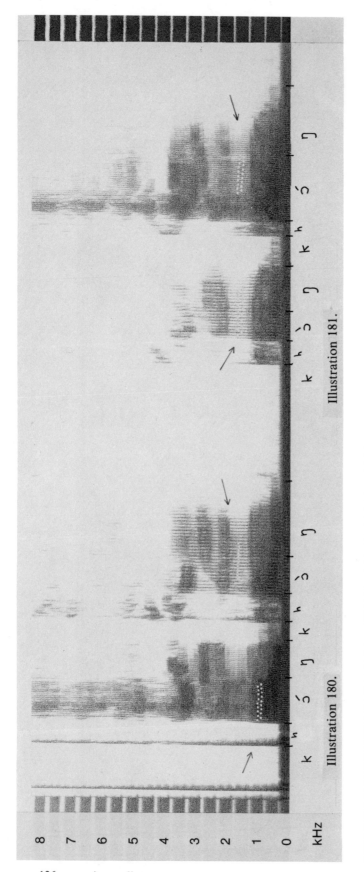

Illustration 180.

Illustration 181.

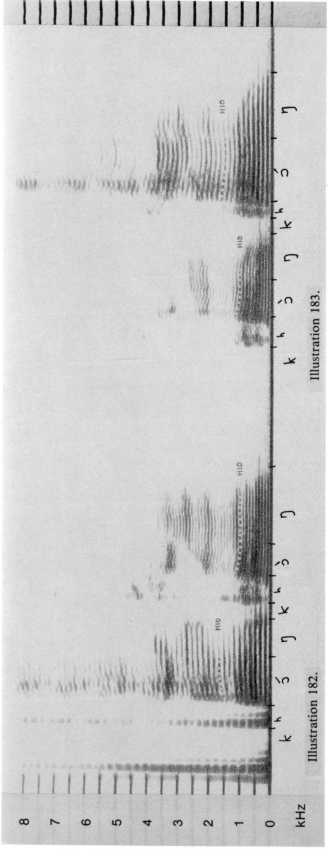

Illustration 182.

Illustration 183.

Illustration 185.

Illustration 184.

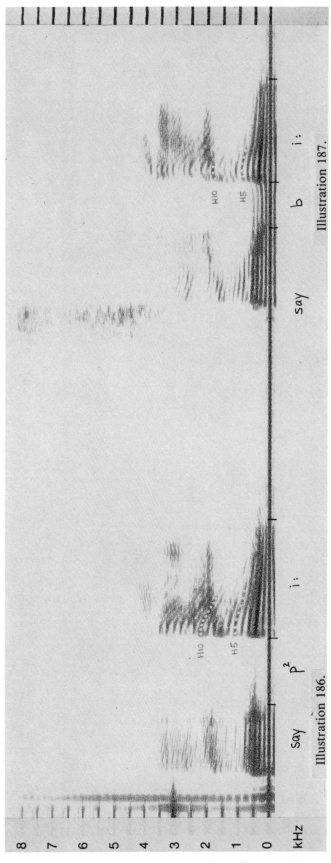

Illustration 187.

Illustration 186.

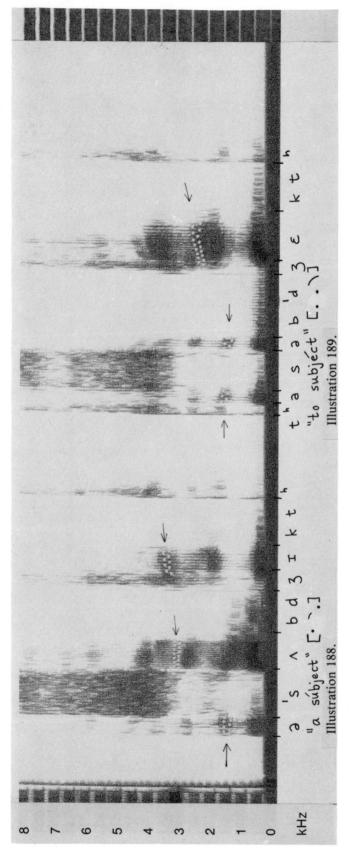

ə ˈsʌ bdʒ ɪ kt ʰ
"a súbject" [˙ ˇ ˙]
Illustration 188.

tʰ ə s ə bˈdʒ ɛ k tʰ
"to subjéct" [˙ ˙ ˇ]
Illustration 189.

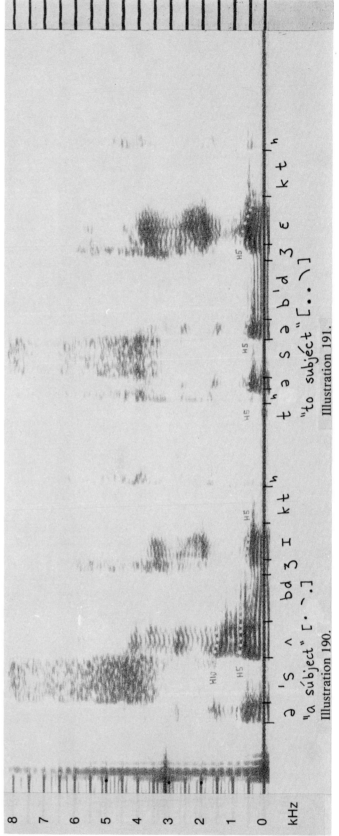

ə ˈsʌ bdʒ ɪ kt ʰ
"a súbject" [˙ ˇ ˙]
Illustration 190.

tʰ ə s ə bˈdʒ ɛ k tʰ
"to subjéct" [˙ ˙ ˇ]
Illustration 191.

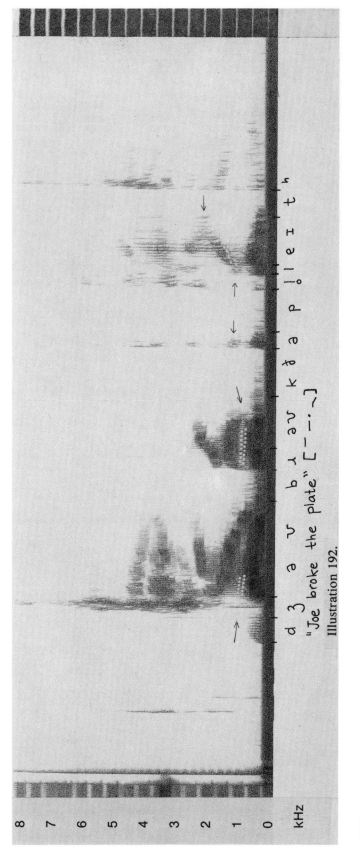

d ʒ a ʊ b ɹ a ʊ k t ə p l̥ e ɪ t h

"Joe broke the plate" [⏤⏑⏑⌣]

Illustration 192.

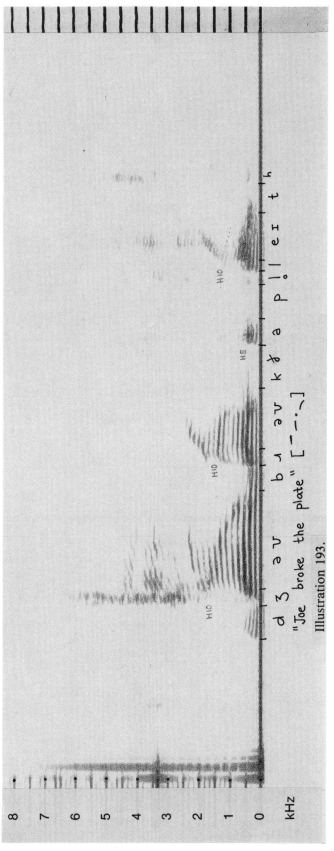

d ʒ a ʊ b ɹ a ʊ k t ə p l̥ e ɪ t h

"Joe broke the plate" [⏤⏑⌣]

Illustration 193.

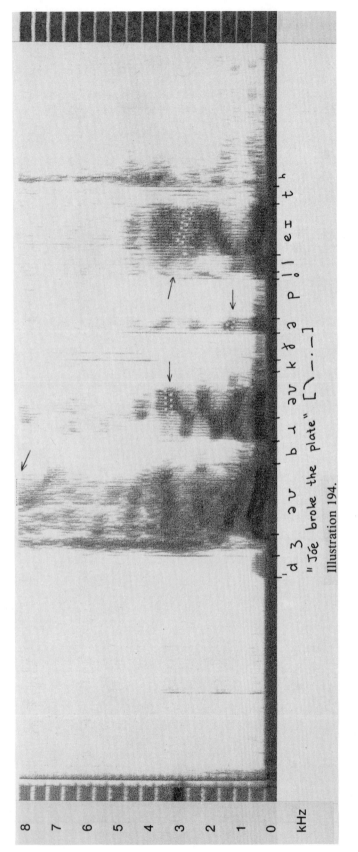

'dʒ ɑʊ brəʊ kɾə pl̥ eɪ tʰ
"Joe broke the plate" [\‿__]

Illustration 194.

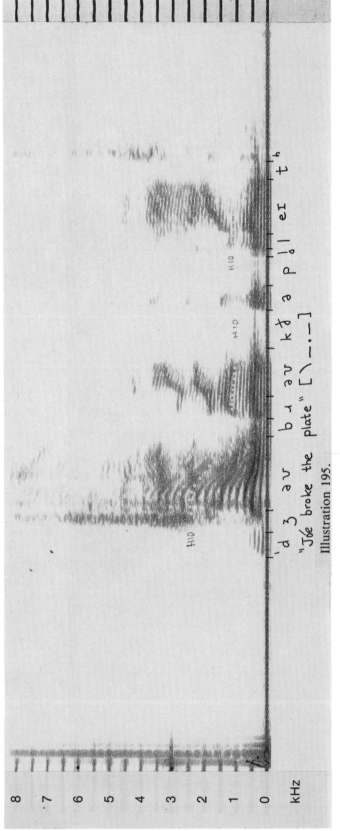

'dʒ ɑʊ brəʊ kɾə pl̥ eɪ tʰ
"Joe broke the plate" [\‿__]

Illustration 195.

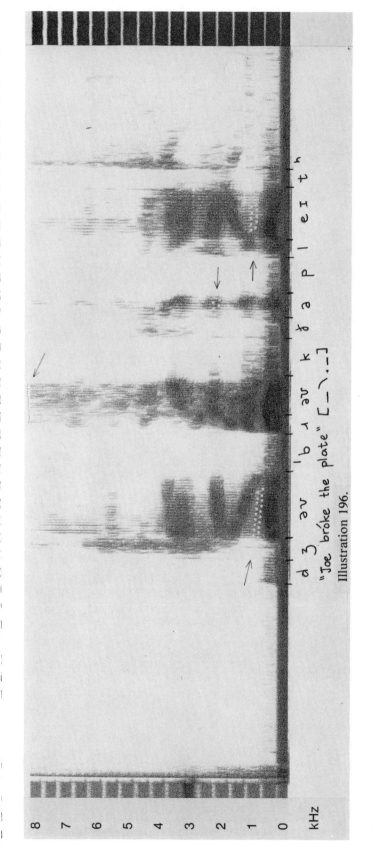

dʒ əʊ ˈbɹəʊk ðə pleɪtʰ
"Joe bróke the plate" [_ ˎ . _]
Illustration 196.

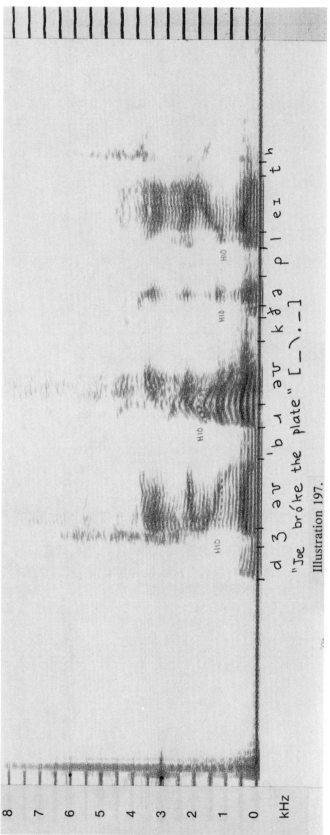

dʒ əʊ ˈbɹəʊk ðə pleɪtʰ
"Joe bróke the plate" [_ ˎ . _]
Illustration 197.

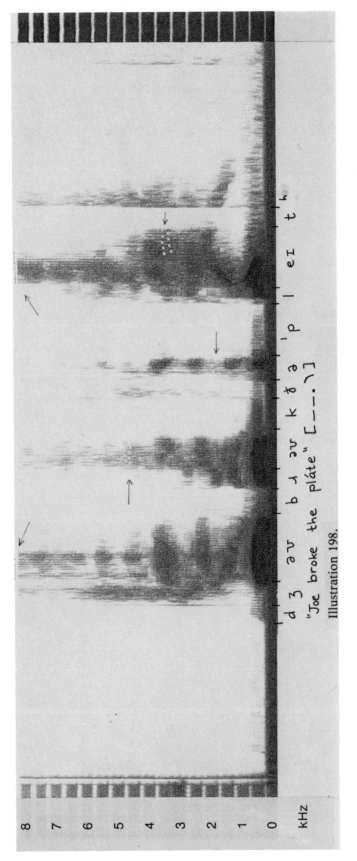

d ʒ oʊ b ɹ oʊ k ð ə 'p l eɪ t ʰ

"Joe broke the pláte" [⌐⌐·⌐]

Illustration 198.

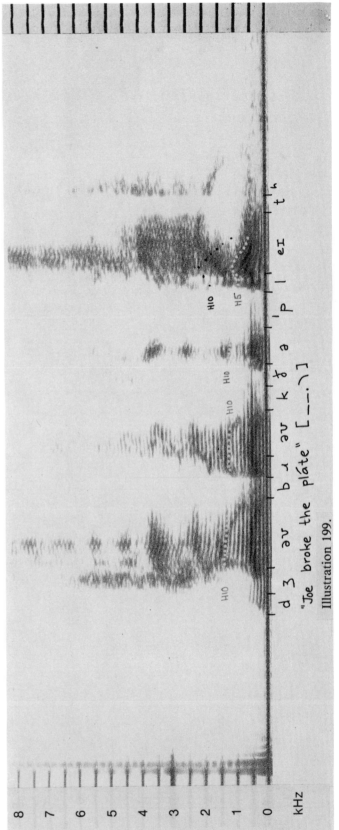

d ʒ oʊ b ɹ oʊ k ð ə 'p l eɪ t ʰ

"Joe broke the pláte" [⌐⌐·⌐]

Illustration 199.

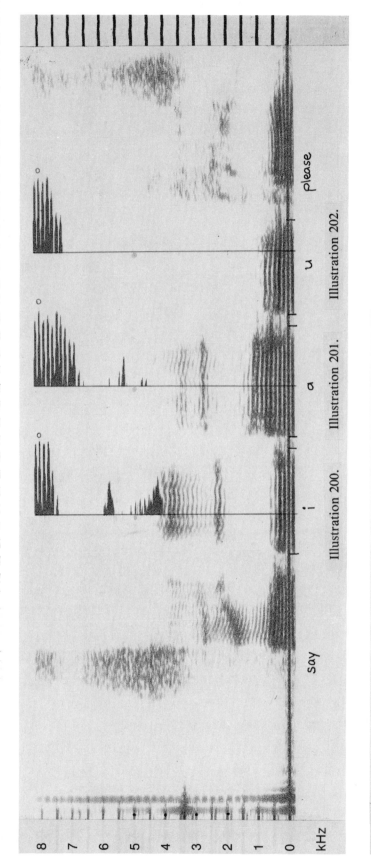

Illustration 200.

Illustration 201.

Illustration 202.

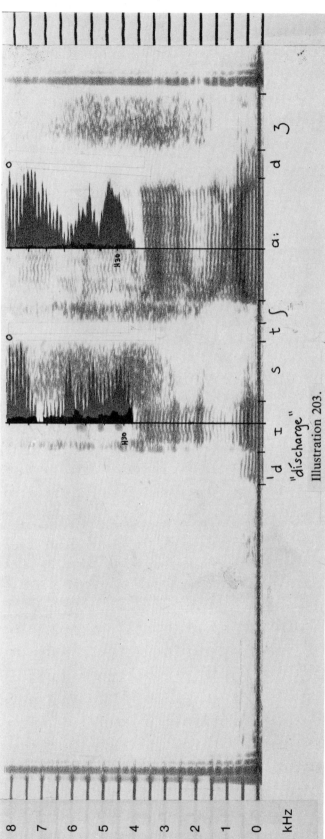

"discharge"

Illustration 203.

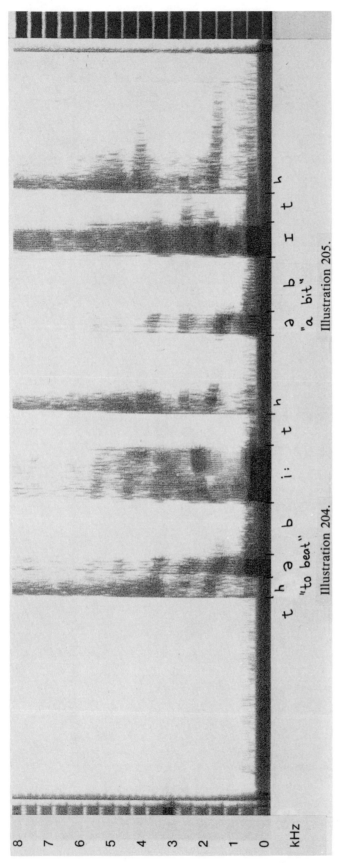

t h ə b iː t h
"to beat"
Illustration 204.

t h ə b ɪ t h
"a bit"
Illustration 205.

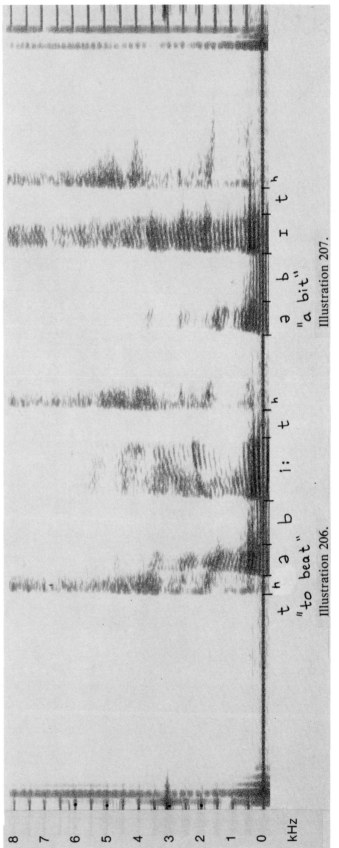

t h ə b iː t h
"to beat"
Illustration 206.

t h ə b ɪ t h
"a bit"
Illustration 207.

kHz

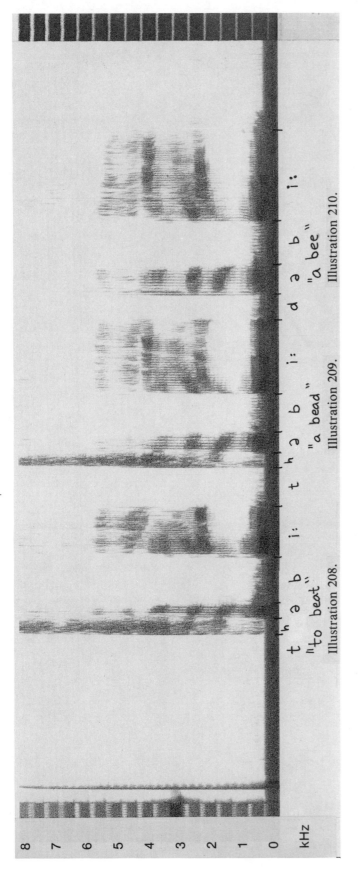

t^h ə b i: t^h ə b i: d ə b i:
"to beat"   "a bead"   "a bee"
Illustration 208.   Illustration 209. Illustration 210.

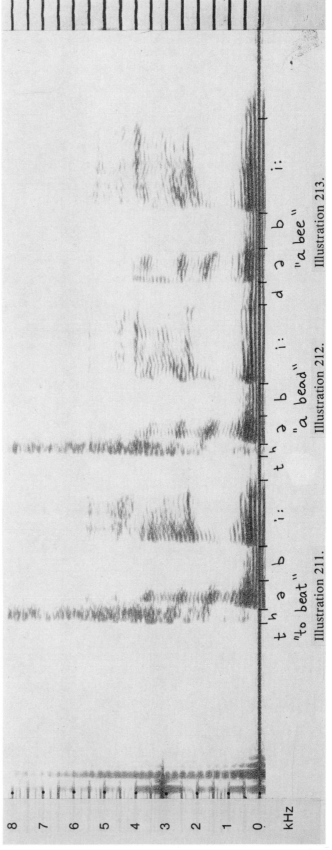

t^h ə b i: t^h ə b i: d ə b i:
"to beat"   "a bead"   "a bee"
Illustration 211.   Illustration 212. Illustration 213.

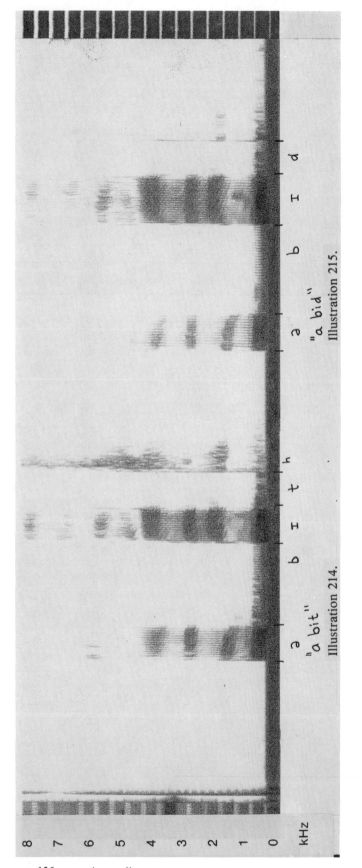

"a bit"
Illustration 214.

"a bid"
Illustration 215.

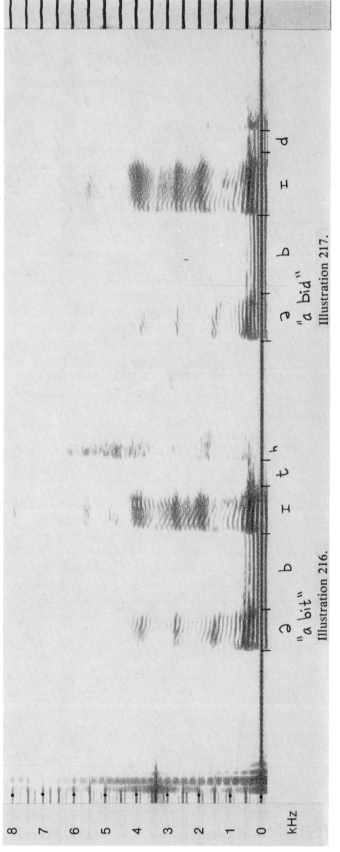

"a bit"
Illustration 216.

"a bid"
Illustration 217.

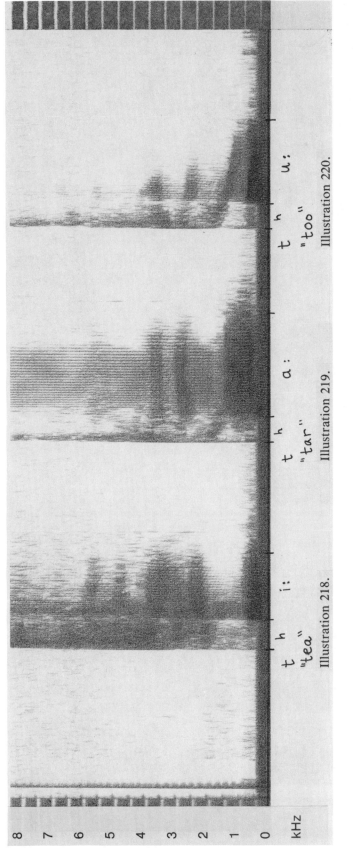

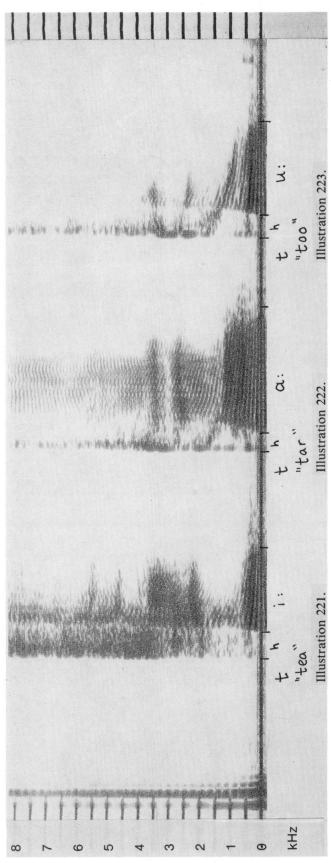

t ʰ i:
"tea"
Illustration 218.

t ʰ ɑ:
"tar"
Illustration 219.

t ʰ u:
"too"
Illustration 220.

t ʰ i:
"tea"
Illustration 221.

t ʰ ɑ:
"tar"
Illustration 222.

t ʰ u:
"too"
Illustration 223.

8
7
6
5
4
3
2
1
0
kHz

8
7
6
5
4
3
2
0
kHz

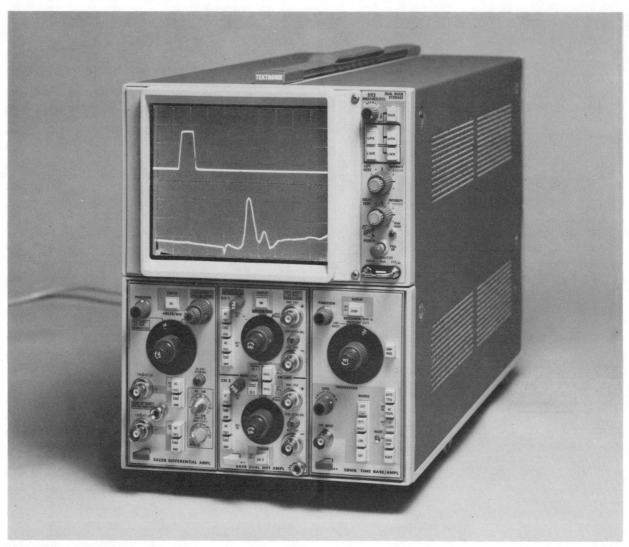

Illustration 224. A dual beam oscilloscope. (Courtesy of Tektronix Inc., Beaverton, Oregon.)

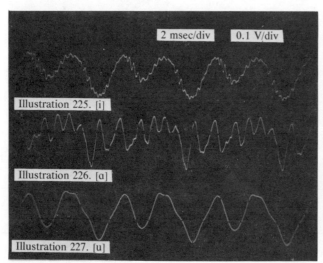

2 msec/div   0.1 V/div

Illustration 225. [i]

Illustration 226. [ɑ]

Illustration 227. [u]

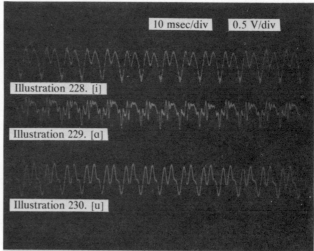

10 msec/div   0.5 V/div

Illustration 228. [i]

Illustration 229. [ɑ]

Illustration 230. [u]

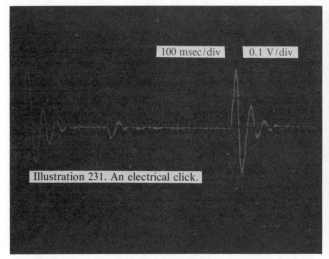

100 msec/div   0.1 V/div

Illustration 231. An electrical click.

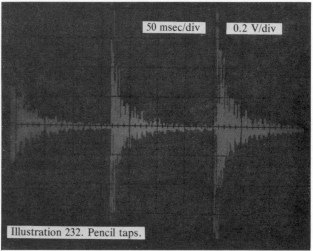

50 msec/div   0.2 V/div

Illustration 232. Pencil taps.

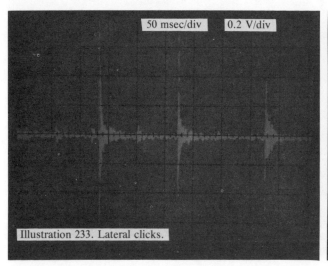

50 msec/div   0.2 V/div

Illustration 233. Lateral clicks.

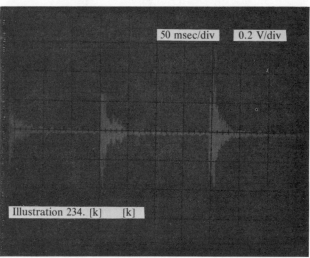

50 msec/div   0.2 V/div

Illustration 234. [k]   [k]

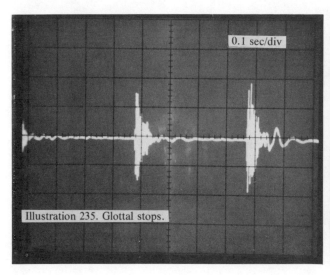

0.1 sec/div

Illustration 235. Glottal stops.

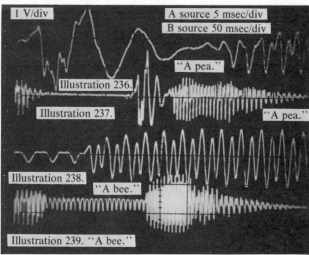

1 V/div   A source 5 msec/div
B source 50 msec/div

"A pea."

Illustration 236.

Illustration 237.

"A pea."

Illustration 238.

"A bee."

Illustration 239. "A bee."

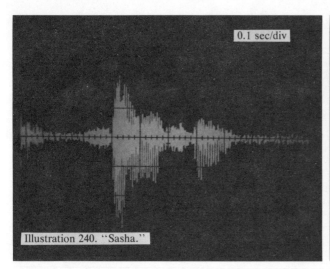

Illustration 240. "Sasha."

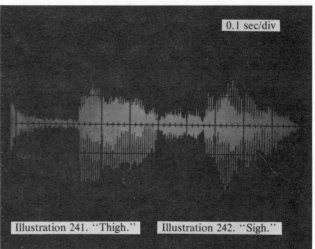

Illustration 241. "Thigh."   Illustration 242. "Sigh."

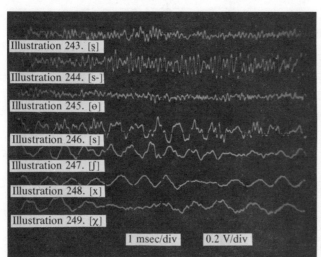

Illustration 243. [ʂ]

Illustration 244. [s-]

Illustration 245. [θ]

Illustration 246. [s]

Illustration 247. [ʃ]

Illustration 248. [x]

Illustration 249. [χ]

1 msec/div   0.2 V/div

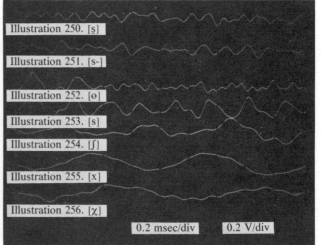

Illustration 250. [ʂ]

Illustration 251. [s-]

Illustration 252. [θ]

Illustration 253. [s]

Illustration 254. [ʃ]

Illustration 255. [x]

Illustration 256. [χ]

0.2 msec/div   0.2 V/div

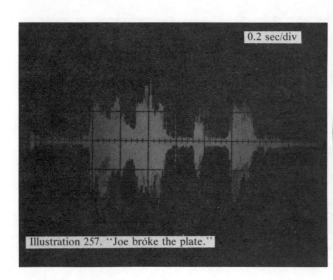

0.2 sec/div

Illustration 257. "Joe bróke the plate."

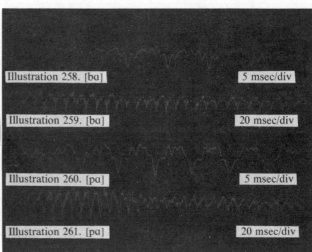

Illustration 258. [bɑ]   5 msec/div

Illustration 259. [bɑ]   20 msec/div

Illustration 260. [pɑ]   5 msec/div

Illustration 261. [pɑ]   20 msec/div

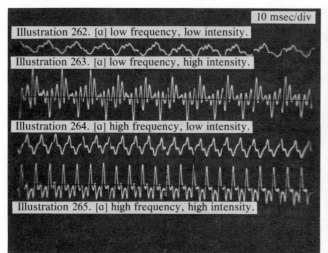

Illustration 262. [ɑ] low frequency, low intensity.

Illustration 263. [ɑ] low frequency, high intensity.

Illustration 264. [ɑ] high frequency, low intensity.

Illustration 265. [ɑ] high frequency, high intensity.

10 msec/div

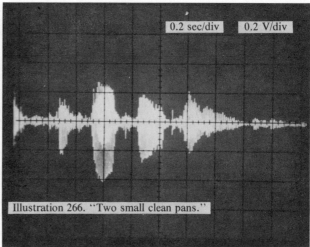

0.2 sec/div   0.2 V/div

Illustration 266. "Two small clean pans."

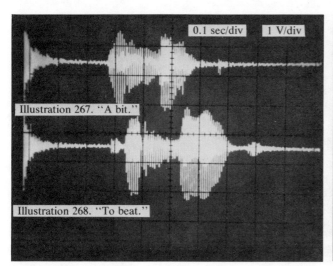

0.1 sec/div   1 V/div

Illustration 267. "A bit."

Illustration 268. "To beat."

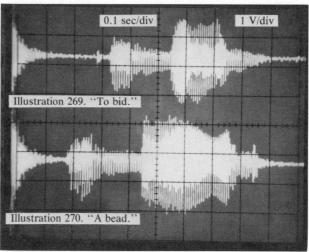

0.1 sec/div   1 V/div

Illustration 269. "To bid."

Illustration 270. "A bead."

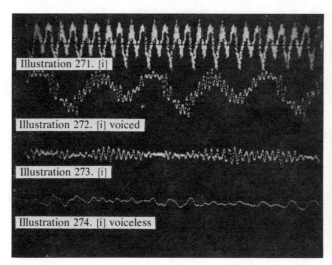

Illustration 271. [i]

Illustration 272. [i] voiced

Illustration 273. [i]

Illustration 274. [i] voiceless

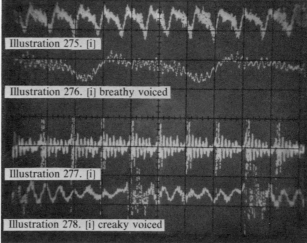

Illustration 275. [i]

Illustration 276. [i] breathy voiced

Illustration 277. [i]

Illustration 278. [i] creaky voiced

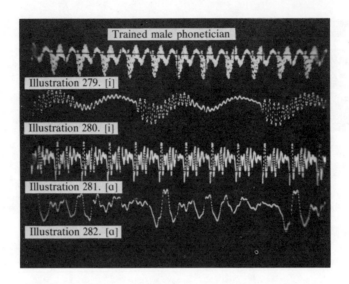

Trained male phonetician

Illustration 279. [i]

Illustration 280. [i]

Illustration 281. [ɑ]

Illustration 282. [ɑ]

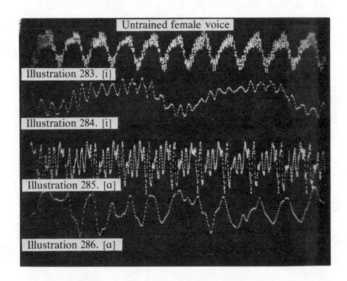

Untrained female voice

Illustration 283. [i]

Illustration 284. [i]

Illustration 285. [ɑ]

Illustration 286. [ɑ]

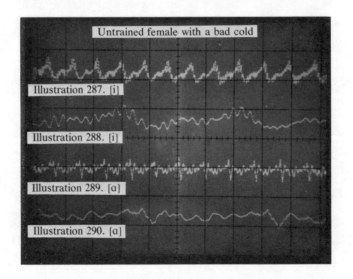

Untrained female with a bad cold

Illustration 287. [i]

Illustration 288. [i]

Illustration 289. [ɑ]

Illustration 290. [ɑ]

Illustration 291. Fundamental frequency meter. F-J Electronics A/S Type FFM 650. (Courtesy of Voice Identification, Inc., Somerville, New Jersey.)

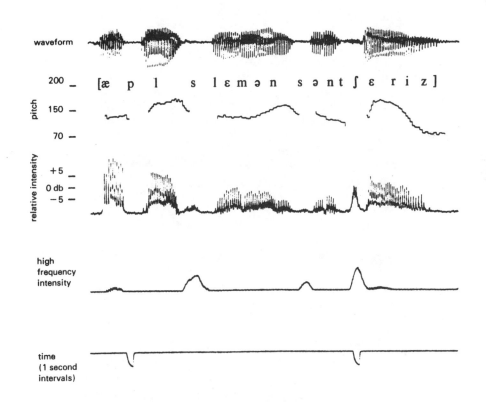

Illustration 292. Oscillomink records of the phrase "Apples, lemons, and cherries," as spoken by an American from California. The top line is the wave form; the second line the fundamental frequency (indicative of the pitch); the third line is the intensity (indicative of the loudness); the fourth line is the intensity of the higher frequencies (the fricatives); and the bottom line is a time marker. (From *A Course in Phonetics* by Peter Ladefoged © 1975 by Harcourt Brace Jovanovich, Inc. and reproduced with their permission.)

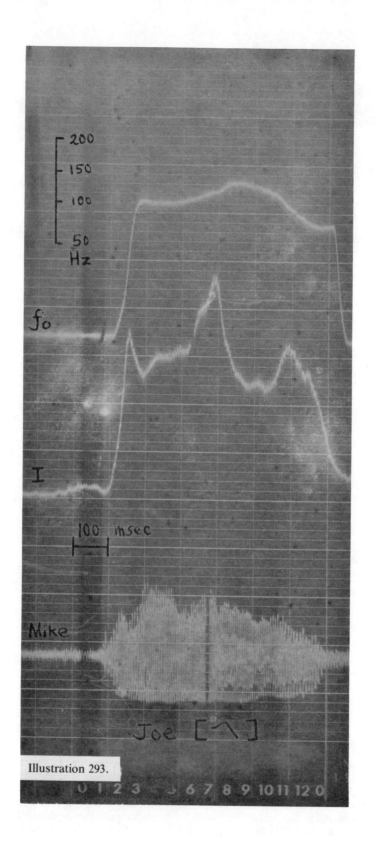

Illustration 293.

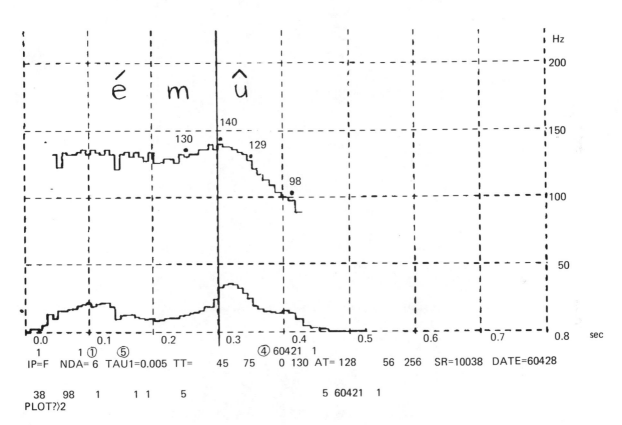

IP=F NDA= 6 TAU1=0.005 TT=   45 75   0 130 AT= 128   56 256 SR=10038 DATE=60428

    38   98   1   1 1   5   5 60421   1
PLOT?)2

Illustration 294.

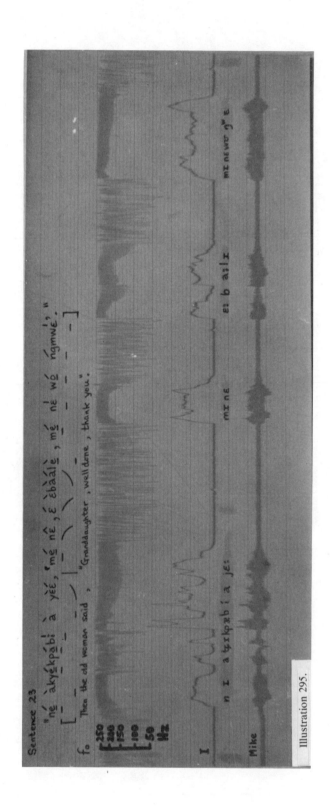

Illustration 295.

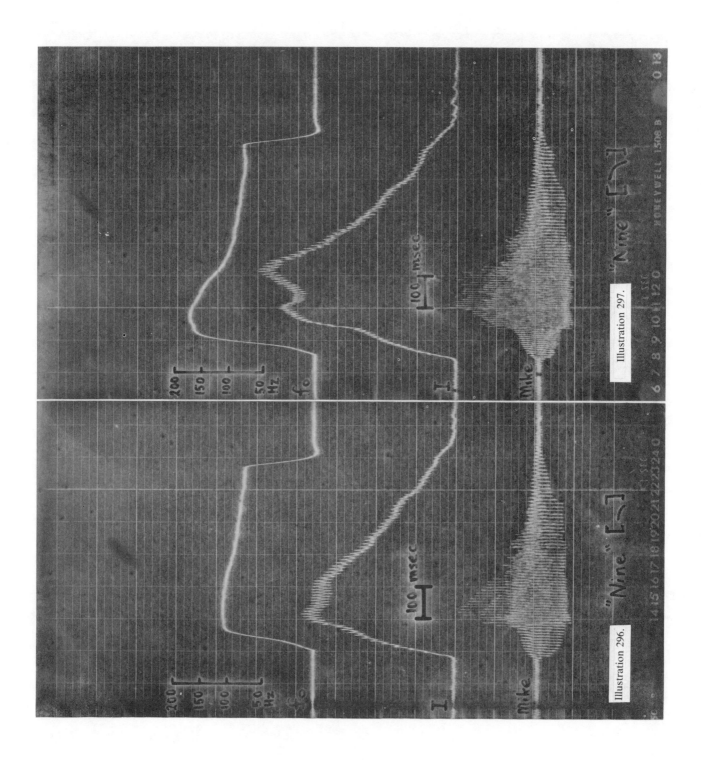

Illustration 297.

Illustration 296.

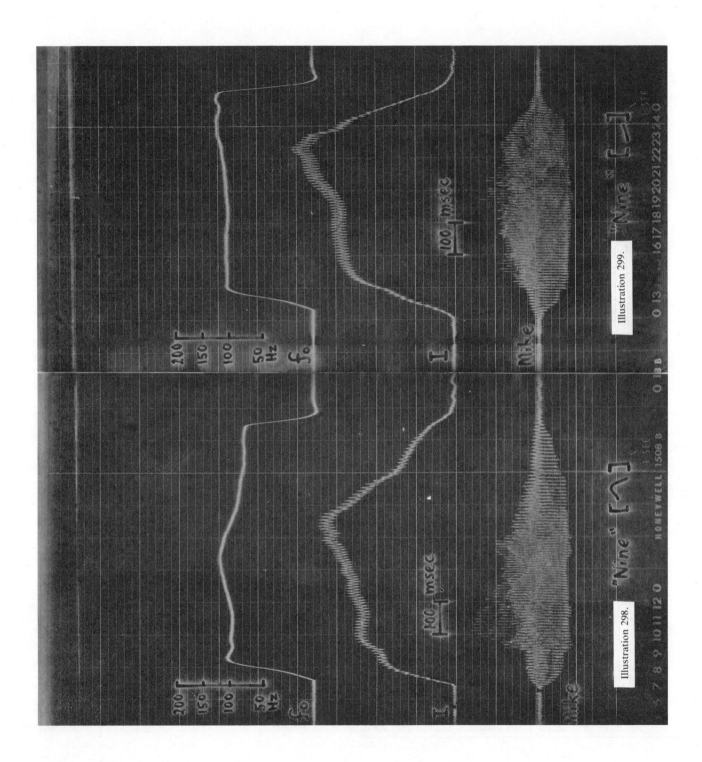

Illustration 298.

Illustration 299.

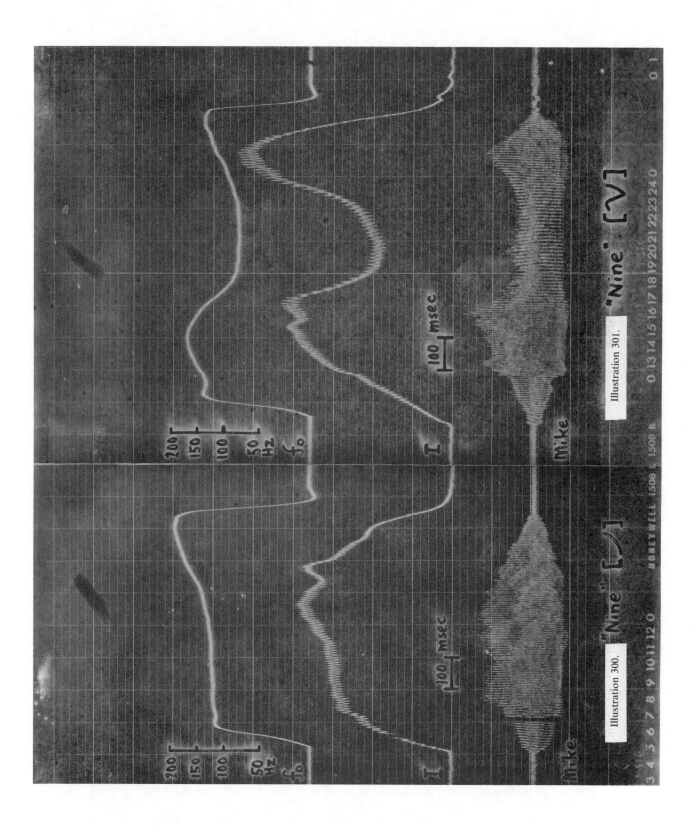

Illustration 300.   "Nine" [✓]

Illustration 301.   "Nine" [✓]

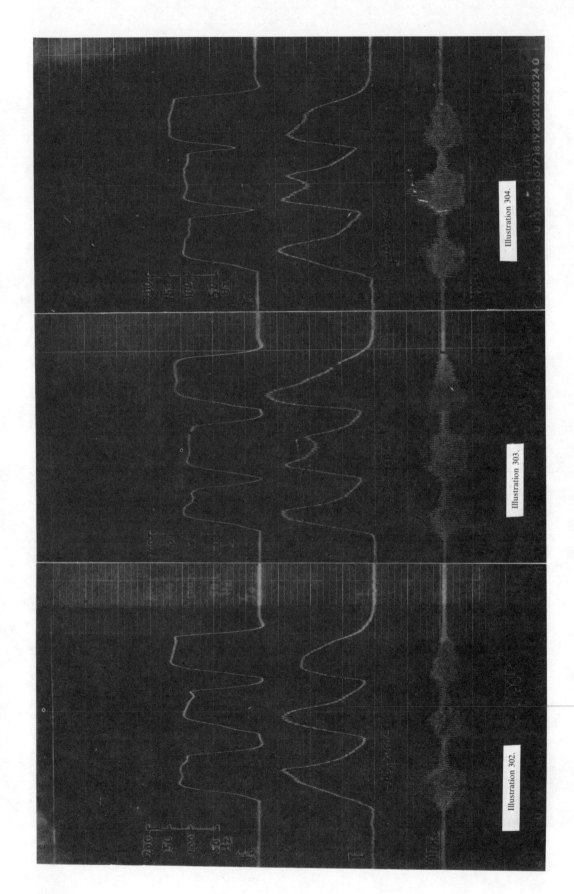

Illustration 304.

Illustration 303.

Illustration 302.

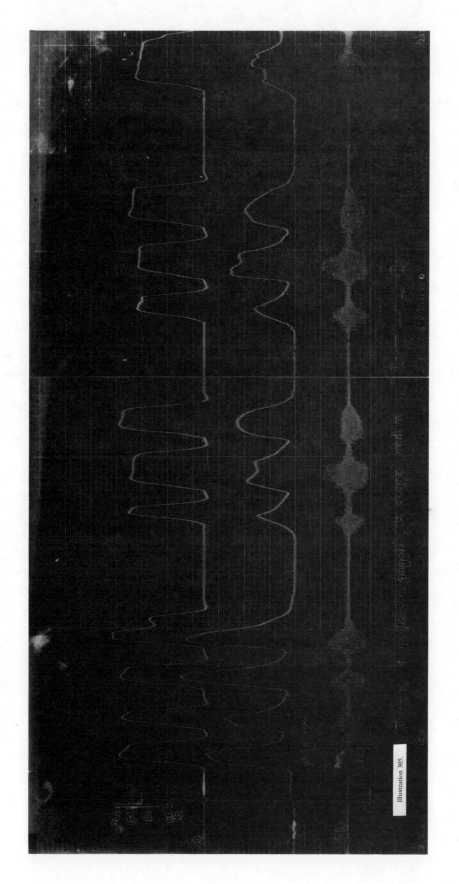

Illustration 305.

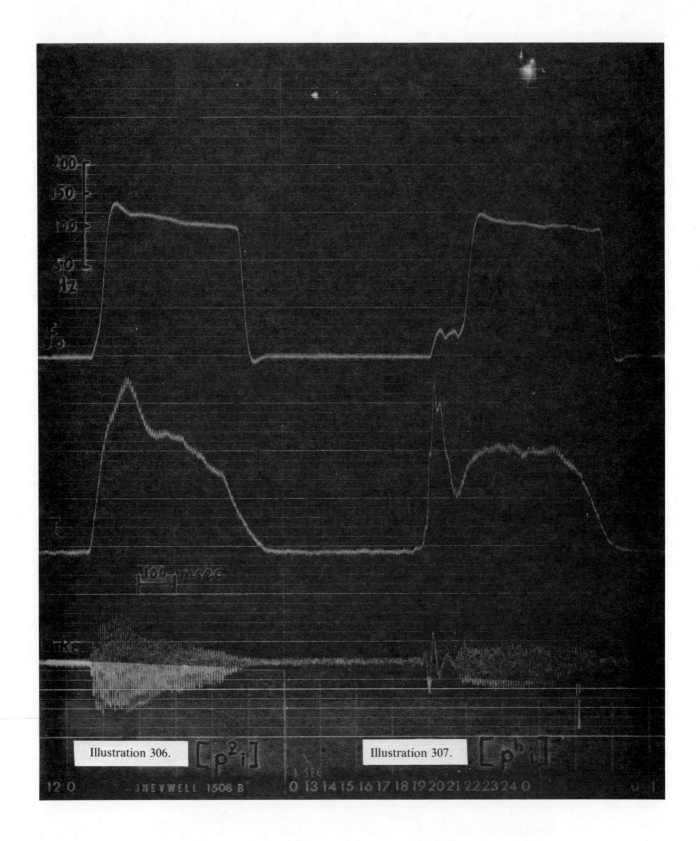

Illustration 306. $[p^2i]$ Illustration 307. $[p^bi]$

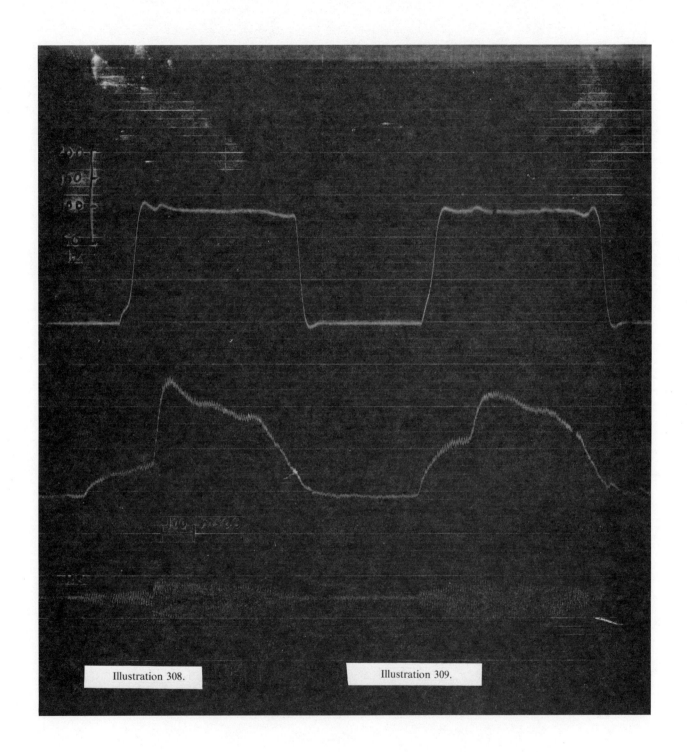

Illustration 308.

Illustration 309.

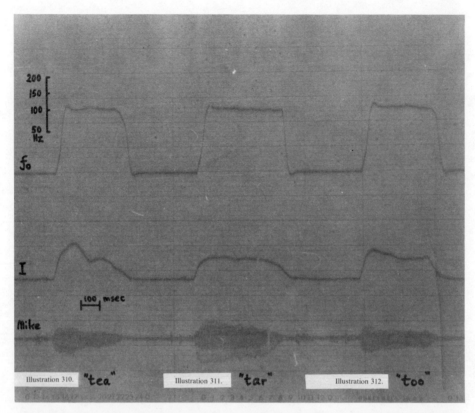

Illustration 310. "tea"   Illustration 311. "tar"   Illustration 312. "too"

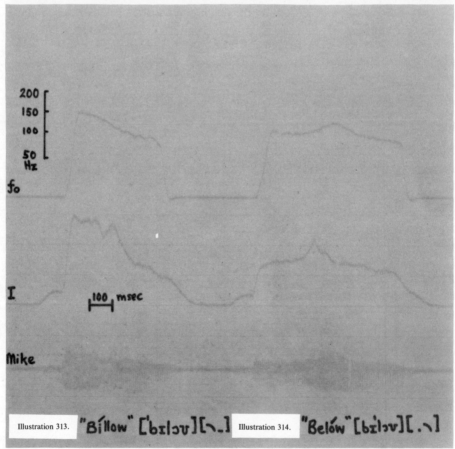

Illustration 313. "Bíllow" [ˈbɪloʊ][ˉˊ]   Illustration 314. "Belów" [bɪˈloʊ][˯ˋ]

154   Appendix

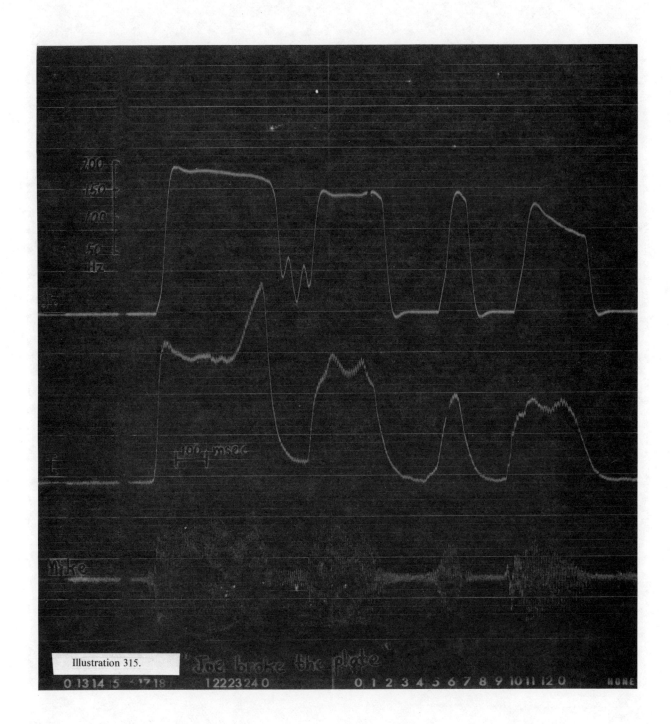

Illustration 315.

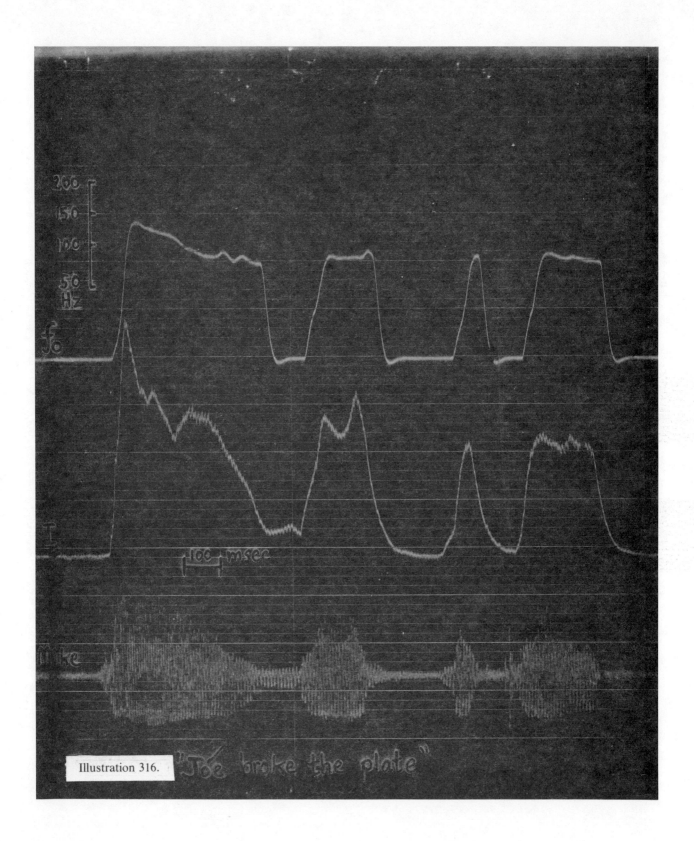

Illustration 316. "Joe broke the plate"

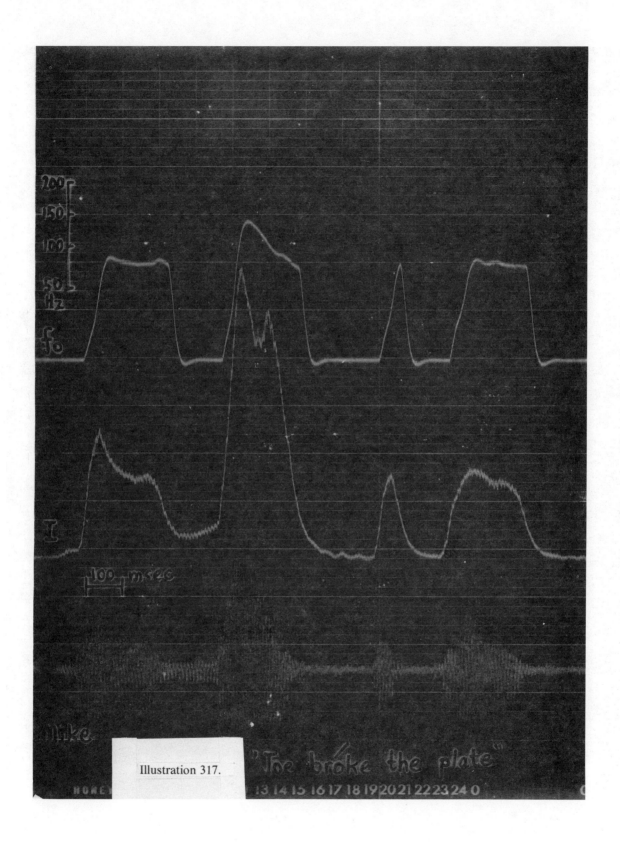

Illustration 317.

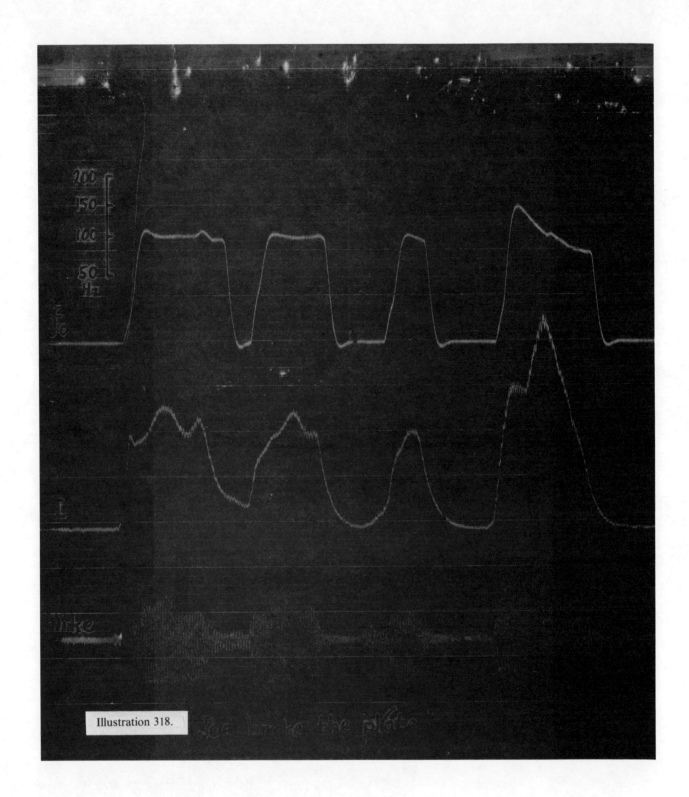

Illustration 318.

Illustration 319. An intensity meter. F-J Electronics A/S Type IM 360. (Courtesy of Voice Identification, Inc., Somerville, New Jersey.)

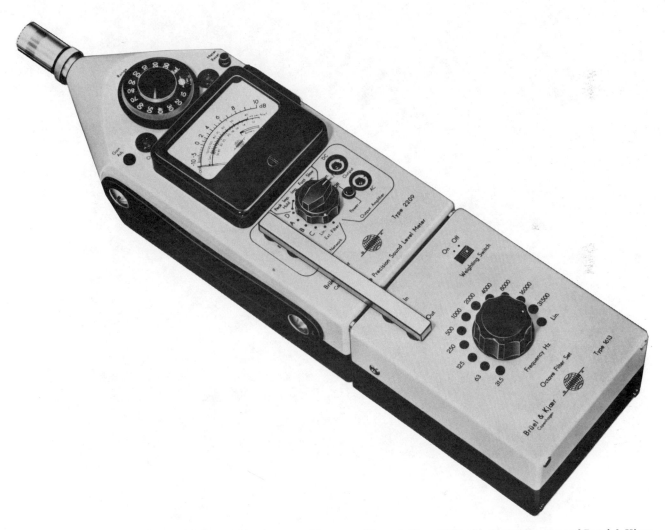

Illustration 320. Impulse precision sound level meter with octave filter set, Type 2209 with 1613. (Courtesy of Brüel & Kjaer Instruments, Inc., Cleveland, Ohio.)

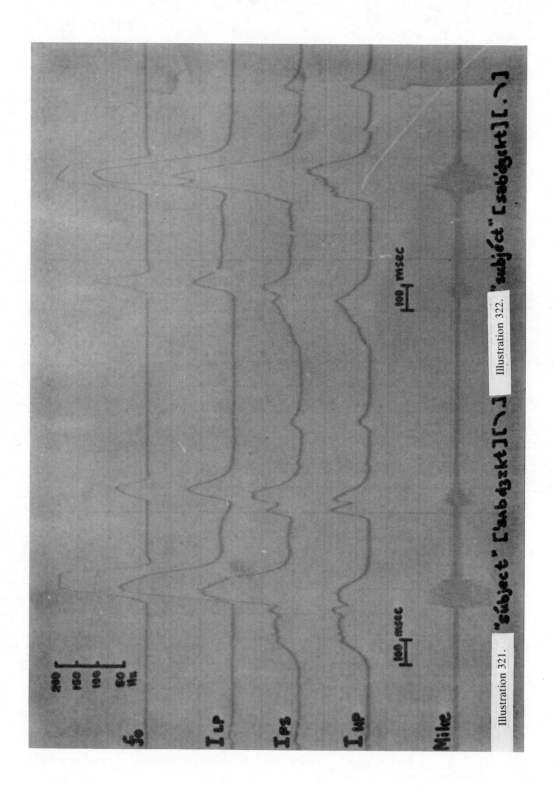

Illustration 321. "súbject" ['sʌbdʒɪkt] [⌐⌐]

Illustration 322. "subjéct" [sʌb'dʒɪkt] [.⌐]

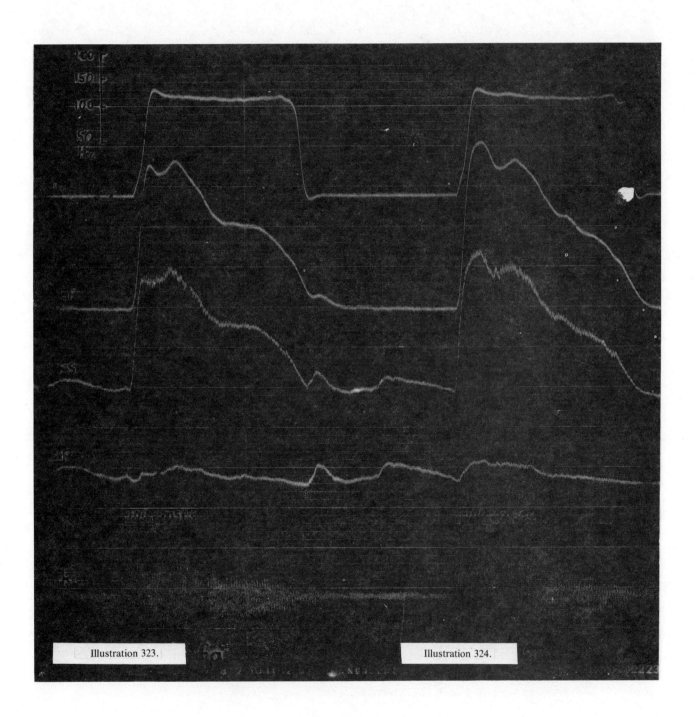

Illustration 323.

Illustration 324.

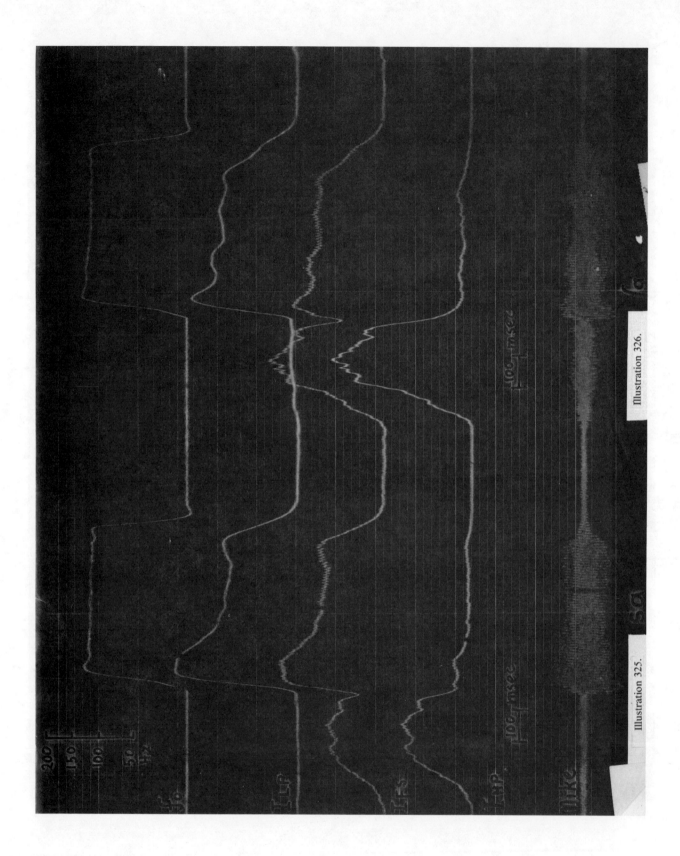

Illustration 325.

Illustration 326.

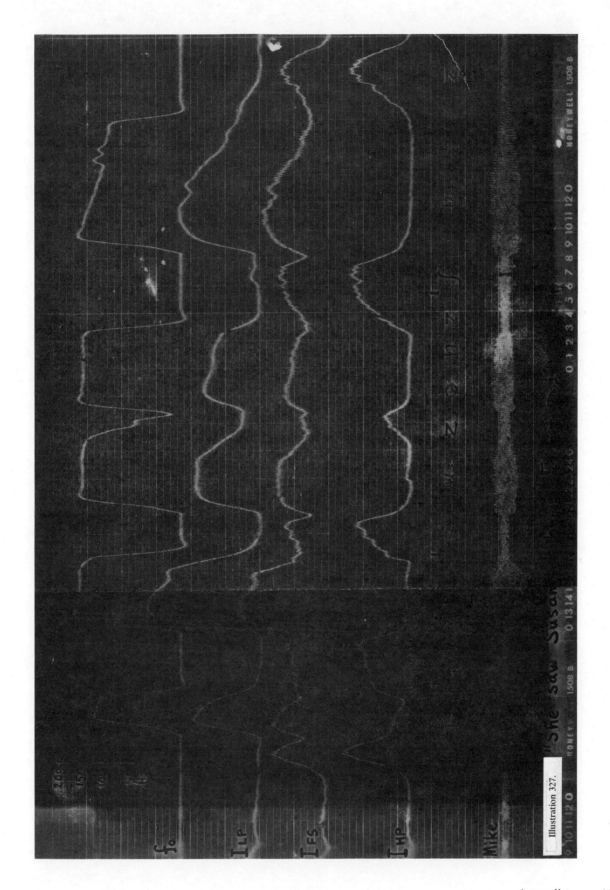

Illustration 327.

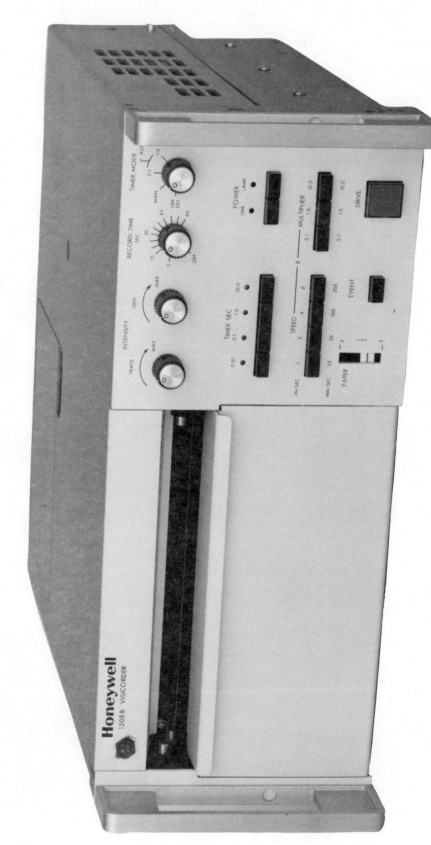

Illustration 328. Honeywell 1508 B Visicorder. (Courtesy of Honeywell, Inc., Newton Highlands, Massachusetts.)

Illustration 329. Honeywell A.C. Amplifier, Accudata 135 A. (Courtesy of Honeywell, Inc., Newton Highlands, Massachusetts.)

Illustration 330. Honeywell Bridge Amplifier, Accudata 113. (Courtesy of Honeywell, Inc., Newton Highlands, Massachusetts.)

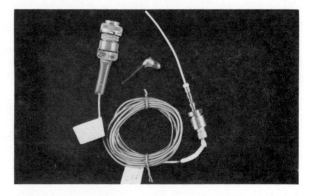

Illustration 331. Statham 55858 pressure transducer and a nasal olive.

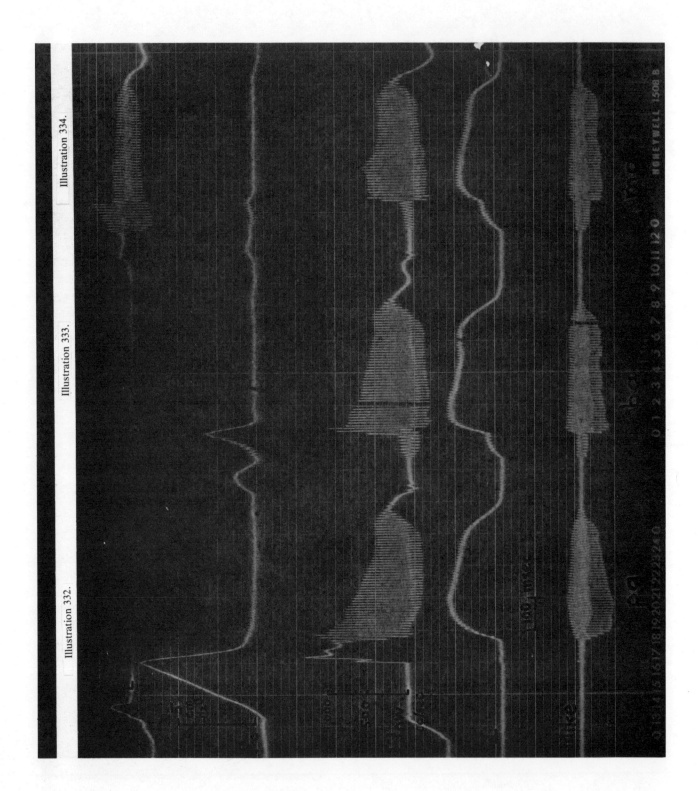

Illustration 332.

Illustration 333.

Illustration 334.

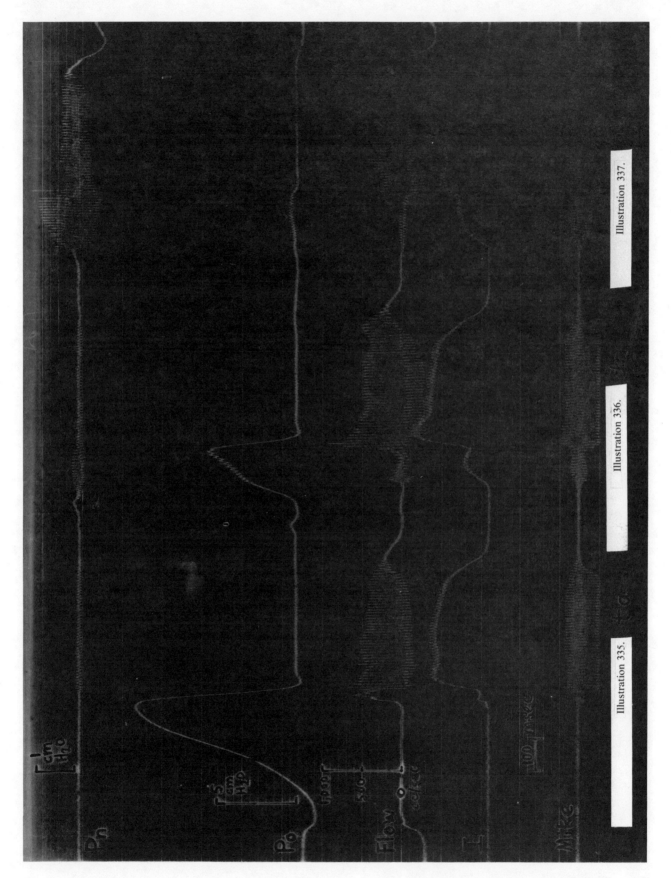

Illustration 337.

Illustration 336.

Illustration 335.

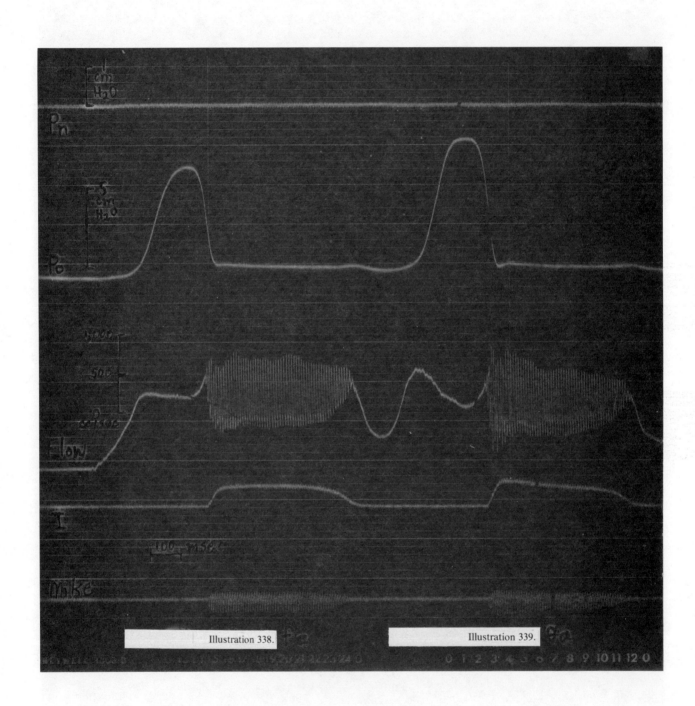

Illustration 338.   Illustration 339.

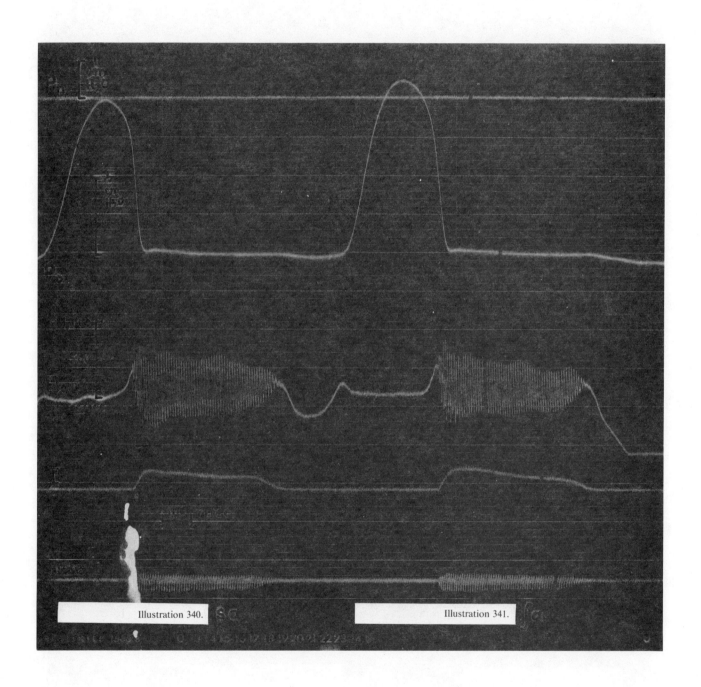

Illustration 340.   Illustration 341.

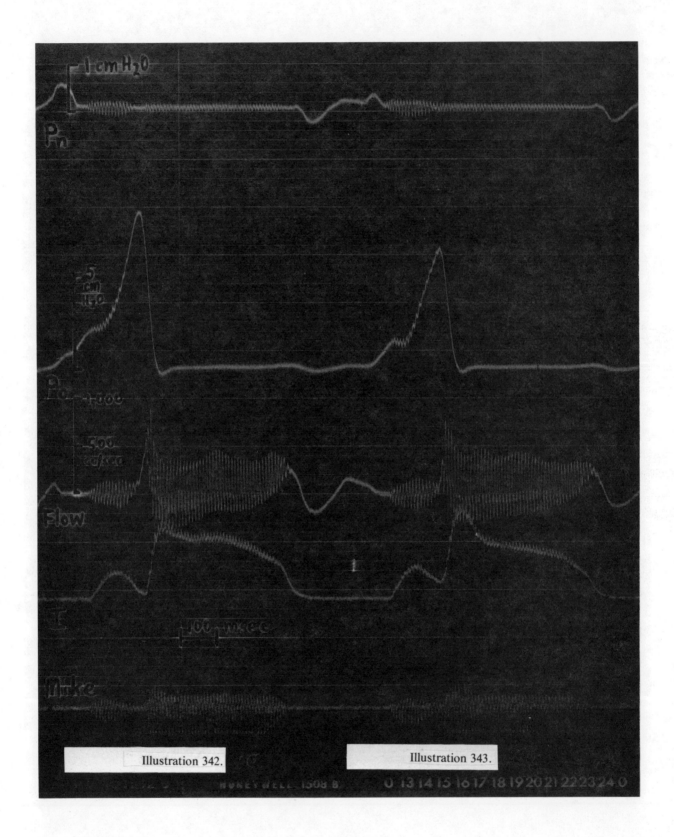

Illustration 342.   Illustration 343.

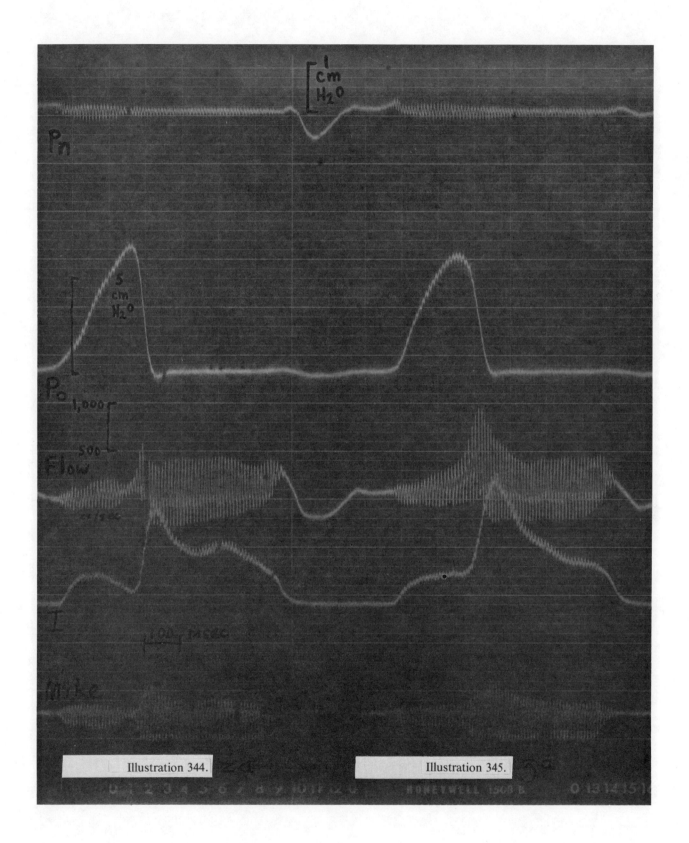

Illustration 344.

Illustration 345.

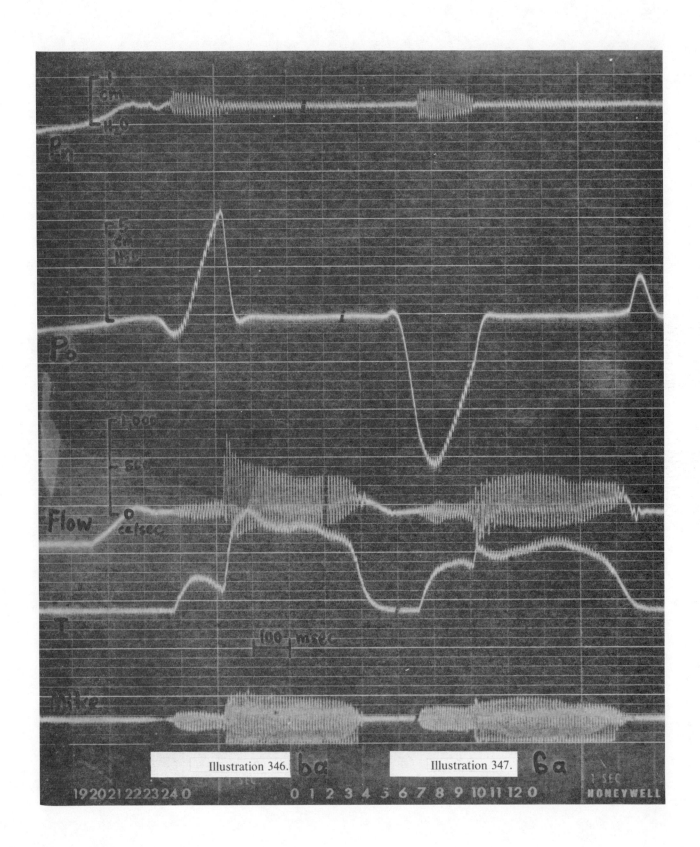

Illustration 346. *ba*   Illustration 347. *ba*

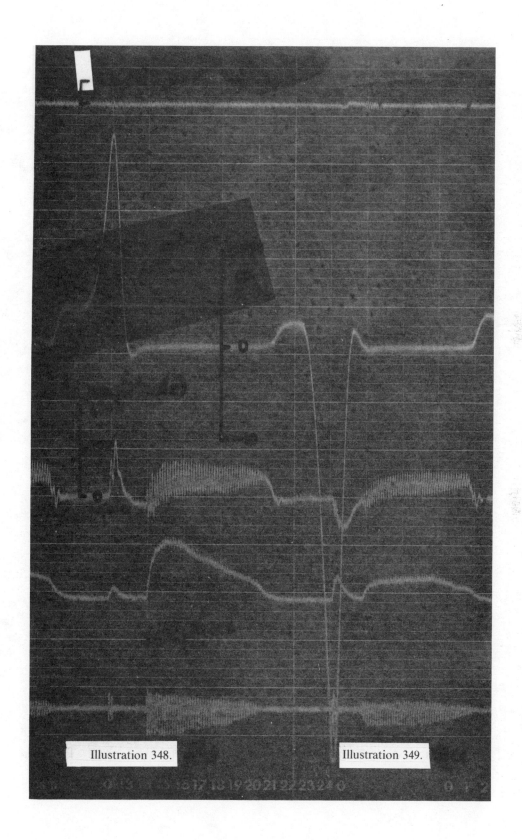

Illustration 348.   Illustration 349.

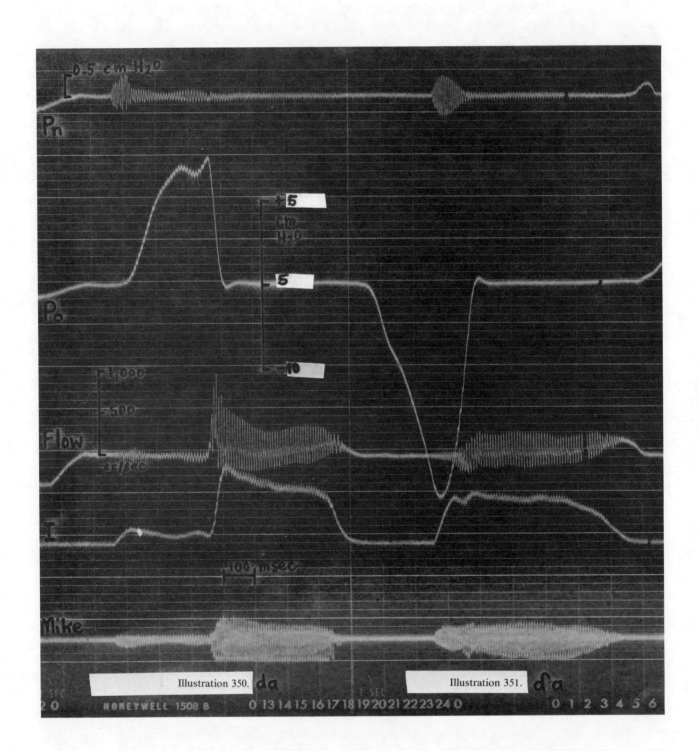

Illustration 350. da   Illustration 351. d'a

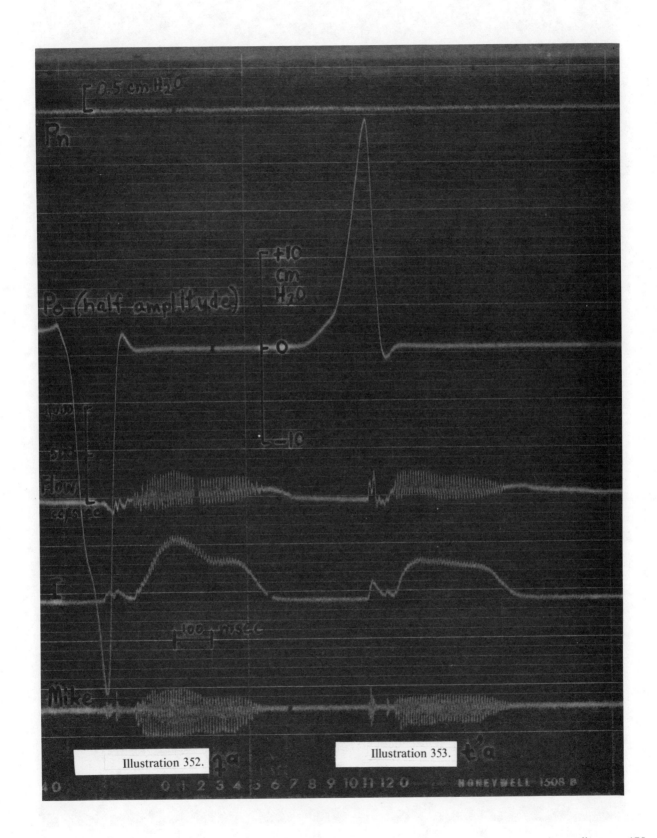

Illustration 352.

Illustration 353.

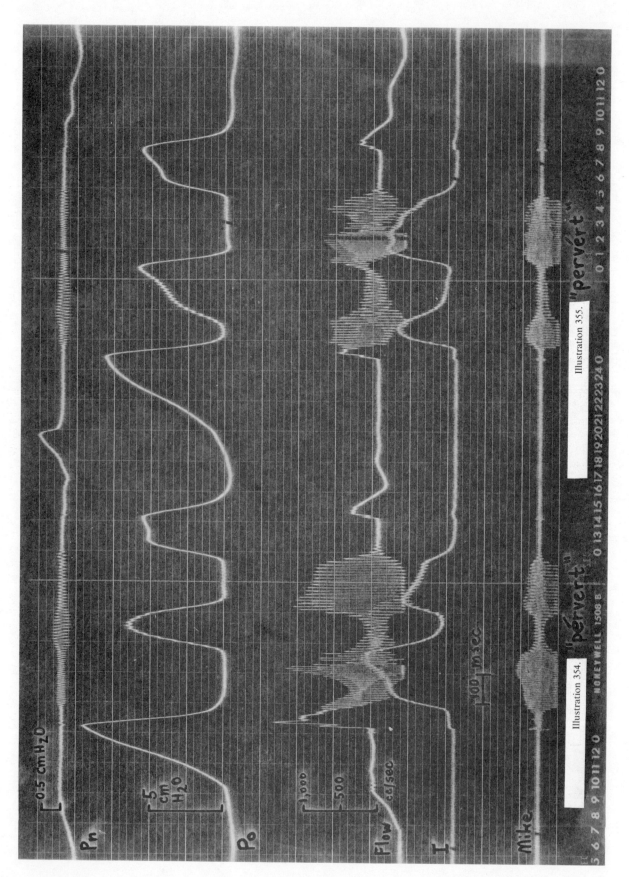

Illustration 354. "pervert"

Illustration 355. "pervert"

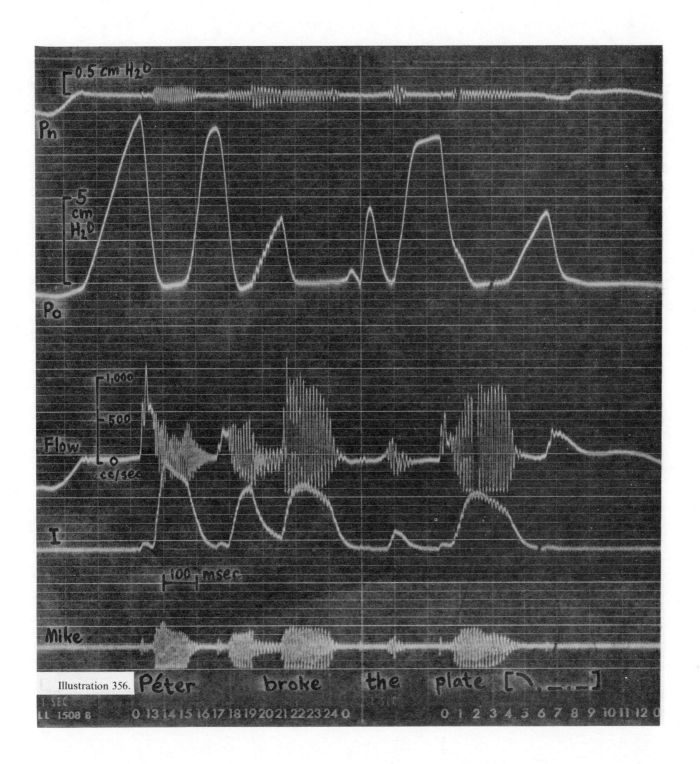

Illustration 356. Péter broke the plate [＼. ___ . __ . __]

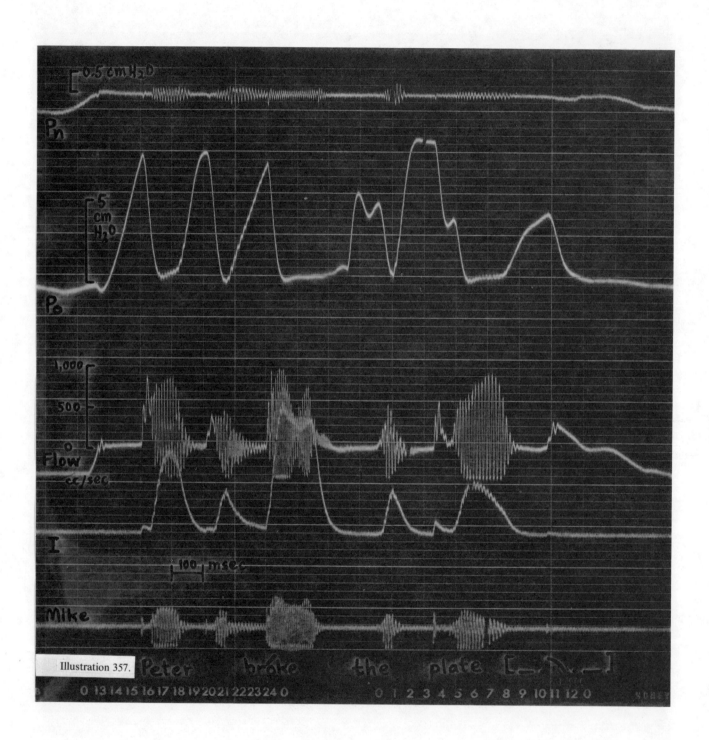

Illustration 357. Peter broke the plate [_ ◠ _]

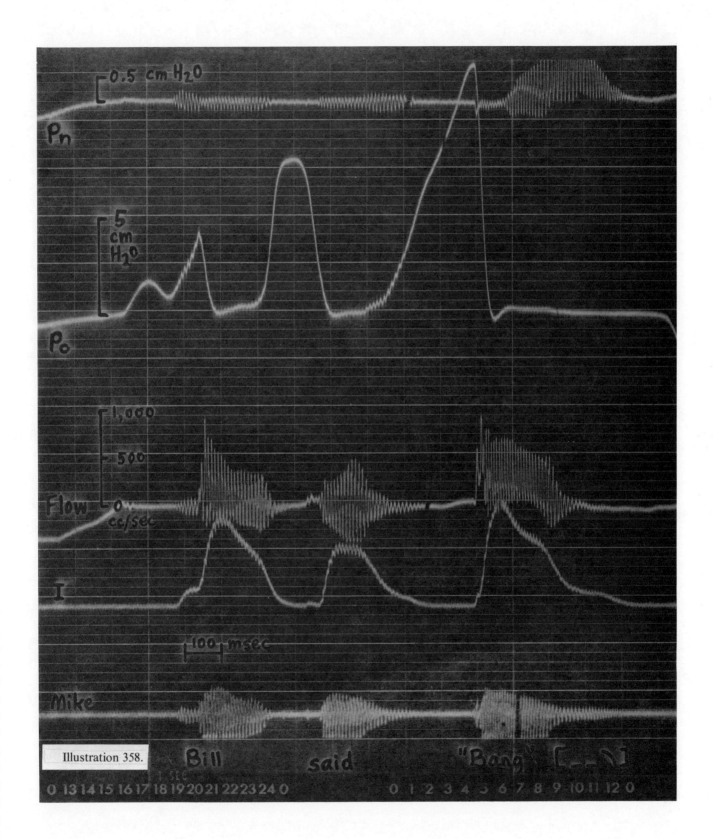

Illustration 358.

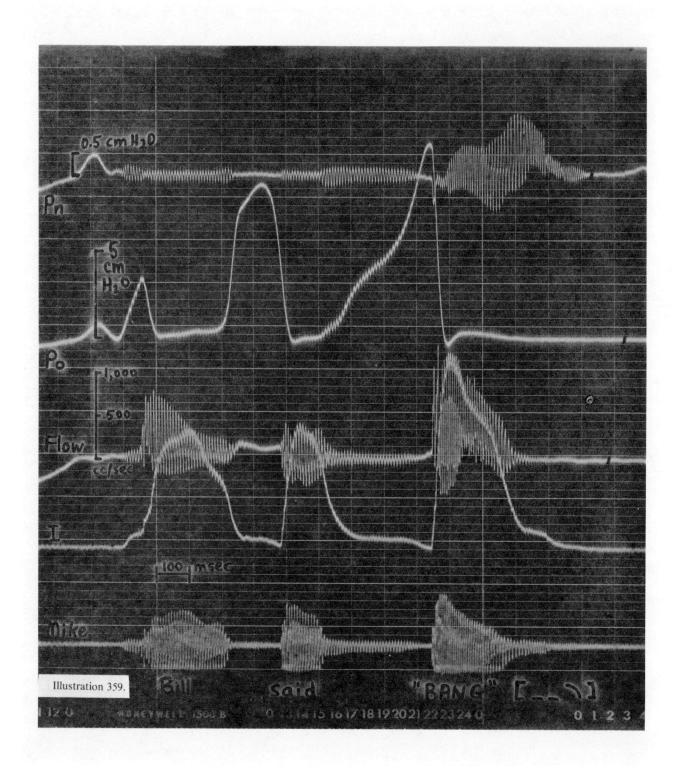

Illustration 359.

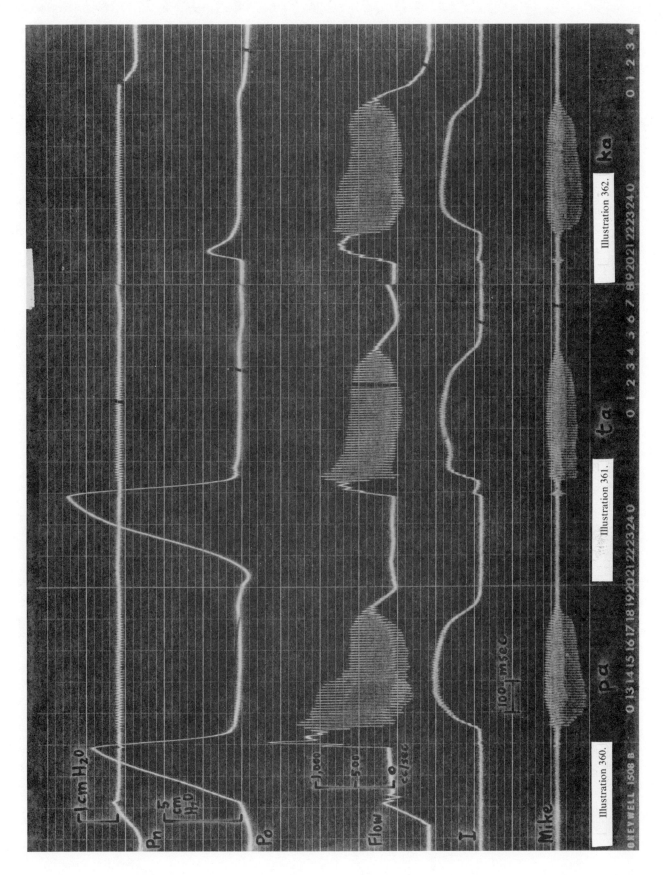

Illustration 360. pa Illustration 361. ta Illustration 362. ka

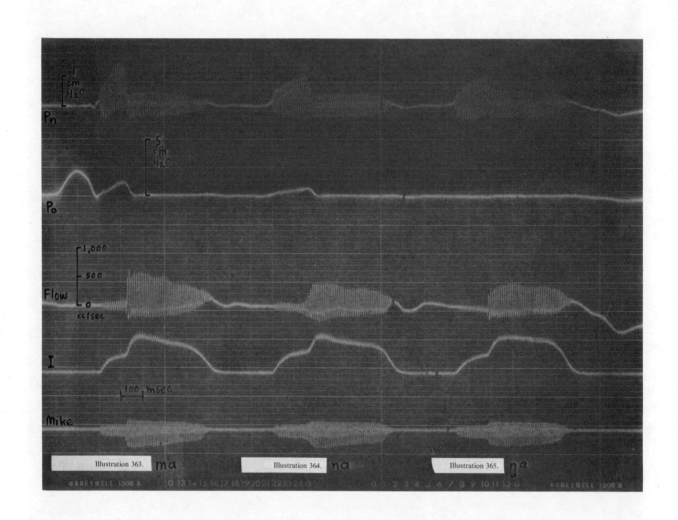

Illustration 363. ma Illustration 364. na Illustration 365. ŋa

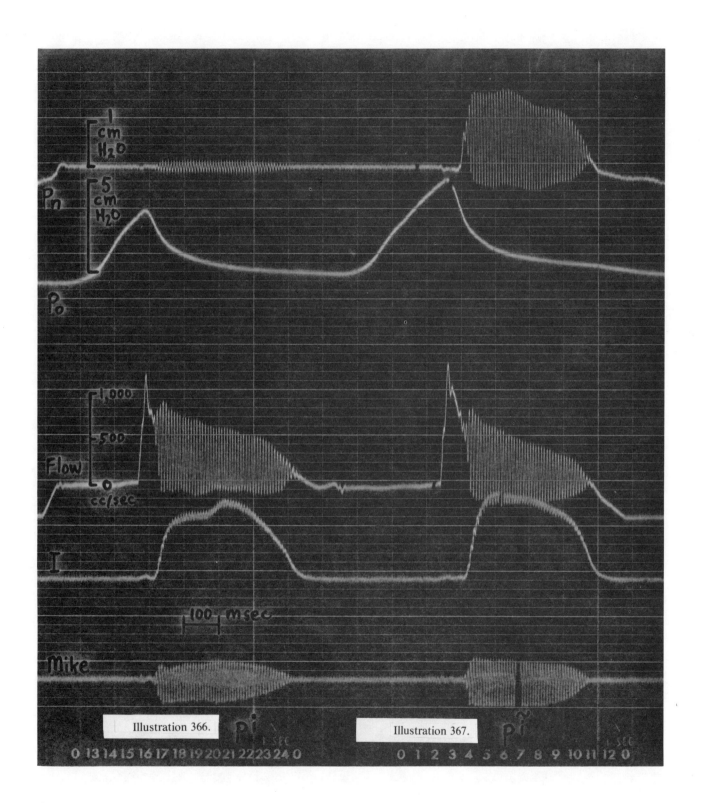

Illustration 366.

Illustration 367.

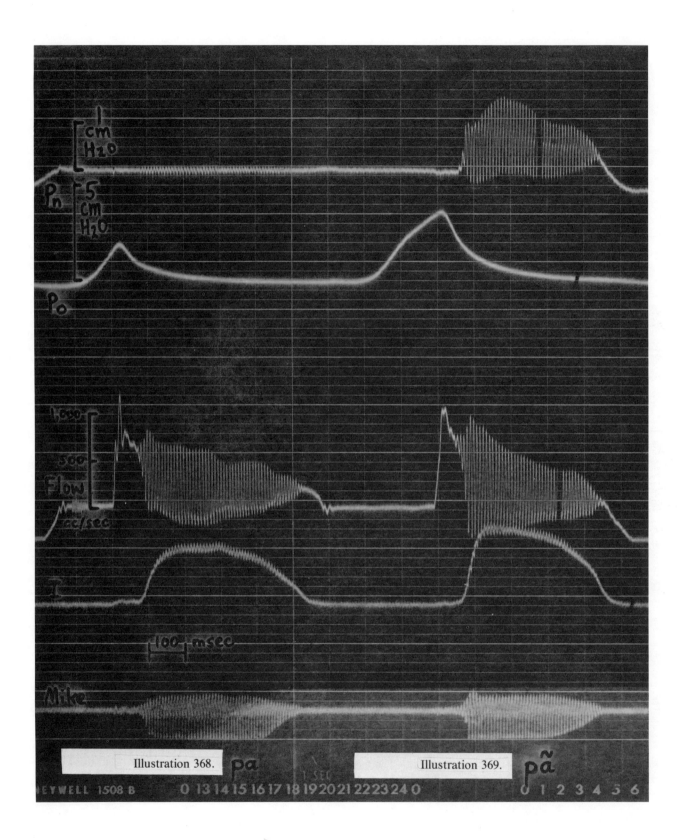

Illustration 368. pa   Illustration 369. pã

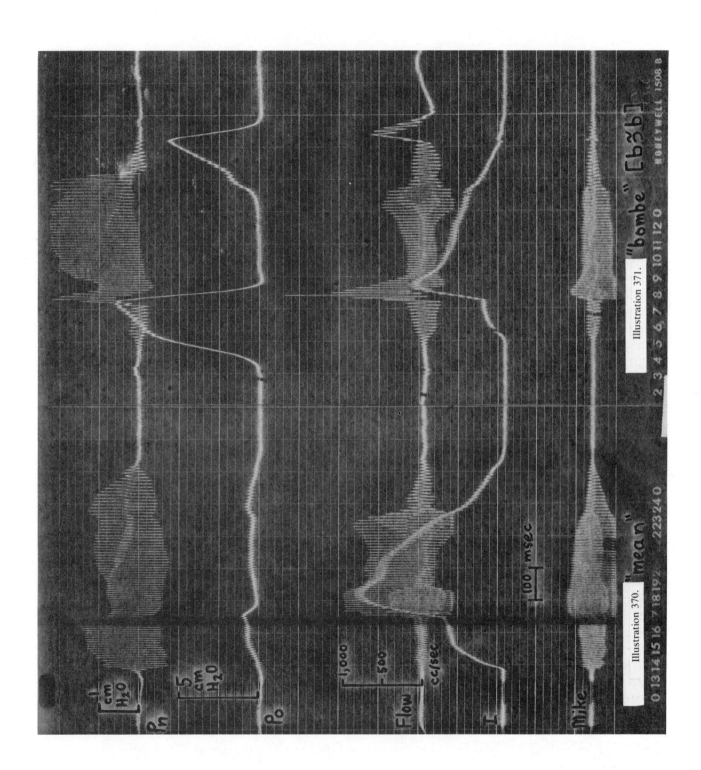

Illustration 371. "bombe" [bɔ̃b]

Illustration 370. "mean"

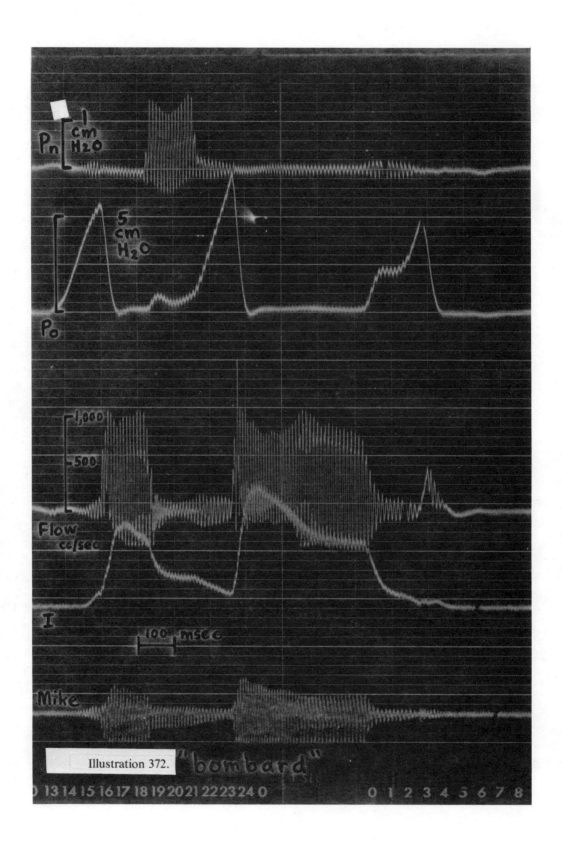

Illustration 372. "bombard"

Illustration 373. Illustration 374.

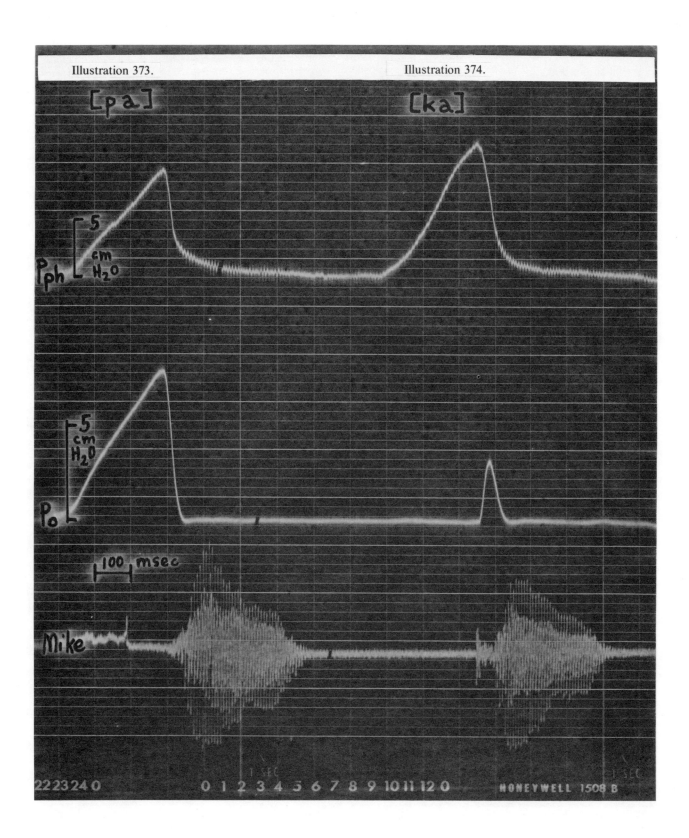

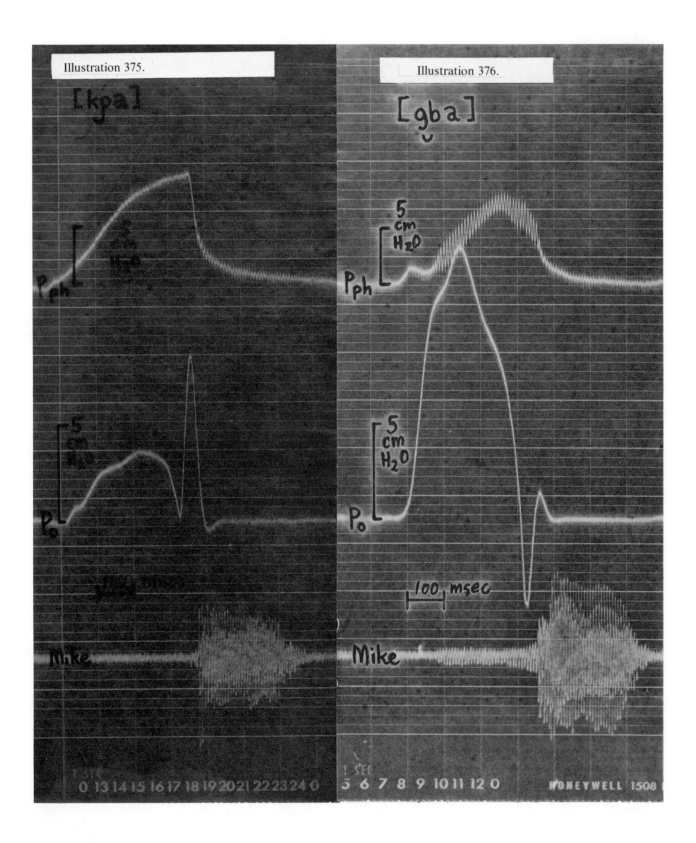

Illustration 375.

Illustration 376.

Illustration 377.

Illustration 378.

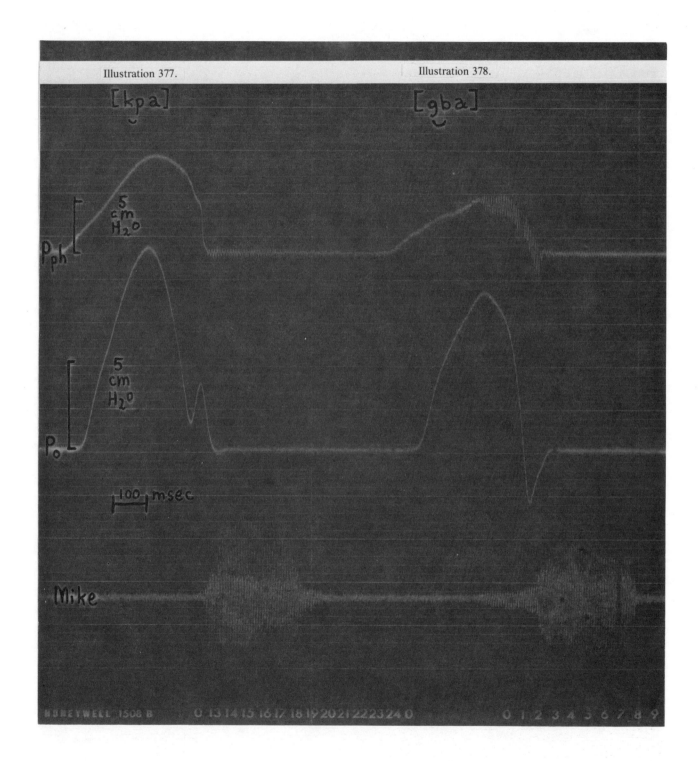

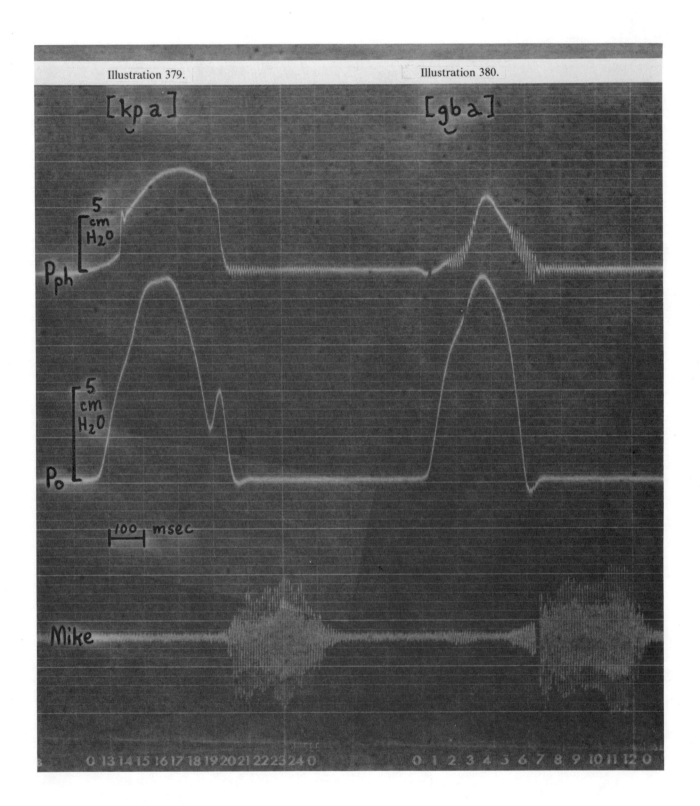

Illustration 379.

Illustration 380.

[kp a]

[g b a]

P_ph

5 cm H₂O

5 cm H₂O

P_o

100 msec

Mike

Illustration 381. Illustration 382.

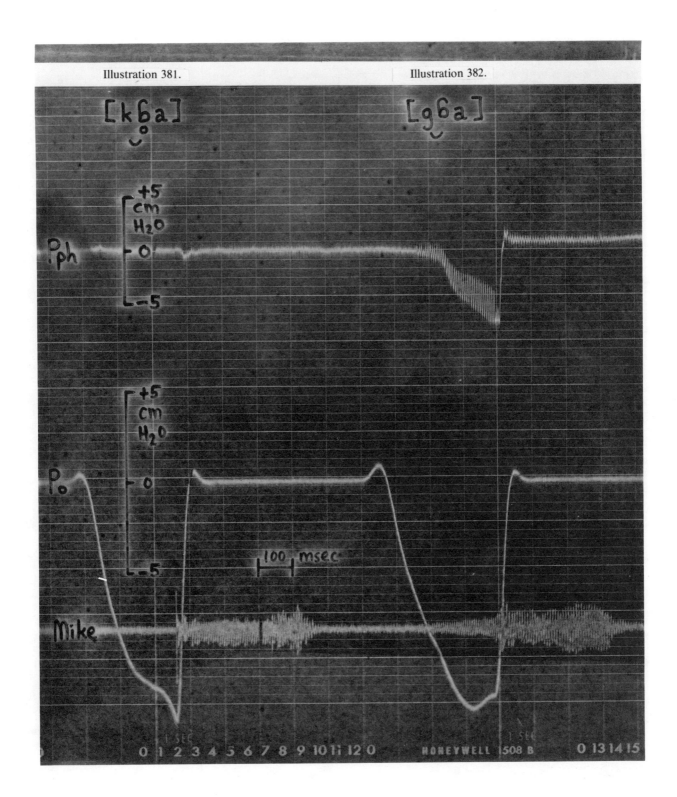

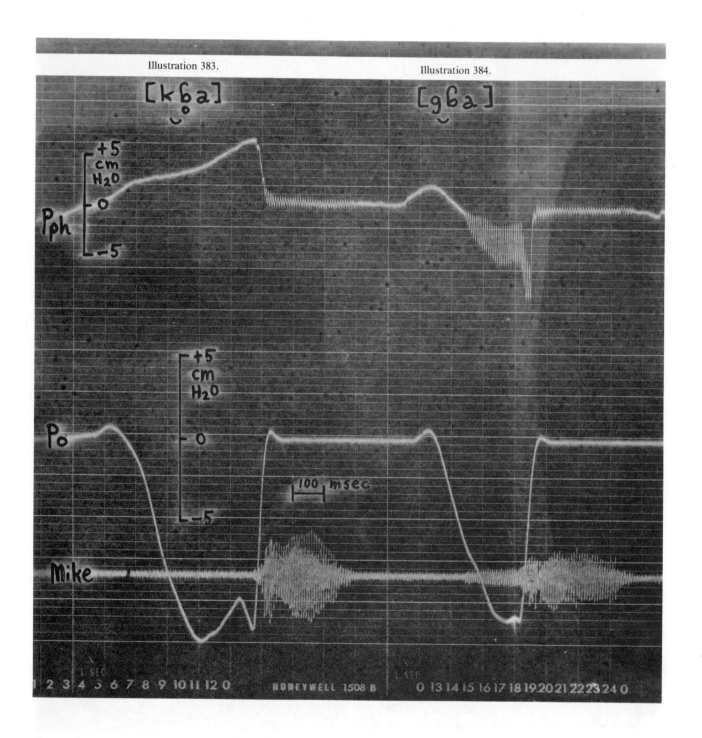

Illustration 383.   Illustration 384.

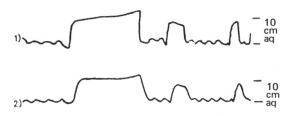

Illustration 385. Simultaneous records of esophageal pressure (1) and tracheal pressure (2) during respiration and speech. (From Ladefoged, P. 1960. The regulation of subglottal pressure. *Folia Phoniatrica 12(3):* 171. By permission.)

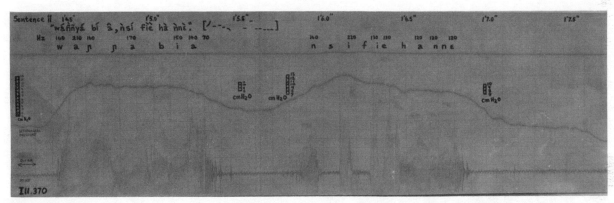

Illustration 386.

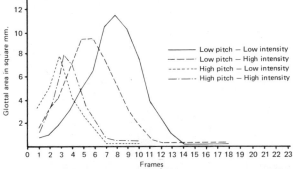

Illustration 387. Glottal area variations during phonation at low pitch and at high and low intensities and at high pitch at high and low intensities for a single subject. (Zemlin, W. R., *Speech and Hearing Science: Anatomy and Physiology,* © 1968, p. 202. Reprinted by permission of Prentice-Hall, Inc., Englewood Cliffs, N.J. Based upon a M.A. thesis by R. Charron.)

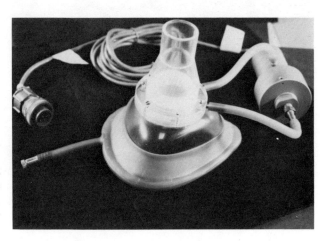

Illustration 388. A pneumotachograph.

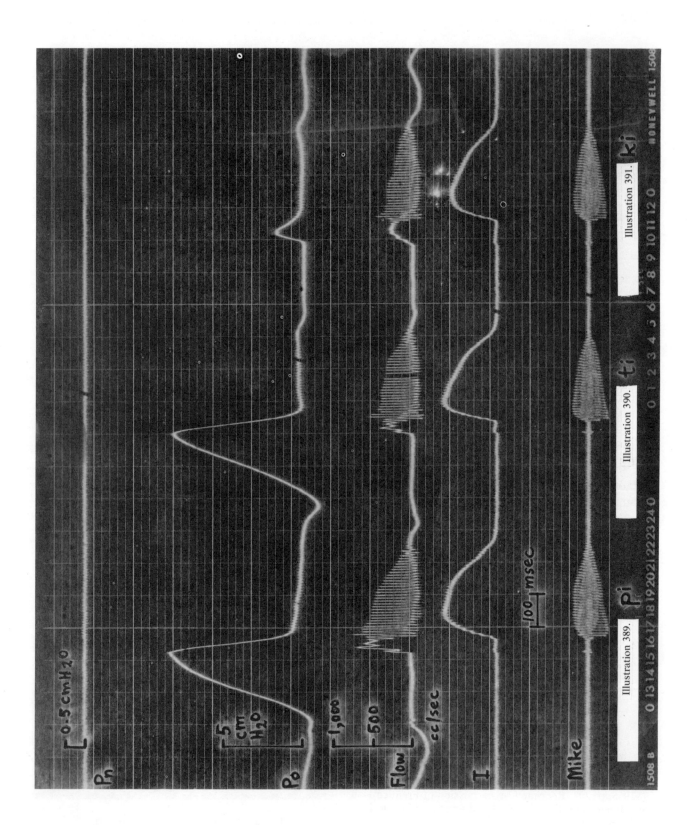

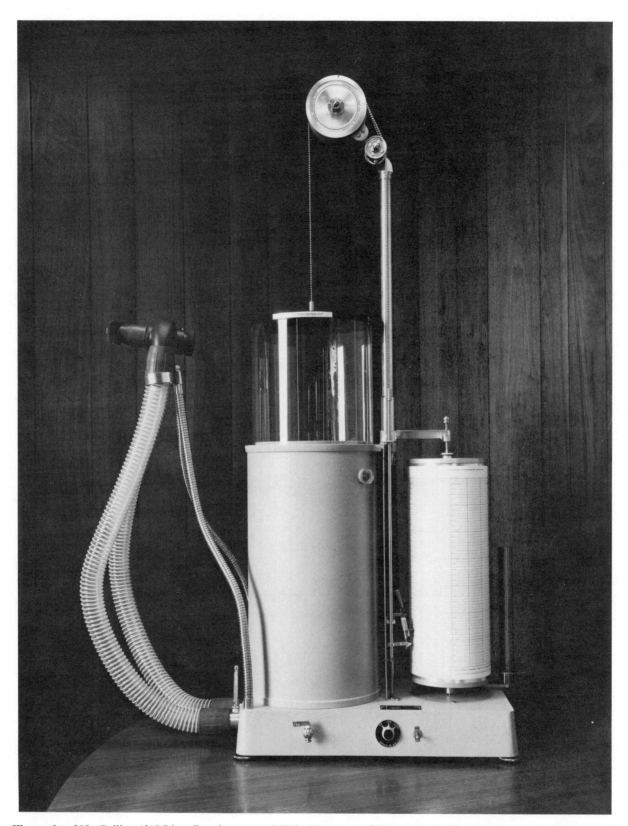

Illustration 392. Collins 13.5 Liter Respirometer, 06003. (Courtesy of Warren E. Collins, Braintree, Massachusetts.)

Illustration 393.

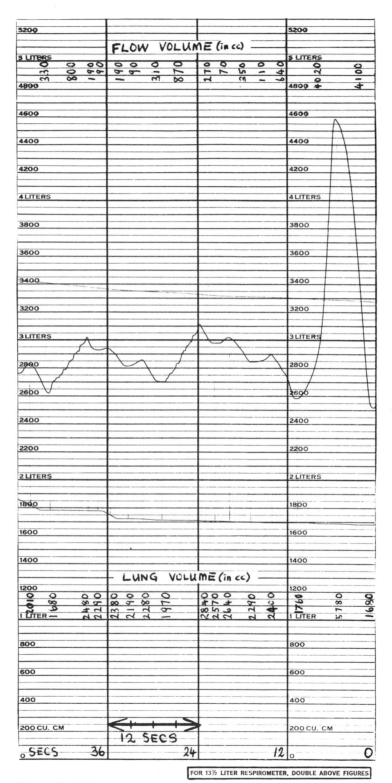

Illustration 394.

Illustration 395. R-D Nasal Manometer. (Courtesy of Stell-Will Products, Grand Island, New York.)

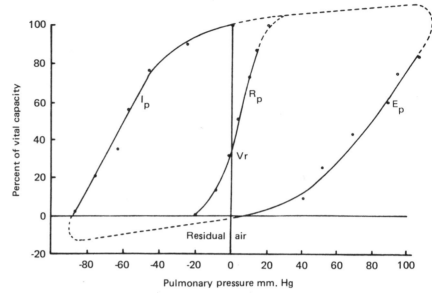

Illustration 396. Pressure-volume diagram of breathing. (From Rahn, H., Otis, A. B., Chadwick, L. E., and Fenn, W. O. 1946. The pressure-volume diagram of the thorax and lung. *American Journal of Physiology 146:*161–178. By permission.)

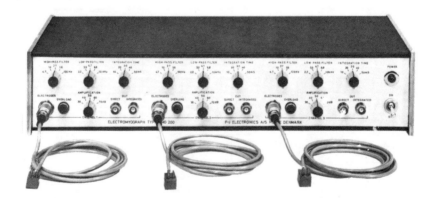

Illustration 397. Electromyograph. F-J Electronics A/S Type EMG 200. (Courtesy of Voice Identification, Inc., Somerville, New Jersey.)

Illustration 398.   A suction cup surface electrode. (From Basmajian, J. V., *Muscles Alive,* Figure 16, © 1974, The Williams & Wilkins Co., Baltimore. By permission.)

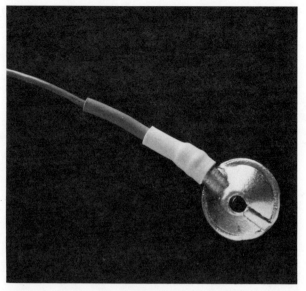

Illustration 399. A nonsuction surface electrode.

Illustration 400.   A hooked wire electrode. Staggered distal ends are folded over needle tip. (From Basmajian, J. V., *Muscles Alive,* Figure 17, © 1974, The Williams & Wilkins Co., Baltimore. By permission.)

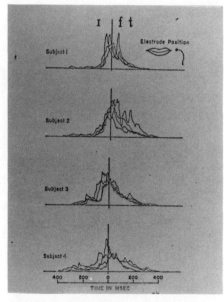

Illustration 401. Tracings of the integrated muscle potentials from each of the four subjects during four productions of the utterance /ift/. The vertical line indicates the offset of voicing. (From MacNeilage, P. 1963. Electromyographic and acoustic study of the production of certain final clusters. *The Journal of the Acoustical Society of America 35:*462. By permission.)

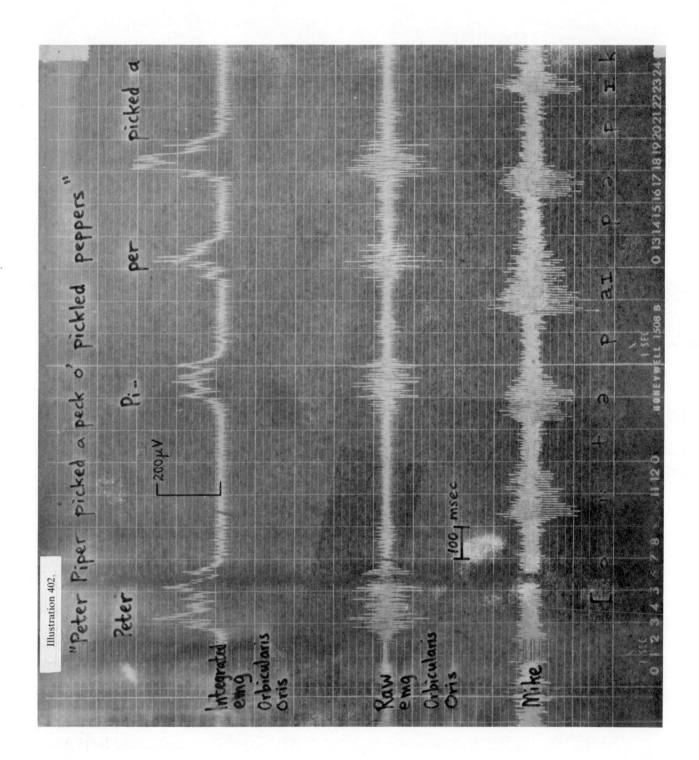

Illustration 402.

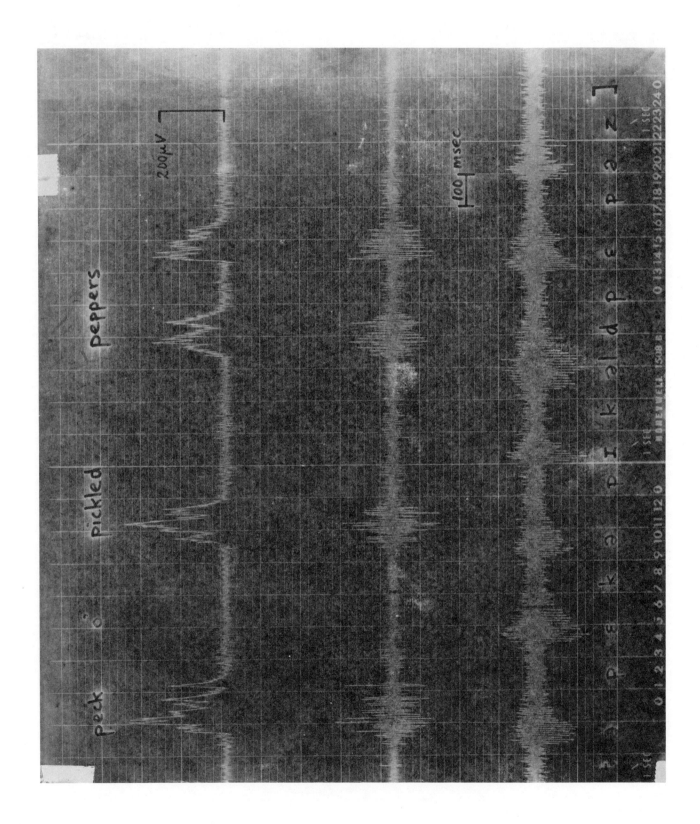

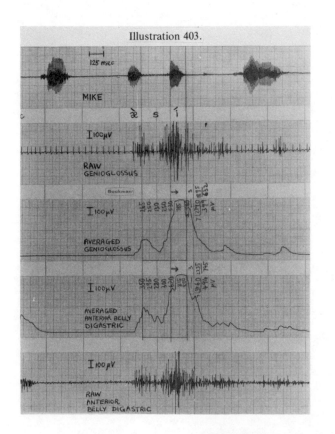

Illustration 403.

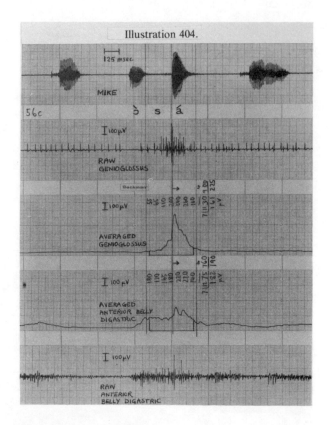

Illustration 404.

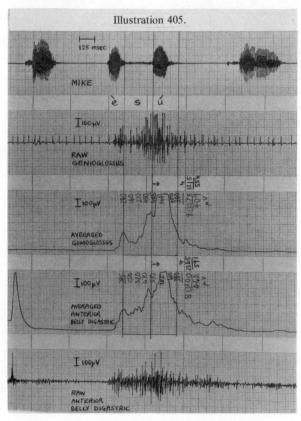

Illustration 405.

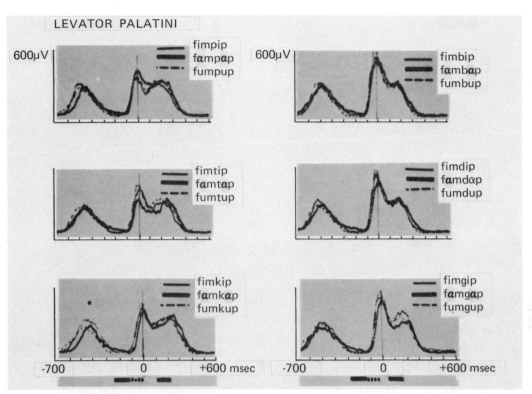

Illustration 406.   EMG signals.   (From Bell-Berti, F. The velopharyngeal mechanism: An electromyographic study. Haskins Laboratories Status Report on Speech Research, p. 70.)

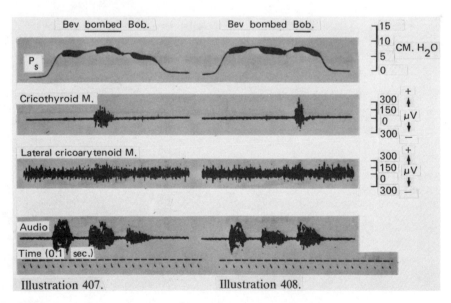

Illustration 407.   Illustration 408.

Illustrations 407 and 408 from Ohala, J. Aspects of the control and production of speech. *Working Papers in Phonetics 15:*36. By permission.

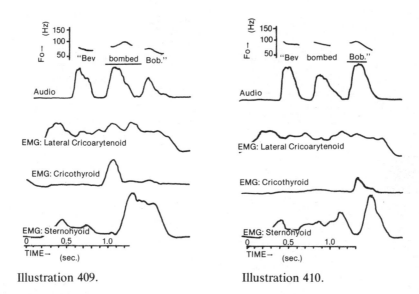

Illustration 409. Illustration 410.

Illustrations 409 and 410 from Ohala, J. Aspects of the control and production of speech. *Working Papers in Phonetics 15:*70. By permission.

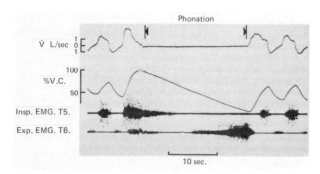

Illustration 411.   Intercostal EMG activity during phonation. (From Sears and Newson Davis. 1968. The control of respiratory muscles during voluntary breathing. *Annals of the New York Academy of Science 155:*183–190. By permission.)

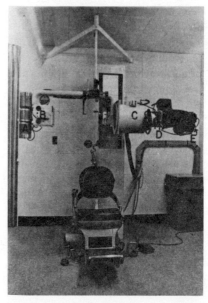

Illustration 412. Cinefluorographic equipment: A, x-ray tube; B, x-ray beam collimator; C, 9-inch image intensifier tube; D, fluoroscopic viewer; E, Auricon, sound-on film, 16 mm camera. (From Moll, K. 1965. Photographic and radiographic procedures in speech research. Proceedings of the conference: Communicative problems in cleft palate. *ASHA Reports 1:*129–139. With permission.)

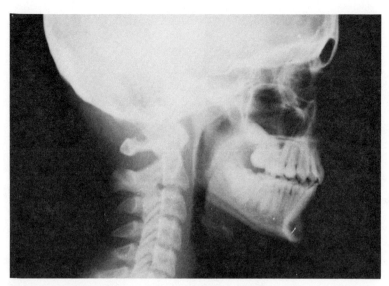

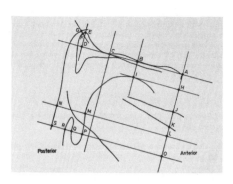

Illustration 414. Tracing of a mid-saggital x-ray with reference points superimposed. (From Painter, C. 1973. Cineradiographic data on the feature "covered" in Twi vowel harmony. *Phonetica 28:108.* With permission.)

Illustration 413. Mid-saggital x-ray of the vocal tract from lips to larynx. (Courtesy of Albert Gray, DMD, Wakefield, Massachusetts. Logotron processed by Ray Sprague of the Massachusetts General Hospital, Boston.)

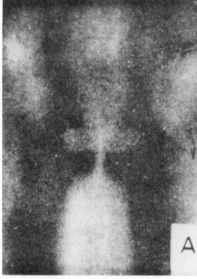

Illustration 415. Frontal laminagram of a male larynx. (From van den Berg, J.W. 1970. Mechanism of the larynx and the laryngeal vibrations. In B. Malmberg (ed.), *Manual of Phonetics,* p. 300. North-Holland Publishing Company, Amsterdam. With permission.)

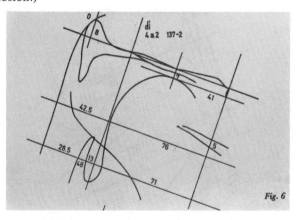

Illustration 416. Steady state tongue position for [i].

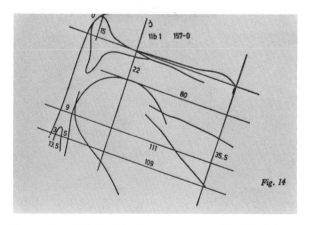

Illustration 417. Steady state tongue position for [ɔ].

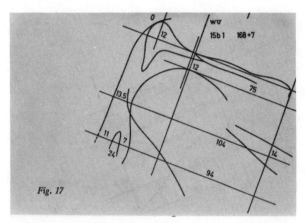

Illustration 418. Steady state tongue position for [ʋ].

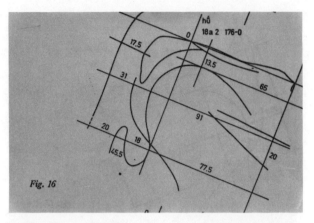

Illustration 419. Steady state tongue and soft palate position for [ũ].

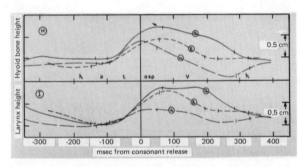

Illustration 420. Comparison of measurements H and I versus time for the utterances /hə′tɑ/, /hə′tɛ/, /hə′tu/. (From Perkell, J. S. 1969. *Physiology of Speech Production,* p. 39. Research Monograph No. 3. The MIT Press, Cambridge, Massachusetts. With permission.)

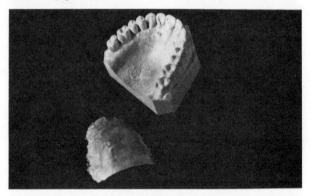

Illustration 421. A plaster impression (top) and an artificial palate (bottom) made for the author by Joseph Perkell.

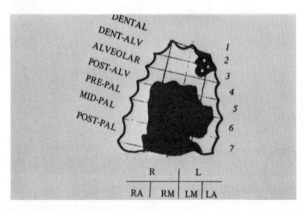

Illustration 422. [tù] to meet.

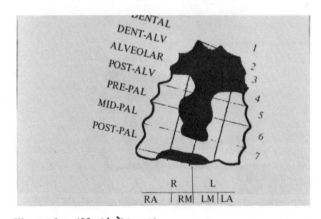

Illustration 423. [dʑì] to eat.

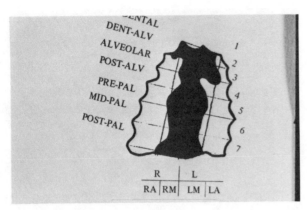

Illustration 424. [ásí] mounds.

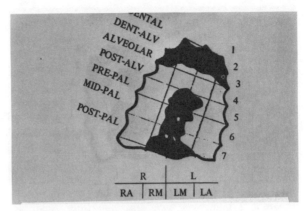

Illustration 425. [ɲɔ́] to dye.

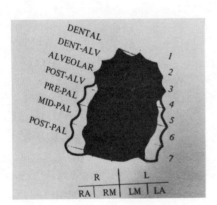

Illustration 426. [épé] home.

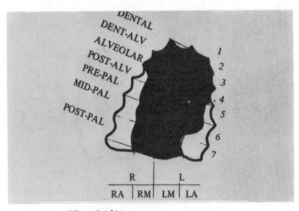

Illustration 427. [àbòjù] corn.

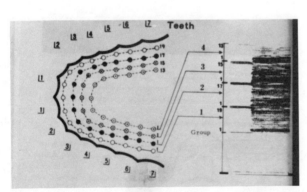

Illustration 428. Selection of electrodes and arrangement of the palatal signals on the recording paper. (Reprinted from Shibata, S. 1968. A study of dynamic palatography. *Annual Bulletin of the Research Institute of Logopedics and Phoniatrics (University of Tokyo)* 2:28–36. With permission.)

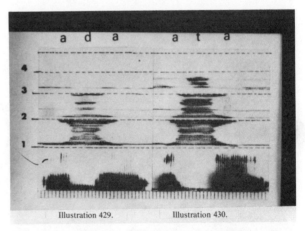

Illustration 429.   Illustration 430.

Illustrations 429 and 430 reprinted from Shibata, S. 1968. A study of dynamic palatography. *Annual Bulletin of the Research Institute of Logopedics and Phoniatrics (University of Tokyo)* 2:28–36. With permission.

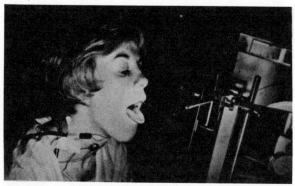 

Illustration 431. Subject in position for laryngeal photography (A) and (B) experimenter prepared to photograph. (From Willard R. Zemlin, *Speech and Hearing Science:* Anatomy and Physiology, ©1968, p. 167. Reprinted by permission of Prentice-Hall, Inc., Englewood Cliffs, N.J.)

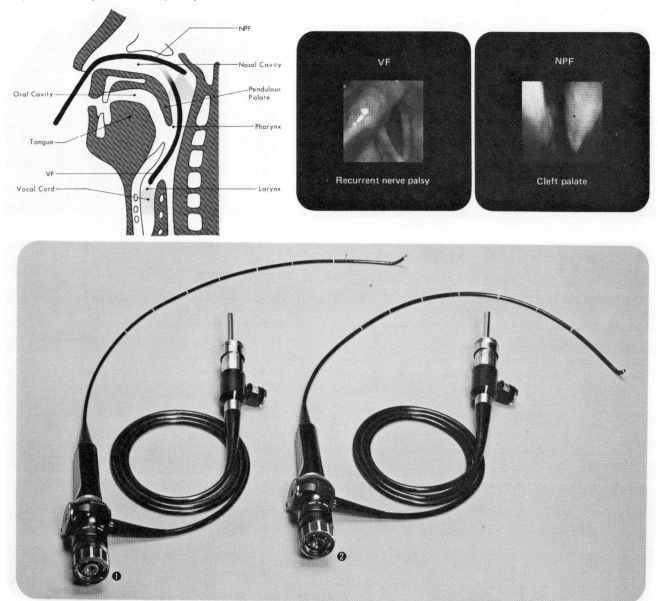

Illustration 432. An Olympus laryngeal fiberscope. NPF type S3 (1) and VF type 4A2 (2). (Courtesy of Olympus Corporation of America, New Hyde Park, New York.)

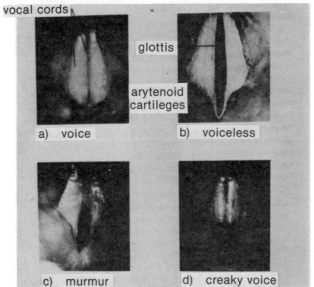

a) voice   b) voiceless

c) murmur   d) creaky voice

Illustration 433. Photographs (by John Ohala and Ralph Vanderslice) of some phonation types. The vocal cords are the white bands running in the vertical direction in each picture. The arytenoid cartilages are clearly visible in the lower part of a and b, and the anterior (ligamental) portions of the vocal cords are in the upper part of each picture. (Reprinted from Ladefoged, P. 1971. *Preliminaries to Linguistic Phonetics*, p. 6. University of Chicago Press, Chicago. Copyright © 1971 by The University of Chicago Press. With permission.)

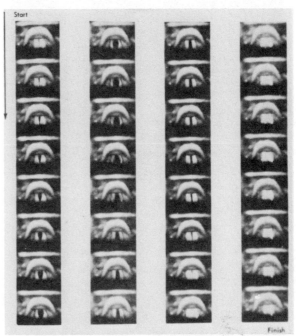

Illustration 434. A cycle of normal vocal fold vibration. (From Willard R. Zemlin, *Speech and Hearing Science: Anatomy and Physiology*, © 1968, p. 179. Reprinted by permission of Prentice-Hall, Inc., Englewood Cliffs, New Jersey.)

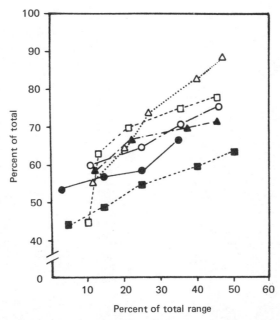

Illustration 435. Variation in vocal fold length with change in vocal pitch. (Reprinted from Hollien, H., and Moore, P. 1960. Measurements of the vocal folds during changes in pitch. *Journal of Speech and Hearing Research 3:*163. With permission.)

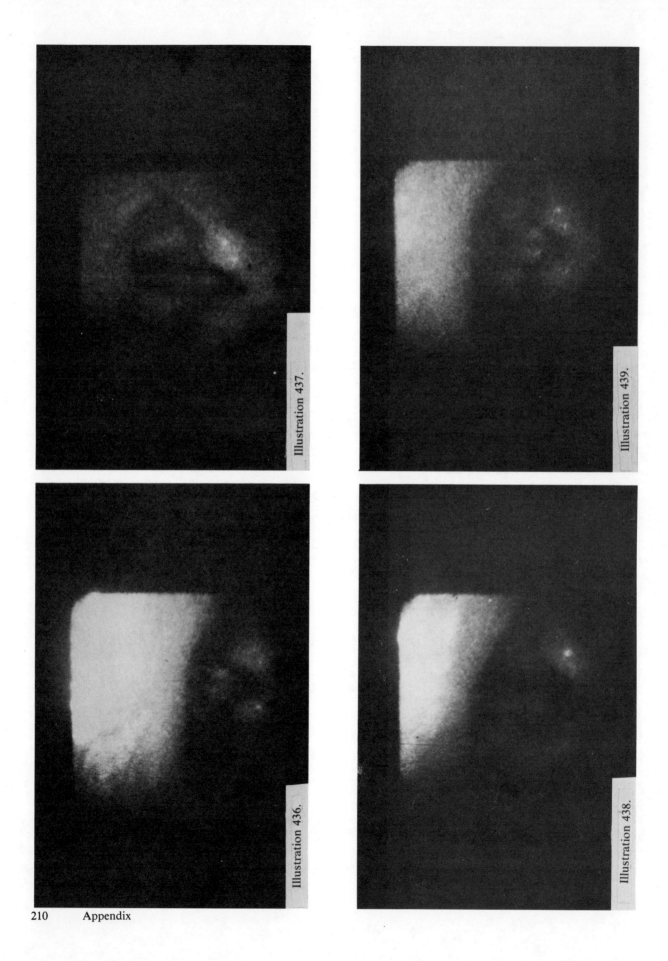

Illustration 436.

Illustration 437.

Illustration 438.

Illustration 439.

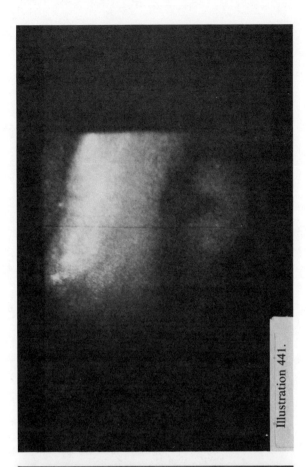

Illustration 441.

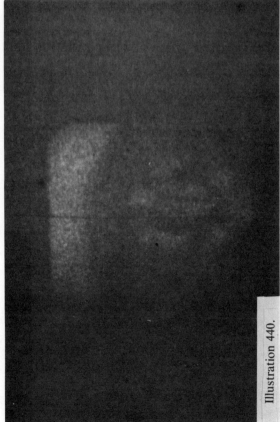

Illustration 440.

Index